THERE'S HOPE FOR THE WORLD

There's Hope for the World

The Memoir of Birmingham, Alabama's First African American Mayor

RICHARD ARRINGTON

The University of Alabama Press • *Tuscaloosa*

Designer: Michele Quinn
Typeface: Minion

∞

The paper on which this book is printed meets the minimum
requirements of American National Standard for Information
Sciences-Permanence of Paper for Printed Library Materials, ANSI
Z39.48-1984.

Library of Congress Cataloging-in-Publication Data

Arrington, Richard.
    There's hope for the world : the memoir of Birmingham, Ala-
bama's first African American mayor / Richard Arrington.
        p.   cm.
    Includes bibliographical references and index.
    ISBN 978-0-8173-1623-5 (cloth : alk. paper) — ISBN 978-0-
8173-8041-0 (electronic) 1. Arrington, Richard. 2. African American
mayors—Alabama—Birmingham—Biography. 3. Mayors—Alabama
—Birmingham—Biography. 4. Birmingham (Ala.)—Biography.
5. Birmingham (Ala.)—Politics and government. 6. Birmingham
(Ala.)—Social conditions. 7. Birmingham (Ala.)—Economic conditions. I. Title.
    F334.B653A773 2008
    976.1'064092—dc22
    [B]
                                                    2008010760

Contents

PREFACE

I promised myself and my friends shortly after leaving political office in Birmingham in July 1999 that I would write about my experiences as mayor—especially as the first black citizen to hold the city's highest and only full-time elected office. Fulfilling that promise has been a long time coming, in part because I vacillated between wanting to write my view of political and public policy analysis and just the mundane memoir. Fearing that if I didn't soon write something time would rob me completely of my thoughts and the opportunity to put them in writing, I opted for the less demanding memoir. I still found it challenging to narrow my experiences down to a reasonable number of topics and pages.

Special thanks go to Nicole Clark, a freshman in the Honors Program at Miles College, for typing the entire manuscript from my handwritten copy. Her diligence and her knowledge of manuscript styles were most helpful.

I am indebted to many friends and supporters for helping me complete this book.

March 2005
Birmingham, Alabama

1

LEAVING CITY HALL
The Last Day

I begin this memoir where it ends—on my last day as mayor of Birmingham.

The northeastern part of the third floor of Birmingham City Hall, which houses the offices and conference rooms of the mayor and his staff, is already deserted. It has been nearly twenty years since I was first elected mayor of Alabama's largest city on October 30, 1979. It is Monday, 5:45 P.M., July 19, 1999. I walk slowly down the hallways, peering into each office and conference room. The only other person present in the complex is police lieutenant Eugene Thomas, who is in charge of the mayor's security staff; everyone else had left by 5:00. Eugene is seated behind the reception desk at the entrance of the complex, waiting to drive me from city hall to my home. Normally Eugene or Sergeant Fred Shaw, the other member of the security staff, accompanies me to my car at the end of the day. On this day, my last as mayor, Lieutenant Thomas will drop me off at home. The city car assigned to me had been checked in to the city garage earlier that afternoon.

As I walked into the reception area where Eugene was sitting, I noticed the space on the glass window next to the door to the complex, which usually read "Richard Arrington Jr.—Mayor," had been changed to "William A. Bell, Interim Mayor." The city's print shop had made the change earlier that afternoon. The walls, hallways, and reception area where a hundred or more plaques and framed recognitions that had been given to me during my twenty-year term as mayor usually hung were bare. My staff had spent much of the day removing the plaques, wrapping them, and placing them in boxes labeled for their next destination—my home or the city archives.

That entire day had been a relatively quiet one for my staff and me. The usually busy schedule of people coming into and going out of the office on city business had been left free of visitors, since I wanted to be able to tie up any loose ends I had overlooked. The staff's farewell party for me, the departing interviews with reporters, the last regular staff meeting, and the like had all been crammed into a very tight schedule during the week of July 12. On Friday, July 16, at 10:00 A.M. I had met with City Council president William Bell and the city department heads for about thirty minutes. I began the meeting by thanking the department heads for their support of my administration and then turned the meeting over to William Bell for his comments and instructions. Bell's comments were very brief. In substance he said, "Business will continue as usual." On July 13, a resolution by City Councilman Aldrich Gunn to rename a street running from the city's southern boundary through downtown to near the city's eastern area airport had been approved by the City Council. On the same day at 2:00 P.M. at Patton Park, a ceremony unveiling a new street sign—"Richard Arrington Jr. Boulevard"—was held.[1]

I walked back into my office, sat behind my "formal" desk, and in a matter of a few minutes I was seized by a surprising lump in my throat. It was an emotional reaction to the realization that I was leaving the mayor's office after twenty years. I became choked up and very teary-eyed. It was a reaction and perhaps a moment I'd never really anticipated. If I had thought about this moment before, I'm sure that I thought I would be leaving with great relief and maybe even joy. But now it was just the opposite. I rose from my seat behind the desk and walked again down the back hallway of the complex past the offices of my staff. The emotional feeling of the moment did not subside but grew in intensity. I thought to myself, "Shoot, this is bull crap." But I couldn't psych myself out of the sadness I felt over leaving. Slowly I walked back to my office, picked up my briefcase, and headed out into the reception area where Lieutenant Thomas waited. He looked up and said, "Ready to go, Boss? Got everything? Need me to get anything for you? Here, let me take your briefcase." "I think I've got it all. Let's go," I said, speaking slowly and avoiding looking at the lieutenant for fear he'd see that my eyes were teary and hear my distinctive, always high-pitched, reedy voice cracking. Then we took the elevator down to the parking area, departing from my usual pattern of walking the back way, sixty-five steps to my car from my office whenever I left city hall, no matter the number of times a day. Eugene continued trying to converse with me as he drove me home. I gave brief responses in a monotone voice while pretending to be peering out the car window. But I was still just trying to hide the emotions I felt about leaving. At home, Eugene carried my briefcase into the house and said, "OK, Boss, I'll see you later." He shook my hand and left. I was relieved that he was leaving because I thought I would cry at any moment. Now at home, with nobody around me for a while, I began to regain my composure. But I spent the next hour reflecting on some of the events that had occurred during my time in the mayor's office. The thoughts came cascading down, converging as if looking at fragments in a kaleidoscope.

On the table in my den, by the couch where I was seated, my attention turned to a small book on the City of Birmingham that I kept there. It was the city's Centennial Celebration book, titled *Portrait of Birmingham*. The book had been published by the 1971 Birmingham Centennial Committee. It contained five pages on the city's first one hundred years and a large number of photographs of notable city sites. I turned to the page that gave a brief synoptic outline of highlights in the city's existence. There was the story of a young city, just turning one hundred, telling how its rich natural resources of coal, coke, limestone, and iron ore and a railroad helped transform it into what it had once been—the leading industrial center of the Southeast, a steel industry giant: the Magic City.[2]

Seeing the city's once beloved but now forgotten slogan, "Birmingham—The Magic City," reminded me of the first time I saw the huge neon sign proclaiming Birmingham as the Magic City. It was erected downtown facing the Terminal Station and welcomed people arriving via the station. As I sat there reflecting, I could see the sign in my mind as clearly as I did the first time my dad took me downtown to the station. I was not yet ten years old and we were there to see a relative off. We found the colored waiting room in the terminal and before long my relative was boarding the train. Walking out of the front entrance of the terminal, one could not help but see the large neon sign standing higher than the terminal and surrounding buildings, attached to a steel-latticed frame reading "Birmingham—The Magic City." The sign, anchored on each side of the street, straddled the Fifth Avenue north subway entrance for cars and railcars and ran directly under the center of the beautiful station. The Terminal Station and the Magic City sign—what a pretty sight for my young eyes! The sign was a gift to the city from E. H. Elliott, a reminder that this young post–Civil War town of the Deep South had grown amazingly fast from a small pioneer town into the leading industrial center of the South.

Both the sign and the station are long gone; both were demolished in the early 1950s. I've heard many citizens express regret that the station was not preserved as one of Birmingham's outstanding structures. But I have never heard an expression of regret that the Magic City sign was demolished—perhaps some thought it tacky or maybe, as I thought on this sad day, no one believed that we could rightfully boast that our city was "magic" any longer. Battered by the economic malaise of the faltering steel economy and the bitter, haunting echoes of racial division, Birmingham saw its magic evaporate and witnessed other, once less affluent, southern cities surpass it in economic growth.

Although it was too late to save the old Terminal Station, perhaps with hard work and vision we citizens could make Birmingham a proud Magic City once again.

My twenty-year administration was certainly a time of positive, significant changes that I hoped would restore some of the magic. My administration and the ones following it are part of our city's search for its magic—to restore its prominence as a progressive city. Indeed, the challenge for Birmingham still is to find its magic.[3]

The book also described crises that seemed to always develop to halt the city's progress and keep it from fulfilling what its critics still call "its perpetual promise." These included the cholera epidemic, the Great Depression, and racial strife. These were called the "storms of change." Under the heading "Century of Storms," the committee wrote, "Even before Birmingham was 50 years old, it was written, 'Our most cherished desires have often been torn to pieces. Sickness, struggle, bereavement, poverty have come to us. These are facts. They have left their mark on all of us. But let us bear in mind that sorrows are stepping-stones to higher things and press forward.'"

How timely, I thought, to have my attention drawn to that book just as I was reflecting on the successes and failures the city had experienced during my twenty years as its mayor. Surely I had my moments of sorrow when some major public policy initiatives had failed. And the collapse of the steel industry shortly after I took office was a storm. I couldn't quite bring myself to see them as "stepping-stones to higher things." But there were noteworthy transitions that occurred during my tenure. I thought both the "sorrows" and the "transitions" were worth writing about and evaluating. I wondered what a Birmingham mayor would say about 1979–99 twenty years later. Would he/she agree with me that it was a time of major transition and reconciliation for our city mixed in with a "stepping-stone of sorrow" here and there? In the pages that follow, I tell my story of my city's efforts during my tenure as mayor to regain its once proud reputation of being a progressive city—a story of transitions, reconciliation, and sorrows.

THE DECISION TO LEAVE CITY HALL

My decision to leave the mayor's office before my fifth term ended had been made two years earlier. While attending a City Council weekend retreat at Point Clear near Mobile, Alabama, I had been approached by William Bell during one of the sessions. He asked if he could meet with me later that evening at the close of the session. We agreed to meet in my room. As soon as Bell asked for the meeting, I knew what was coming. Donald Watkins, my attorney and a close friend, had alerted me to the fact that Bell was going to ask me to leave office early so that he could become interim mayor and have what he thought would be the advantage of his running for mayor as the incumbent. Under the state law that established Birmingham's mayor-council form of government in 1963, in conjunction with the ouster of the city's commission form of government and the infamous Eugene "Bull" Connor, the president of the Birmingham City Council would become mayor of the city if a vacancy existed in the position of mayor for any reason. The law further stated that in case of such a vacancy, a city election for mayor must be held within ninety days of the date the vacancy occurred.

In our meeting that evening Bell asked whether I would be willing to resign from the office of mayor early. We discussed different scenarios about my possible resignation and how the entire matter might play out. Bell, who had been elected to the City Council in 1979, had shared with me his interest in seeking the position of mayor at the end of my first mayoral term. At that time he had inquired about my interest in seeking another term, saying that he wanted to seek the office but would not do so as long as I ran for reelection. He was always true to his word. Even when I sought my fourth and fifth terms as mayor, after earlier stating I would not seek reelection, Bell reiterated his interest in running for mayor but not against me. I even encouraged him on two occasions to run even though I was running for reelection. He said, "No, I'm never going to run against you. I'll just wait."

Our conversation that evening at Point Clear ended with an understanding that I would likely resign early when I no longer wanted to seek reelection. Bell had emphasized that he was in no way urging me not to seek reelection.

I'm sure that he was remembering that I had told him on two other occasions that I would not seek reelection as mayor but later ended up doing just that. We never spoke again about this matter until two years later in 1999 when I told Bell I was not going to run for a sixth term. Following one of our council meetings I asked him whether he was still interested in becoming interim mayor and being in the position to seek the office of mayor as the incumbent. He said that he was. Before mentioning this to Bell, I had decided not to seek a sixth term. I had also had the city attorney quietly research the law on filling a vacancy in the position of mayor to be certain that my understanding of the law was correct. This done, I decided I could resign as mayor about three months before the regular 1999 mayoral election, which permitted Bell to serve as mayor until the 1999 election. By timing my resignation as such, it also avoided the necessity and expense of a special election to fill the vacancy for the position of mayor.

"OK," I said to Bell, "here is the game plan, but please don't mention it until I make a public announcement of my intention to resign. And remember, if we do it this way, politically speaking, I'll be the albatross around your neck. Do you still want me to do it?" He did. We then talked about how his opposition for the office would probably accuse me of trying to handpick my successor—which, in fact, I was. But Bell thought that the positives of our plan outweighed the negatives and was completely supportive. I was certain William Bell would be the next elected mayor of Birmingham. I was to learn, however, that the best laid plans sometimes go astray—especially in politics. On April 15, 1999, I announced my plan to retire early. On July 19, I retired and the next day Bell was interim mayor.[4]

SETTING THE TABLE FOR THE NEXT MAYOR

It was my desire and intention to leave office with the city clearly on an upward course. I wanted the city to be fiscally strong, which it was. But I also wanted to have in place several well-funded programs that the next mayor could preside over and implement. The new mayor could then get off to a positive start and would have time to lay his own plans for a year or two down the road. I spoke of this as "setting the table" for the next mayor, but perhaps the desire to leave city hall with the city clearly on an upward course was of equal importance to me. If I could achieve this goal, it would be an important stepping-stone for the transition to a new administration. I believed that I had benefited from the well-funded projects I inherited from my predecessor, David Vann. Vann had not begun the implementation of his program for business and residential rehabilitation but he had laid the groundwork and put the funding in place. No doubt he thought that he would implement them in his second term as mayor—a term that never came. Foremost among my plans to "set the table" for the new mayor were two projects: the 1998 Metropolitan Area Projects Strategy (MAPS) and the 1999 endowment of a lifetime capital funds program for Birmingham's public schools (from the proceeds of the sale of city's water works and sewer system).

Metropolitan Area Projects Strategy (MAPS)
MAPS was an ambitious metro-wide program that had as its theme "Building the Foundation for Our Future." I believed MAPS would do just that for our city. Implementing MAPS became one of my fondest dreams as mayor. If approved by a countywide vote, MAPS would undoubtedly be the biggest single economic development project undertaken in metro Birmingham.

I am not suggesting that MAPS was a unique Birmingham creation; quite the contrary. As I pointed out repeatedly during the campaign for the MAPS referendum, at least thirteen other cities had successfully funded and implemented MAPS-type programs, including Phoenix, Cleveland, Detroit, Cincinnati, Oklahoma City, Houston, Tampa, Seattle, Chattanooga, Milwaukee, Indianapolis, and Atlanta.

From its very inception as a metro Birmingham project, MAPS faced many hurdles. But let's first outline the economic development projects that made up MAPS.

1. A 200,000-square-foot, $280 million domed public convention and entertainment facility to be connected to the existing Birmingham-Jefferson Convention Complex; $8.7 million for upgrading the existing convention center

2. $75 million for the Public School Education Capital Fund; $2.5 million for enhancement of technology in the regional library system (40 public libraries; $23.5 million for expansion of the McWane Science Center and Imax theater)

3. $20 million capital fund for police and fire protection needs

4. $25 million capital fund for regional cultural and historic facilities

5. $40 million for a regional zoo; $10.3 million for development of a 69-mile linear greenway system, including bicycle and pedestrian trails; and $21 million for a multipurpose recreational center (aquatic center, tracks, tennis courts, therapeutic center, and soccer complex)

6. $590 million in temporary retail sales; $590 million in construction retail sales; $114 million per year in convention income; and 1,239 new permanent jobs

MAPS was put together by a steering committee of leading business, civic, and political figures. It proposed a twelve-year countywide one-cent sales tax funding plan: three-quarters for MAPS and one quarter for regional transportation. According to Ernest and Whinney, a leading CPA firm, the economic impact of MAPS would be 39,895 temporary construction jobs, $778 million increase in personal aggregate income, $19 million increase in retail sales, 87 new retail outlets, and an annual permanent impact of $370 million.

The first hurdle was mobilizing Birmingham's corporate community behind MAPS. The corporate community gave leadership and $1.5 million in promotional funds for the MAPS campaign. The support of the corporate community was also instrumental in getting the Alabama legislature's approval to permit a countywide referendum. Under Alabama law the MAPS program triggered a constitutional requirement for a statewide referendum—unless the enabling legislation for MAPS passed both legislative houses without a dissenting vote. This miracle was accomplished through heavy lobbying by Birmingham's corporate community. The MAPS referendum was scheduled for August 4, 1998. Much to our disappointment, the president of the Jefferson County Commission, Mary Buckalew, who had been a leading member of the MAPS steering committee, abruptly resigned from the committee and withdrew her support. Commissioner Buckalew had not told the other steering committee members of her plans to back away from MAPS and simply told a local television station. Perhaps the position taken by some corporate members of the MAPS steering committee—that the chairperson of the county commission and the mayor of Birmingham were leading the MAPS campaign—

caused Buckalew to rethink her position. During my nearly twenty years as mayor, I had found no elected white official in the county government or sub-urban government who felt politically comfortable being allied with me.

The campaign for and against MAPS was waged with intensity. The op-position to MAPS was led by a group calling itself Real Accountability Prog-ress (RAPS), led by Birmingham City Council members Jimmy Blake, Bill Johnson, Don McDermott, and Bernard Kincaid. These four council members of the nine-member council formed the opposition to most of the Arrington administration initiatives, including MAPS. Blake, Johnson, and McDermott represented Birmingham's predominantly white voter districts. Kincaid, the only black in that group, represented the predominantly black City Council District with the largest percentage of white voters, largely blue collar. I men-tion race here because like so many important issues in Birmingham's history, the MAPS issue would become a racial issue. The Blake-led opposition pitched its opposition mainly to the overwhelmingly white suburban communities, appearing at the meetings of suburban governing bodies to call for the defeat of MAPS and to promise voters that RAPS had a better alternative, called Plan B. I interpreted the message to be one aimed at whites and the anti-Arrington sentiments of whites: they were asked, why do you want to put your tax money in projects that will largely benefit Arrington's black Birmingham? In an ef-fort to offset this appeal to whites, the MAPS steering committee made two moves late in the campaign. It persuaded Donald Hess, a young, white, success-ful business executive who headed Parisian, a retail department store chain, to come aboard as chairman of the MAPS campaign effort. It also recruited Larry Langford, mayor of the overwhelmingly black suburban city of Fairfield, to become a vocal supporter of the MAPS program. Langford, who was black, a former Birmingham City Council member, and a onetime Birmingham may-oral candidate who later changed his residency to Fairfield, was clearly the most popular local black elected official among Jefferson County white vot-ers. He had run for mayor of Birmingham in 1979 as the candidate backed by the local Fraternal Order of Police (FOP). A former television news reporter and a gifted motivational speaker, Langford clearly avoided and dodged ra-cial issues, saying they were not about black or white but right or wrong. It was the hope of those of us on the MAPS steering committee that Langford's pro-MAPS stand would help offset some of the anti-Arrington sentiment of white voters. For the last couple of weeks before the August 4 vote we flooded the local television stations with ads promoting MAPS. I met for several hours with the editorial staff of the *Birmingham News* explaining the project in detail, answering questions from the staff, and seeking the paper's endorsement of the MAPS project. I believed that the state's largest newspaper would be important in getting voter approval of the project. In the week leading up to the vote, Larry Langford, a white child in his arms, solicited support for MAPS. I saw the ad as designed to appeal to white opposition. The stage was set and it was racial: the predominantly black (65 percent) city of Birmingham was pitted against the predominantly white (75 percent) suburbs—the inner city against the suburbs.

Early in the referendum on MAPS, the *Birmingham News* endorsed the project. Although it cited its reservations about funding the project with a sales tax, it recommended that voters support it. The editorial staff of the city's afternoon paper, the *Birmingham Post-Herald*, recommended that voters reject the project. I had sought an audience with the *Post-Herald* editorial staff several weeks after visiting the staff of the *Birmingham News*. The *Post-Herald* staff had appeared to me to be opposed to MAPS, especially the idea of funding the project with a sales tax. While I sought the *Post-Herald*'s endorsement, I did not think it was critical to getting voter approval. Its circulation was significantly less than that of the *News*. Aside from that, I viewed the *Post-Herald* as a much stronger critic of my administration than the *News*.

At a July breakfast meeting with corporate leaders, where I made my major pitches for MAPS, the editors of both newspapers were present. I thought my presentation in support of MAPS was the best among dozens of presentations I had made before numerous groups during the MAPS campaign. I had been on the hustings for MAPS for weeks, and I felt supremely confident as to why MAPS was a "must" for Birmingham. By the time I made the July breakfast presentation, I felt I was a "walking encyclopedia" on MAPS. The corporate group threw many questions at me that morning, but I felt that I handled each well and was doing an outstanding job selling them on MAPS. I felt good, believing I had solidified the corporate support for MAPS. But as I left the breakfast I ran into Jim Willis, the *Post-Herald* editor. He came over to me and with a slight grin said, "Good job, Mayor. You almost sold me on MAPS." His remark was a clear message that the *Post-Herald* was not going to endorse the MAPS project. The August 5, 1998, editorial of the *Birmingham News* wrote of the outcome of the MAPS referendum: "Jefferson County voters Tuesday turned out in the largest numbers since the 1992 Presidential election to reject MAPS. In unofficial returns, 96,490 or 57% voted NO, mostly in the suburbs, and 71,495 or 43% voted YES, largely in Birmingham. Race split the referendum according to the *Birmingham News* analysis. Predominantly black polling places and those in the inner city voted heavily for MAPS, while most predominantly white polling places rejected the proposal."[5]

Birmingham was split once again along racial lines on an issue important to its well-being. In Mountain Brook, the area's wealthiest community—and one of the nation's wealthiest—the vote was 47 percent for and 53 percent against. Turnout in mostly black polling places was about 38 percent, while white voter turnout was about 50 percent. A few days later a RAPS spokesman said that his group never had a Plan B, as earlier claimed; they just wanted to kill MAPS.[6] There were about fifteen months left in my four-year mayoral term and I had to concede that metro Birmingham was still very much a "status quo" area, resistant to change. In fact Growth Strategies Organization, Incorporated, a nationally recognized planning group used by the Birmingham Area Chamber of Commerce for its economic planning strategies, had labeled Birmingham as an area unwilling to take risk. "It likes to stick its toe in the water occasionally to sample the water but not wade into it," the study reported in 1998. There was little point in arguing against this characterization of metro Birmingham, which had steadily fallen behind other prominent Southeastern metro areas in urban development over the preceding two decades. In 1947, Birmingham had ranked second among Southeastern metros in population and economic strength, surpassed only by New Orleans.[7] By 1998, Charlotte, Atlanta, New Orleans, Nashville, and several other metro areas had surpassed Birmingham according to the "Economic Development Strategy update for the Birmingham Metropolitan Area," a study used to rank the quality and economic viability of metropolitan areas. Growth Strategies Organization's report ranked Birmingham thirteenth among Southeastern metros in its 1998 study, noting that it had moved up several positions since its study of the area ten years earlier. Of course Birmingham had been mired in racial confrontation during a significant period of those years. In Birmingham race seemed always just beneath the surface, waiting to be scratched a little to raise its divisive head. Ron Boyles of the Growth Strategies Organization told the *Birmingham News* on June 22, 1998, "Birmingham has come a long way since I conducted a similar study [for it] ten years ago and found it to be among the worst cities in the region. Birmingham has made great strides in economic development over the past decade, but some other southeastern cities have done even better."[8] MAPS had been a key part of my strategy to move Birmingham to the top five Southeastern cities in economic development within seven to ten years.

The defeat of the MAPS project was a significant blow to that strategy. Indeed Birmingham was just "sticking its toe in the water" one more time. But it was not ready to take the leap.

Owning a Water System versus Educating Children

A day after the MAPS defeat I announced that I would turn my attention to finding ways to better fund Birmingham's public schools. Funding the public schools was an issue that I had neglected for too long, though that is not to say that nothing was done about it during my tenure as mayor. Every city bond issue during my tenure included funds for capital improvements for schools. Several new schools were constructed and a dozen or more got support for significant renovation projects. Also, each of the city's annual operating budgets included funds for enrichment and safety programs for schools. In Alabama the public schools are largely funded by the state, primarily through the State Education Trust Fund. Municipal governments that provide any support for public education do so largely through capital projects. Public schools are also administered by an appointed or elected school board that has near total authority for staffing and operating the system.

One so-called advantage of this arrangement is that it is supposed to limit politics in the system. In Birmingham the mayor has no authority to operate schools. That point had been brought home to me when I had tried to intervene in a dispute over the retention of the system's first black superintendent. A *Birmingham Post-Herald* editorial had called for me to stop interfering in the system's business. Keep politics out of the system, it said.

During my mayoral tenure there was not a single request to the city from the Board of Education or its superintendent that the city failed to meet. In fact it was city government that always approached the system about including funds for the system in city bond issues, not the reverse. And even though the city provided a fair amount of funds for schools, the amount was relatively insufficient based on the system's total needs.

One might ask what a mayor with no authority in a school system does about the system. The Birmingham mayor's office is at least a bully pulpit for education, if the mayor chooses to use his office in that way or understands the importance of good schools. I always understood the latter but chose to busy myself with the hundreds of other problems confronting our city. I believe that was my greatest failure as a mayor. Two developments brought this point home to me. The first occurred when the system was operating under an acting superintendent. By 1997 the system was in serious difficulty over the poor administration of its federal lunch program and was faced with losing the multimillion-dollar program. I intervened to help save the program and got my first inside glimpse of how poorly administered our school system was. The system was riddled with administrative deficiencies. The greatest concern I saw at the Board of Education was its fear of the powerful teachers union, the Alabama Education Association (AEA). The union was very good at protecting its members, but I never learned what it did to improve the school system overall. The union would probably argue that education begins with the teachers, and I agree. But it also includes ridding this system of underperforming teachers and administrators. But the union protects the poor-performing union members as well as the good performers, as many unions do. In fact I was soon convinced that it was the poor teachers, poor administrators, poor lunchroom managers, poor janitors, poor bus drivers, and so forth who needed and relied on the union for job security. But the powerful AEA has such undue influence with Alabama legislators that no one dares oppose it. If the school administration failed to weed out poor teachers during their probationary period, it became very difficult to do so after tenure was attained.

There was a refreshing change in the Birmingham system when the Board of Education hired Dr. Johnny Brown, a Texan, as superintendent about two years before I left office. Brown demanded accountability throughout the system. Under his administration measurable progress was evident. The large numbers of schools labeled by the state as academically deficient dropped drastically, leaving only a couple of the sixty or so schools in academic difficulty. Student performances on national tests in reading and mathematics rose steadily. But the source of the greatest difficulty for Dr. Brown aside from inadequate school funding, including midyear state budget cuts for the system, was the opposition he encountered from the teachers union. Under Brown, poorly performing personnel were being dismissed and the local union fought Brown at every turn. Two years after I left office and after the union had succeeded in its long struggle to get an enlarged and elected school board rather than the one appointed by the City Council, Brown left Birmingham to head a larger school system in Georgia and things were gradually returning to the way they had been prior to Brown's arrival.

The second development that got my attention was the increasingly vocal complaints from a small group of parents about the quality of the school system. As is always the case with politicians, the loud criticism about the school system got my attention. After all, it was 1995, an election year for Birmingham's mayor. In fact it was quite clear to me that the number one issue in the 1995 mayoral race was the public school system. It was a long time coming, but it had finally arrived and it had my attention. I met several times with then superintendent Cleveland Hammonds to develop a strategy for greater city aid for our schools. Hammonds developed a priority list, which I agreed to help him implement as soon as I was reelected. We even went as far as working out an agenda that he and I would take up with the board, down to choosing a place and time for the meeting. Within weeks after I was sworn in for my fifth term I was on the phone with Hammonds to finalize the plans for meeting with the board. When he had not gotten back to me after a couple of weeks, I called the president of the Board of Education to talk about the planned meeting. She told me in no uncertain terms that the board was not interested in the proposed meeting since it had notified Hammonds that his contract was being terminated. It was a total surprise to me. Hammonds sought to get a more "orderly termination" such as one that would come at the close of the school year or, at worst, at the end of the midyear semester. I think Hammonds believed that I had enough influence with the board to persuade it to postpone his termination to at least the end of the semester. I had tried and been rebuffed by the board. Sadly, I believe Hammonds left Birmingham under the impression that I was a party to his firing. I had nothing to do with it.

I wish I could tell you that the outcry for better schools came from parents and others who saw the need for better schools, and maybe some of them did. But the catalyst for "the better schools movement" was the failure of a group of Birmingham high school seniors to pass the required exit exam. Angry parents of the students had petitioned the board and superintendent to let these students march in the graduation ceremonies while their diplomas were withheld until they passed the exit exam. The superintendent, whose position I supported, refused to grant their requests, which led to several small protests on the steps of the Birmingham Board of Education building. From this spark, "a better schools movement" flared and became an issue in the 1995 mayoral election. The movement to replace the five-member school board with an elected board of nine members gained momentum. I had led the fight in the state legislature to beat back legislation to change the Birmingham board to an elected board for the past ten years. By 1997 the AEA, led by the Birmingham affiliate, had gained the support of the Jefferson County legislative delegation for an elected board. Eventually Birmingham state senator Roger Smitherman joined AEA's president and vice president, Paul Hubbard and Joe Reed, respectively, to push the bill through the local delegation. With Jefferson County's Senate now onboard (as the House delegation had been for some time), I saw the handwriting on the wall and made a last desperate, unsuccessful attempt to get an elected board limited to five members. A public hearing on the proposed legislation to authorize an elected nine-member board was held at Birmingham's Sixth Avenue Baptist Church. I attended the meeting to speak in opposition to the proposed bill. The hearing room was packed with AEA members who hooted and hissed when I stood to speak. Senator Smitherman showed every courtesy but the bill was on a fast track.

In late 1998, after the defeat of the MAPS referendum, I was looking for ways the city could provide significant additional capital support for our schools, which had been one of the items rejected in the MAPS defeat. The City Council suggested that I research all assets of the city and recommend how any of them might be used to generate greater city financial support for our schools. With the assistance of outside financial consultants, I reported to the council that the only city asset that could be readily converted into an adequate source of capital support for the schools was the city-owned Water Board and Sewer System. By selling the system to a private operator the city could immediately generate at least $600 million and, through certain terms in the sales contract, accrue additional annual funds from a tap-on fee for every new home or business added to the system. I made a point of saying little publicly about the proposed tap-on fee. From these funds we could establish a lifetime endowment for capital school needs and have money left for other city needs.

I had been misinformed by our consultants that the system could be sold to a private firm on the majority vote of the City Council. I set out to secure five council votes for the proposed sale, only to learn later that such a sale would require approval by a majority of city voters. It turned out that the city could sell the system to another governmental entity on a City Council–only approval, but a sale to a private entity required the citywide referendum. In order for the referendum to take place, the five-member Birmingham water board would have to vote to transfer assets of the system to city hall for sale. With great pain and reservation the board voted 5–0 to return the assets. Without their concurrence the proposed sale was dead. Following considerable and often bitter debate by the council, the citywide referendum was approved, 5–4, by the council and a June referendum was set.

I headed into the referendum campaign confident that the city voters would approve this sale. Race was again a factor in my thinking. Nearly 70 percent of the city voters and 95 percent of the city's schoolchildren were black. I reasoned that black voters would embrace an opportunity to improve the financing of city schools by selling the water system. I was never more wrong about a matter or more disappointed about an outcome. The council opposition group of Blake, Kincaid, Johnson, and McDermott led the assault against the proposed sale. Kincaid was especially effective in convincing the city's black voters that a sale of the water works system would be a fatal mistake. It would be like selling "your seed corn," he told them. Still, I thought a strong appeal to black voters to support better schools for an overwhelmingly black school system would succeed, even though polls were showing that the referendum would not pass in the black community. In desperation I turned to a supporter of the administration, Alton Parker, an attorney in one of the city's oldest and largest law firms, to head up a late effort aimed particularly at white voters to support the referendum. Given the short time period, Alton made a gallant effort to mobilize white support for the referendum. The referendum was overwhelmingly defeated, losing badly in the city's predominantly black boxes. If I had any doubt about it being time for me to leave the mayor's office, it was swept away by the referendum results. Not only had I failed to deliver for the schools, but I had lost the hold on the majority of the city's black voters.

My brand of race politics, adopted after successful campaigns for mayor in 1979, 1983, and 1987, was swept down the drain. During those races I spent considerable time and resources trying to increase my white support. Still, it remained at about 10 percent. Convinced I would never gain more white support, I decided to pump that time and those resources into expanding my large black support base, especially in working for a higher black voter turnout. The strategy had worked in city-only elections but clearly failed in the referendum on the water system sale. Thinking black voters would rally to support an overwhelmingly black school system was a miscalculation. Also, despite good black voter support in the MAPS referendum, it was a major tactical error not to work harder for the majority white vote until late in the campaign.

Working with our consultants and council president William Bell, we got the council to approve (5–4) a plan to borrow $260 million against the water system to fund the school board's capital plan for new schools, including three new regional high schools. But the bitter taste of two major political defeats—MAPS and the water system sale—would not go away. I sought some consolation in focusing on some of the political successes I had experienced during my twenty years as mayor, but to little avail. I knew it was time for me to leave city hall and politics. Some of the successes are the subjects of some of the following chapters. But first it is appropriate to give an overview of my life leading up to my entry into politics as a candidate for public office.

2

Early Life Overview
The Journey from Sharecropping to City Hall

Memories of the Farm

One's memory, especially very early in life, can be tricky, I'm told. Family stories of experiences one had in early childhood might become imprinted in the mind as one's own recollections. I spent many summers with my grandparents in Livingston (a Black Belt town near the Mississippi border) after my family moved away to Birmingham, but I never visited the old home place of my birth.

Nevertheless, I have vivid memories of my early childhood days when my family lived near Livingston. Although I was born in October 1934 as our nation weathered a severe economic depression, I have no recollections of the tough times my family and others must have endured during those years. For the first five and a half years of my life I lived with my parents on a farm just outside of Livingston in the house where I was born. My father, Richard Arrington Sr., was a sharecropper and rented the farm from a Mr. Mellon. I clearly remember the house, with its open-air window spaces that were shut off from the outside by solid wooden shutters hinged to the inside wall and latched from the inside. Two of the rooms in the three-room house had walls plastered with pages torn from old mail-order catalogs. These pages were glued to the wall with a flour-based glue, much as wallpaper is hung today. There was a fireplace in the living room–bedroom, a second bedroom, a hallway, and an open porch leading to the kitchen. The smokehouse, where meat, mainly pork, was cured, stood a short distance from the kitchen, beside a fenced-in chicken pen. The outhouse was a short way from the house. On the side of the house across a narrow strip of land bearing a couple of trees, a wooden chopping block, and some black wash pots, were our barn and a cow pen. A few feet down a modest slope was my dad's blacksmith shop where he sometimes shoed horses. I remember some of our fields, especially the cotton, watermelon, and corn fields.

My parents and my mother's younger sister picked cotton in the field, each dragging a large burlap sack with a cloth shoulder strap along to place the cotton in. Our drinking water came from a spring nearly a half mile from our house that we shared with several other local families. Wash water was caught in large wooden barrels in rain runoff from the house's tin roof. I remember that my father almost single-handedly dug a well near our house. But before long its water went bad and was not fit for drinking. My father built a wooden cover over the well.

While the adults worked in the fields, chopping, planting, or picking cotton, I often fetched buckets of drinking water from the spring. I would ride one of our horses, bare-backed, to the spring, slide off the horse, fill a bucket of water, and then struggle mightily to climb back on the horse, grabbing its mane with one hand and holding the bucket in the other. Sometimes I led the horse to a tree stump on which I could stand to mount it.

Our mailbox was down the road on the highway in the opposite direction of the spring, about a half mile or so from the house. I often fetched the mail from the box and still recall the day that our dog that accompanied me to the mailbox ran onto the highway and was killed by a passing vehicle.

There were no lights in our house except for kerosene lamps lit at night that burned until bedtime. The family graveyard that I visited with my mother and aunt when they went to clear the graveyard of weeds was located off the narrow road between the home and the spring.

In my adult years I often wanted to go back to visit the old home site to see if it looked as I remembered it. But my dad said the place had become all woods; it was owned by the American Can Company and used for growing timber. So I abandoned the idea of the visit, but it did cross my mind many, many times.

On some Saturdays I rode in the wagon with my dad to downtown Livingston, which was about ten miles away. In town the people usually sat around talking after purchasing items from the store in the town square—blacks near the black café and whites in the park area.

Our church, called either Shiloh or Pilgrim's Rest, was about five miles from the house and reached by wagon, buggy, or horseback on the Sundays worship service was held. A small wooden elementary school, where my grandmother taught, was near the church.

The memories of my farm home still linger: my dad's baby sister, Lizette, "talking about religion" as new converts did back then; the nights of hog killing with the help of neighbors; cooking molasses down at the molasses mill; fishing with my mama with a cane fishing pole at a creek that was within walking distance of the house; roasting sweet potatoes in the hot ashes of the fireplace in the winter; and heating our quilts in front of the fireplace before heading off to bed on cold nights.

Life on the home place ended in the summer of 1940 when my dad returned and moved his family to Birmingham after having gone there for a short while to work in the steel mill. My father gave up his life of sharecropping in Sumter County, Alabama, and moved my mother (whose name was Ernestine), my younger brother, and me, as well as my mother's younger sister and brother, to seek his fortunes in the steel mills in the metro Birmingham valley. We were part of the great migration of black farmers, mostly sharecroppers from the South, to the urban centers of places like Birmingham, Pittsburgh, Chicago, and Gary, Indiana. The exodus from the farmlands had been in the making for several years. Mechanized farming, a declining market for cotton, and sharecropping, which permitted people like my family to barely make a living, were factors in the migration. Sharecropping, which the Southern agrarian economy had relied on since the emancipation of black slaves in the mid-1860s, was in reality nothing but another and slightly less harsh form of slavery. Most freed black slaves owned no land or valuables of any kind, aside from themselves, and worked for former slave owners as sharecroppers. The plight of the early freed slaves is emphatically underscored by W. E. B. Du Bois in his 1903 book, *The Souls of Black Folk:* "The most piteous thing amid all the ruin of war-time, among the broken fortunes of the masters, the blighted hopes of mothers and maidens, and the fall of an empire—the most piteous thing amid all this was the black freedman who threw down his hoe because the world called him free. What did such a mockery of freedom mean? Not a cent of money, not an inch of land, not a mouthful of Victuals,—not even ownership of the rags on his back. Free!"[1]

Blacks had spent 244 years in slavery in a land of plenty and were suddenly freed with nothing. Through the failed Reconstruction of the South, opportunities for black slaves and their descendants improved only slightly and only for a short period of time. Efforts to provide a form of reparation for former slaves, including the Freedmen's Bureau, though well meaning, were short-lived and unproductive. The Civil Rights Acts of 1866, 1870, 1872, and 1875 and the Reconstruction amendments of 1865, 1868, and 1870 (Thirteenth, Fourteenth, and Fifteenth Amendments), all of which were aimed at cloaking newly freed slaves with constitutional protection, fell far short of their goals at the time.

From 1880 to 1889 the unfavorable racist federal court rulings on civil rights for blacks doomed equal treatment and political influence for blacks. By 1890 the states of the old Confederacy, led by Mississippi, moved swiftly through state conventions to strip blacks of their new voting rights, rapidly removing nearly every black from Southern states' voting rolls within two to three years and often within mere months.

So by the early 1900s black Southerners, especially those who were part of the South's agrarian economy, like my family, found life quite bleak. We had little property, few constitutional protections, and no voting rights.

Adding to their impoverished state was the poor state of America's economy. Under Republican president Herbert Hoover, who was elected in 1928, the country languished in the Great Depression. By 1932 when Democrat Franklin D. Roosevelt defeated Hoover, twelve million Americans were jobless and dependent on government welfare for subsistence. Roosevelt got Congress to enact the New Deal, a package of legislation aimed at bringing economic recovery to the nation.

Jimmie L. Franklin, in his discussion of the depression and segregation, in *Back to Birmingham,* notes that the "New Deal . . . progress of the 1940s did not significantly affect the Arringtons' lives as farm tenants. Like other blacks, they had reason to hope that the dawning of a better day would come with the institution of new government policies. The Arringtons indirectly participated in the new [Agricultural Adjustment Act] Program but it netted them little."[2]

With cotton production curtailed by government policy, my father and his family turned to raising watermelons, sweet potatoes, beans, corn, and other garden crops. He also continued to operate his small blacksmith shop and worked under the new federal Works Projects Administration (WPA), repairing rural roads for $3 per day. His work with the WPA lasted only a month.

In the summer of 1940, my father borrowed the Model T belonging to his brother Jonathan, tied our bed mattresses to its top, packed his family into the car, and headed to the Birmingham area 120 miles away to join Jonathan and several of his other brothers to work in the steel mills in Fairfield, a suburb of Birmingham. That move brought down the curtain on a chapter that covered nearly a third of my parents' existence.

My mother had grown up on a large former plantation generally known as the Bell Place. Bell was my mother's family name. Her father and several of his brothers lived on and farmed much of the former plantation land and raised their families there. Most blacks in Sumter County at the time assumed that the Bells owned the property, but they did not. At the time of the emancipation of the slaves, Lula DeGraffenred owned the plantation. My maternal great-grandfather, Oliver Bell, was three years old at the time of the Emancipation Proclamation. He and his mother were slaves on the DeGraffenreds' planta-tion. After emancipation my great-grandfather's family, former DeGraffenred slaves, changed their family name to Bell. The white DeGraffenreds, who even-tually moved to another site, allowed the Oliver Bell family to continue to live on the land. I am not sure of the details of this arrangement, but Oliver Bell grew up there and raised seven of his children there. One of his sons, Ernest, was my mother's father. Eventually the plantation became the property of the white Mellon family.[3]

The Bell family had a high regard for education. Several of Ernest's younger brothers had some college training at Tuskegee Institute and Alabama A&M College and taught school in Sumter County. My mother's maternal grand-father was D. S. Jones, the first black to graduate from Selma University.

My mother attended boarding school at the Sumter County Training School for Negroes where she earned a high school diploma. She met and began dat-ing my father, Richard, in 1929.

My father's family lived in a Sumter County home near Boyd and later moved to the town of York. His parents, Matthew and Barbara Arrington, had fourteen children. After Barbara's death, Matthew married Willie Gray, who bore him five more children.

Despite having had only a third grade education in a one-room school-house, which housed several grades, my father was a man of many talents and an avid reader. He was an accomplished brick mason, a carpenter, a black-smith, and a mechanic. He built a few homes in Sumter County and dozens of homes in Fairfield that are still standing. He built the Fairfield houses while also working a full-time shift at the steel mill after the family moved to Fairfield.

In 1933, at the age of eighteen, my mother lost her mother; she had what appeared to have been a heart attack. Six months later her father was killed in a logging accident while cutting timber. In December 1933 my parents married. My father moved into my mother's home and became the head of the family, which included my mother's younger brother and sister. He immediately became the husband and father of the household, raising his sister-in-law Eloise Bell and brother-in-law Clyde Bell, and shouldered responsibility for them into their adulthood.

My New Home—Birmingham

We arrived in Birmingham from Sumter County just after dark one night in the summer of 1940. I would turn six in October but I had never traveled out of Sumter County before. We moved into one side of a duplex, which my father rented from a neighbor by the name of Sturdivant. Our side of the house had three rooms. The outdoor dry toilet was in the backyard. A single water faucet and sink were in the kitchen, which also contained a wood-burning stove, a table, a cabinet, an icebox, and four chairs. Baths were taken in a large tin tub, usually on Saturday. A few years later we got a modern water toilet in an unlit small closet on the back porch. The house, which is still standing much as it was in 1940, was located in the suburb of Fairfield, the site of the Birmingham area's largest steel mills. The all-dirt street on which we lived divided the city limits of Fairfield and Birmingham. My playmates across the street rode the streetcar to attend Birmingham public schools. I walked about seven blocks to the Fairfield public school.

The black community of Fairfield resided largely in the Interurban Heights area of the city. There were two other very small remote and somewhat isolated pockets of blacks living in communities called Englewood and Anisburg in Fairfield. These two adjacent communities were about three miles northwest of the Heights. The total population of Fairfield, which is now about 12,000, was then about 8,000, the majority of whom were black and blue collar. In the black community about 99 percent of the men worked in the steel mills. Working women were largely in the maid service. The rigid racial segregation that circumscribed blacks and whites to separate areas, not unlike apartheid, kept the few black professionals of Fairfield—a physician, a pharmacist, ministers, and a few educators—thoroughly integrated into the blue-collar black community. The Italian American families operating small neighborhood grocery stores also lived in the black area. The smoke and soot that was belched out of the prospering steel mills polluted the air—a fact we were all aware of even though nobody thought of the environment in a formal sense. Yet Fairfield was, for its blacks, a safe community with little or no violence. Its elementary and high schools and the dozen or so churches shaped its social agenda and, to a great extent, its values, which I believe led so many of its children to high achievement.

In Birmingham I saw a number of things I'd never seen in Sumter County. Sitting on the porch of my new home one evening shortly after we arrived, I heard an unfamiliar sound about two blocks away. After hearing it a second time, I went into the house and asked my mother what was making the sound. She said to me, "Oh baby, that's a streetcar." "Streetcar," I thought to myself. "What in the world is a streetcar?" I could hardly wait until the next morning to go out on our porch and see a streetcar. From our porch I could see railcar number 7, which ran from downtown to the end of the Vinesville line, which was in sight of my house. I thought that the streetcar looked a little like a train, which I had seen on two occasions when I had accompanied my parents to the train station in Livingston to see off some relatives. I was nearly equally excited about the electric lights in our house. Back in Livingston I had never been in a home with electric lights. In our new home each room had a single light bulb at the end of an electric cord that extended about two and a half feet from the ceiling.

Starting Elementary School

Our relative isolation back on the farm had restricted my social contacts to just a few children who lived a few miles from our farm with whom I visited on occasion. Now I was somewhat hesitantly making friends with children next door and across the street. Yet when it was time to enroll in school that September, about a month from my sixth birthday, I was frightened. My mother walked me to the 61st Street Elementary School, later to be named Robinson Elementary in honor of the woman who was then its principal. On my first day I cried something awful when my mother sent me into the building and began her walk back home. The children thought I was such an oddity and poked fun at me for crying. I was also the only redhead in the entire school and that, too, was a source of jokes from the other pupils in the elementary and high schools. Many of the males in the Bell family had bright red hair, which only turned dark as we reached adulthood. But after a week of being escorted to and from school by my mother and after stern warnings from my teacher and my mother that I had "better stop crying," I ceased doing so. But it took weeks more before I actually felt comfortable in school. I gave strict attention to Mrs. Wilhite, my first grade teacher, watching her so intently that she began to kid me about it. She would sometimes forget where she placed some objects and would turn to me and say, "Richard, I know you can tell me what I did with that eraser." Most of the time, I could.

In December 1941 Japan bombed Pearl Harbor and the United States was drawn into World War II. When my father was drafted for service he was sent to Fort McClellan for his physical. Because of near deafness in one ear and partial deafness in the other, he was turned down for military service. Several of his brothers served in the armed forces during the war. All returned home after the conflict.

My days in elementary school turned out to be good ones and I was consistently on the honor roll. My fourth grade teacher, Mrs. Mary Williams, thought I was too advanced for the fourth grade and persuaded the principal to skip me to the fifth grade. It worked out fine except that unlike the other fifth graders, I had not mastered my multiplication tables and had great difficulty doing so for the first six weeks.

My mother was always very attentive and strict about my doing my schoolwork. Each weekday she sat with me on the porch, reviewing my homework with me for the next day. She drilled me in reading and arithmetic, sometimes into the early evening. Many times when I was distracted by other children out playing, she swiftly pulled a switch from a nearby tree and used it to strike me as punishment. At a very early age she had ingrained in me that I was expected to do well in school.

Fairfield Industrial High School and E. J. Oliver
From 61st Street Elementary School I went to Fairfield Industrial High School (FIHS), just a block from 61st Street. It offered grades eight through twelve. Its principal was one of the best, most respected, and most feared educators I

ever met in my educational career. Professor Edmond J. Oliver ran his school, including his handpicked faculty, with stern discipline and high expectations. He inspired us with assembly speakers who were role models. Honor students, of whom I was one, were brought to the auditorium stage before the student body for recognition every six weeks. Each year several juniors and seniors at the school were selected to compete in the statewide high school academic competition at Alabama State College in Montgomery in several disciplines. The top five performers in each discipline were awarded place ribbons. Fairfield Industrial students always did well in the competition. The glass exhibit case in the principal's office was filled with ribbons students had earned over the years. One of my greatest disappointments and embarrassments in high school was my failure to win a ribbon in my year of competition.

Prominently displayed in the first floor hall across from the principal's office was a glass-enclosed bulletin board containing pictures of graduates who had been inducted into the Fairfield Industrial High School Hall of Fame. The inductees were those who had been the first to achieve some worthy milestone after graduation, for example, the first physician, the first attorney, or the first Major League Baseball player. We all longed to be in the Hall of Fame. When I became the school's first Ph.D. in zoology my dream of being a Hall of Fame inductee was fulfilled.

E. J. Oliver inspired us in numerous ways. Sadly, the school fell victim to racial integration under Oliver's successor and was closed. Today's FIHS graduates from throughout the world still meet every July 4 in Fairfield for a reunion. Hundreds attend and recall the glory days at FIHS and repeat stories about E. J. Oliver, who attended each reunion until his death.

A Guy Named Willie Mays

The best known of many talented athletes to graduate from FIHS is Willie Mays, a member of the Baseball Hall of Fame and without a doubt the most electrifying athlete I ever saw. In high school we all knew Willie as "Buck Duck," his nickname. In fact all male students and some female students had nicknames by which they were better known. I graduated knowing everybody's nickname but not everybody's real name. My nickname was "Papa," which had been given to me in early childhood by my mother. While in high school Willie Mays was an All-County first team Most Valuable Player in basketball and football and played baseball on the local sandlot team called the Fairfield Graysox. In the spring of eleventh grade he turned professional and began playing baseball with the Birmingham Black Barons. The Barons were managed by another FIHS great, Lorenzo "Piper" Davis, a three-sport athlete from Piper, Alabama, who played Triple A baseball for the Boston Red Sox. Only his relatively advanced age at the time blacks were allowed to compete in the Major League kept him from the big leagues. He was one of the Negro Baseball League's greats.

Mays, who was two years ahead of me in high school and who lived with his father, known as "Cat" Mays, two streets over from my home, was a community hero because of his great athletic talents. Although I played sandlot basketball and football with Mays on occasion, I was never one of his gang. I followed his career closely, however. When I lived in St. Louis and Mays's Giants team came to town, I went to the ballpark early to get a centerfield seat, just to watch Mays warm up. He was just that exciting. When I began my second campaign for mayor in 1983, Willie Mays came to Birmingham as the guest speaker for my fund-raising dinner. He packed the ballroom at the Birmingham Convention Center and raised about $270,000 for my campaign. He returned to Birmingham at my request on several other occasions during my tenure as mayor. I was his overnight houseguest at his New York City condominium on two occasions. Mays remains an athletic hero to me and I feel the same exciting twinge and tug of heart when around him today as I felt when I was around him back in our high school days.

Angelina Ray

Two other memories of my high school days should be mentioned. Among the fine faculty E. J. Oliver assembled was an attractive young English teacher named Angelina Ray. Her equally attractive young sister, Mattie, was my brother's teacher in elementary school. Several times during the year the Ray sisters visited our home to discuss our academic progress with our parents. I have vivid memories of those two beautiful women seated on our front porch glider talking to my parents. But aside from her beauty and talent as a teacher, Angelina Ray was the English teacher who taught me all of the grammar I know today. Until I reached her classroom during my first year at FIHS, I did not know how to conjugate verbs or write properly. After studying under her I was never again without a consciousness about either. A few years later Angelina Ray married the Reverend John Wesley Rice, who coached my brother in basketball at FIHS and pastored a Presbyterian church in Birmingham. The Rices had a daughter, whom they named Condoleezza. Condoleezza Rice, of course, was the former provost at Stanford University and the national security advisor of foreign affairs in President George H. W. Bush's administration. At this writing she serves as secretary of state under President George W. Bush. On a couple of occasions in Birmingham I spoke with Condoleezza about my fondness for her mother as one of the best teachers I'd ever had.

My curriculum at FIHS included a course in Negro history that E. J. Oliver required every student to take. How he persuaded an all-white school board in those days to adopt Negro history as a required part of the curriculum when it was done nowhere else in Alabama I don't know. But after all, the man was an extraordinary educator. As seniors we were all required to write an essay on Booker T. Washington's book *Up from Slavery.*

Despite its fine academic program, the school had no academic counselors so I and many other students who planned to attend college spent our last two years in a vocational program rather than the pre-college academic program the school offered. At the end of our sophomore year, Oliver met with us in the auditorium and asked who was going to college. The few who said yes were directed into the pre-college program. The others were directed into one of the vocational programs. FIHS, like most other black U.S. high schools, emphasized vocational training. Blacks were thought not intellectually equipped to study liberal arts. Booker T. Washington was a major proponent of "trades" education for blacks, while his nemesis, W. E. B. Du Bois, argued for liberal arts training for blacks, especially for what he called "The Talented Tenth." In my case, even though I knew I was going to college because my parents had mandated it, I was not sure at the time how I would be able to afford college. I was also greatly influenced by my closest school buddy, Thomas Harden, who suggested we go into the vocational program. So we both opted to go into the tailoring trade. But so many students wanted to go into tailoring that Professor Oliver decided to allow us to put our names in a hat and the first fifteen names drawn got into tailoring. Thomas and I were not in the fifteen. So at Thomas's suggestion we both opted to study dry cleaning, which we did in the afternoon during our junior and senior years. However, both Thomas and I ended up in the 1951 freshman class at Miles College.

Miles College and the University of Detroit

During the summer after my junior year of high school I worked as a mortar mixer for a plasterer at fifty cents an hour. For several summers prior to that one I worked as a mortar mixer and carpenter's assistant for my dad. He never paid my brother or me one red cent. So earning fifty cents an hour was a great advancement. Those earnings paid for school clothing for my senior year. The summer after my senior year I began working at Howard Cleaners, a downtown dry-cleaning and laundry facility. I continued to work there for the next three years while I attended college, doing every job at the plant, including firing the boilers, cleaning clothes, and driving the truck for branch deliveries. The earnings from part-time work during the school year and full-time summer work paid my expenses for college. After nearly four years at the cleaners I got fired during my senior year in college for reporting to work late one day.

At Miles College Thomas and I and the other FIHS graduates had no problem passing the college's mathematics and English entrance exams. Those failing the exam were not denied admission to the college but were required to spend their freshman year studying remedial English and mathematics, for which they received no college credit.

At Miles I was again blessed to come under the influence of some good teachers. Mrs. Verdell Martin, a psychology teacher, asked me during my sophomore year what discipline I had chosen as a major field. I admitted that I had not made a decision. In fact, I had no idea what I was going to major in. She told me that she thought I had a strong aptitude for sciences and sent me to talk with a biology teacher, Emmett Jones. As a result I majored in biology. Mr. Jones took a special interest in his majors and encouraged some of us to seek graduate degrees. Before he mentioned graduate school, I had no idea what it was. He encouraged me to apply for admission and a teaching fellowship at his graduate school alma mater, the University of Detroit. I did so and with his strong reference, I was admitted and given a teaching fellowship, which carried a monthly salary and tuition reduction for teaching freshman laboratory classes in biology.

In the fall of 1955 my wife, Barbara, whom I had married during my sophomore year, and I took a Greyhound bus from Birmingham to Detroit where we lived with Barbara's sister and her husband, Gertrude and James Huby, while I studied at the University of Detroit. It was my first trip outside Alabama. We lived with the Hubys until January 1957, when we were expecting our first child, Anthony. I then secured an apartment in one of the city's public housing projects located at the intersection of West Canfield and the Edsel Ford Freeway.

During my tenure at the University of Detroit I combined my incomes from my teaching fellowship and my work on the 3–11 P.M. shift at the Ford Automobile Foundry with reimbursement from the State of Alabama under a program that paid black Alabama residents a tuition differential for graduate study at out-of-state graduate schools. (Barbara also worked for a while at a local senior citizen facility as a dietician.) The program was designed to keep Alabama's white state graduate schools racially segregated by paying black Alabama graduate students for the extra cost they incurred in having to leave their home state to take graduate school courses offered or available at Alabama white state colleges.

The University of Detroit was a new experience for me in several respects, but the most significant for me was that it was my first experience in a racially integrated school. Of the 12,000 students enrolled at the university, fewer than twenty were black. I was the lone black graduate student in the biology department during my first year. A second black, Sue Chapman, a Detroit native, became a graduate student in the department during my second and final year there and eventually became a dentist.

The integrated environment was stressful to me, a black from rigidly segregated Alabama. During all of my years in Alabama the only whites I knew were those I worked for at Howard Cleaners. I felt quite uneasy among the white graduate students. On some weekends in the office assigned to graduate teaching fellows, during horseplay between the male graduate students, one of them would suddenly grab me and beginning jostling or wrestling. I was bewildered. They apparently thought nothing of it or even suspected that I did. In my classes I felt as though I were carrying the weight of the entire black race on my back. I had to know the answers when the teachers asked me questions. If I didn't, I felt I had let the black race down. That is the kind of insecurity and feelings of inferiority twenty years of racial segregation in Alabama had left me with. Young American men were being drafted to fight in the Korean War between 1955 and 1956. I avoided this because I was a student and married. With a newly earned master's degree in biology from the University of Detroit, my family and I, now totaling three, returned to Birmingham where I went to work as an assistant professor of biology at Miles College. My salary was $390 per month for nine months.

Marriage, Children, and Divorce

I met Barbara when she was a high school senior at Westfield High School, which was located in a steelworker's camp adjacent to the city of Fairfield. I was a freshman at Miles College at the time. Barbara was a beautiful girl, a very popular student, and a talented athlete. She was an all-state first-team girls basketball player and a majorette in the Westfield High band. Even today I marvel at how I, a shy, seventeen-year-old college freshman who had never had a girlfriend, began dating such a well-known and popular local girl. But I remember how it began, almost as if it were yesterday. One night at the Greystone, the local social gathering spot and dance hall for high school students, Barbara Watts made a rare appearance. It was my first time seeing her outside the marching band or off the basketball court. All of my friends were very much aware that the "great Barbara Watts" was at the dance. I sat across the dance floor from where she was seated, slipping long glances at her when she didn't notice. When several guys approached her and asked for a dance, I noticed that she refused. Summoning all the courage I could muster, with my heart in my throat, I weak-kneed it across the floor and asked her for a dance. She readily accepted.

After that dance I watched as she turned down requests from several other guys for a dance. But each time I asked she consented. I was suddenly "dancing on clouds." Now I wanted to know if I could call her. "Yes," she said and gave me her phone number. After the dance on my way home with my friends Thomas and George, we talked about nothing else but how I, "Papa," as they called me, the quiet bookish kid, had caught the eye of Barbara Watts. In the weeks that followed, I was constantly on the phone with Barbara. Eventually her parents consented to my dating her at her home on Wednesday and Friday nights. I never missed a single date night, taking the "nickel Willie" bus between Interurban Heights and Westfield. The last bus from Westfield to Interurban Heights ran each night at 10:00, and I had to be on that bus. One evening I lingered in Barbara's living room, with both of us hating to part and with her mama calling out from the bedroom, "Bobbie Jean, let that boy go." As I went out to the front porch to leave, the bus passed by and I had to walk the four or so miles to my home. I took off at a fast pace, alternating walking and running, trying to make it home before my 11:00 curfew. I was about four blocks from home when I met my dad in his car, out looking for me. It was past 11:00 and my mom insisted he go look for me. I didn't get a tough time from my dad. But boy did my mama chew me out when we reached home. I never again missed that 10:00 bus.

When Barbara and I first started dating, I learned that she had been attracted to me because of my bright red, bushy Afro-style hair. She told me that when she went home that first evening we met, she told her mama she had met a boy with red hair. Her mother's reply was, "Aw girl, you know that boy dyes his hair." Our relationship became so intense that Barbara's mother, Corene, was anxious to get Barbara away to Alabama State College in Montgomery, a hundred miles away from Birmingham, in order to put distance between Barbara and me. But I constantly begged my dad to let me use his car to drive to Alabama State to visit Barbara, where she was a majorette in the college band and played basketball on an athletic scholarship. Whenever I visited her at the college, she skipped classes and hung out with me at the Hornet Café on the corner of the college campus until it was time for me to leave to arrive back home before dark. At the end of my sophomore year, at age eighteen, on June 20, 1953, with parental consent, Barbara and I went to my minister's home and were married. She moved into my parents' home with me. She would eventually matriculate and graduate from Miles College, my alma mater.

Our oldest child, Anthony, was born in 1957, just before I completed my work for my master's degree in biology at the University of Detroit. Back in Birmingham, where I went to teach at Miles College, we were blessed with two more children, Kenneth and Kevin. Angela was born while I studied at the University of Oklahoma, and then Erica, our last child, came along once we were back in Birmingham again.

School and raising children kept us busy. But after nearly twenty years of marriage, Barbara's and my interests had diverged. She had become devoutly religious and read the Bible constantly, while my interests were in academics and politics. Barbara decided to leave the Baptist church we had worshiped in and join the Holiness Faith. On my birthday in 1974, Barbara and I agreed to dissolve our marriage by divorce. A month later the divorce decree was granted. Barbara would later marry a minister of the Holiness Faith and I would marry Rachel Reynolds Gilmore, formerly of Montgomery, Alabama.

I met Rachel when she joined my staff at the Alabama Center for Higher Education in 1973, just after she had obtained a divorce in her first marriage. With a master's degree in business, she worked as the finance officer of the center. Prior to that time she had taught in the Birmingham Public School System as a supply teacher and later worked on the local staffs of the Federal Reserve and the Federal Bureau of Investigation. In the fall of 1974 we began dating, and we were married on July 18, 1975. We had two children, Matthew and Jennifer Rose, and were married for twenty-seven years, until Rachel filed for divorce in August 2002.

A Registered Voter at Last

The major political focus of blacks in Alabama up through the mid-1960s was gaining the right to vote in a very hostile environment where whites used every means at their disposal to prevent blacks from voting. The question asked of blacks from the members of the Board of Registrars ranged from valid questions about the Constitution and local government to the ridiculous and the preposterous. In addition, in many places in the South, especially in rural Alabama and Mississippi, blacks who dared to register to vote or encourage other blacks to attempt to do so were the targets of intimidation and violence from whites.

During those years black civic leagues drew up and circulated throughout the black community of Birmingham a list of the questions registrars often asked black applicants when they sought to register. Through this method the leagues were able to produce a study list of most of the board's questions. But even knowing the answers to the questions, something most blacks doubted the registrars knew, did not assure one of the right to vote. Blacks were totally at the whim and mercy of a hostile white Southern society, determined that blacks would never have any significant voice in politics.

In October 1955 I turned twenty-one. Returning home to Birmingham in December of that year for the short Christmas recess, my first priority was a visit to the Jefferson County Board of Registrars. Holding a bachelor's degree and currently studying for a master's degree, I went nervously to the Jefferson County Courthouse in downtown Birmingham and into the first-floor office of the Board of Registrars. I was greeted by a very kind, white, middle-aged female registrar. She spent about five minutes asking me questions about my background and education. And then, just as I readied myself for her questions about the Constitution and government, she surprised me by saying, "Please raise your right hand" and swore me in as a registered voter. She then congratulated me and let me sign my oath—not a single question on government. But even though more blacks were being permitted to become registered voters in Birmingham by 1955, my experience was still an exception to the general practice of registrars in Birmingham and was still virtually unknown in rural Alabama.

EXPANDED EDUCATION OPPORTUNITIES

In October 1957 Russia launched Sputnik I, the first satellite in space. It was a clear sign that Russia, a major communist power, was ahead of the United States in space exploration. That event had a major impact on federal public policy regarding higher education in the United States, especially in the sciences. Congress soon enacted legislation, which it called a new national defense act. Among other things, this act made loans available to college students and provided special financial incentives for college science teachers to further their education. Through programs of the National Science Foundation (NSF), competitive grants were available to teachers in the sciences for further graduate study. Several NSF grants made it possible for me to leave the Miles College faculty in the summer of 1959 for further graduate study. I first attended New Mexico Highlands University for research study in genetics. From there I went to the Medical College of the State University of Iowa (Iowa City) to study radiation biology. After spending the 1960–61 academic year studying molecular biology at Washington University (St. Louis), I returned to Miles to teach for two years. In the summer of 1963 I was accepted into the doctoral programs in zoology at several universities. I chose to attend the University of Oklahoma. In August 1963 I moved my family, now including three children, to Norman to pursue a Ph.D. in zoology. Norman was largely a university town with a permanent residential community of 25,000, which included only one black family. By the time I arrived at the university, the institution had been permitting blacks to enroll there for a decade and a half. In 1948 a federal court had compelled the university to admit black students in the famous *Sipuel v. Oklahoma State Board of Regents* case.

My life at the university was pleasant and productive. I matriculated there from 1963 to 1966. Aside from academics, I have several recollections about that period. First, about a month after I arrived at the university from Birmingham, the tragic 16th Street Baptist Church bombing in Birmingham took place. It occurred on the morning of September 15, 1963, killing four young girls who were attending Sunday school. I learned of the bombing that Sunday afternoon while watching television with my family at our Norman apartment. I was shocked and sickened. I knew the families of two of the young girls. That heinous act made me as bitter as I have ever been about any crime. Leading up to that tragic Sunday there had been more than forty unsolved dynamite bombings of black churches and homes in the City of Birmingham.

The year of 1963 had been a year of vigorous black protests against racial injustices in Birmingham. In the months leading up to my departure from Birmingham for the University of Oklahoma there had been bitter clashes between largely black citizens peacefully protesting Birmingham's bedrock racial segregation and the city's racist city commission led by Eugene "Bull" Connor. Daily civil rights protests had taken place on the streets of Birmingham and hundreds of protesting children had been jailed. Connor had employed police dogs and high-powered fire hoses in an attempt to break up demonstrations. His tactics attracted negative international attention to Birmingham. In addition, George Wallace, the new fiery segregationist governor of Alabama, had stirred the pot of racial hatred with speeches made in Birmingham and elsewhere in Alabama during this period.

Biracial Dialogue in Birmingham

Although I had not participated in any of the civil rights marches held in Birmingham, I had attended meetings of local black leadership in Birmingham in 1962 and 1963 at which strategies for petitioning local city government had been formulated. Students from Miles College had begun to protest segregated lunch counters in downtown Birmingham in 1962. The president of Miles College, Dr. Lucious Pitts, had become a leading spokesperson for the protest movement and Birmingham's black community. Students and black clergy of the city led protests. Dr. Pitts drafted me to attend the early strategy sessions of blacks who were attempting to get white city fathers to rid the city of its segregation laws. My assignment was to keep a record of the discussions at the meeting and to draft public statements setting forth black requests and demands, which he and other members of the group like Dr. James Montgomery, a physician, issued at news conferences. The group of about fifteen persons instructed me to draft a "Statement of Concerns of Birmingham's Black Community," which it adopted and forwarded to members of Birmingham's corporate community and city government. As a result of this statement of concern and petition, white corporate leaders consented to meetings between black and white leaders. In their brief written acceptance to meet, the white group suggested that each group have ten members to participate in these biracial discussions. At this point few biracial discussions took place in Birmingham and if they did, it was done with the utmost secrecy. It was against city law for blacks and whites to meet in the same room. A U.S. senator from Idaho who dared walk through a door marked "colored" to speak to blacks was arrested by Connor. I still remember the black group's meeting at Dr. A. G. Gaston's office on the morning the group received its acceptance from the corporate community for biracial discussions. There were about a dozen of our group present at this particular meeting. Those I recall are Gaston, Montgomery, Pitts, Peter Hall (civil rights attorney, later to become the city's first black municipal judge), Arthur Shores (civil rights attorney), Abraham and Calvin Woods (brothers and clergy), W. C. Patton, and Edward Gardner.

The acceptance statement from the white corporate group named the members of its group's committee who would participate in the discussions and also named the members of the black group's committee. This bold action of the whites naming the blacks to speak for the black community insulted the black leaders. They agreed to do two things—to accept the invitation for the proposed discussions and to inform the white group that the day had passed for whites deciding which blacks spoke for the black community. They would, they said, choose their own representatives. Montgomery and Calvin Woods were dispatched as couriers to the white group to deliver this message and the acceptance of the biracial discussions.

On that afternoon or the next morning the black group met again at Dr. Gaston's office to read the response the white group had sent back with Montgomery and Woods. They reported that the white group had agreed to arrangements for the initial meeting of the biracial group and had sent an apology for its inappropriate action of naming the committee members of the black group. They did, however, request that our group inform them as to who we planned to have represent our committee in the discussions. Our group quickly began to name its members for the discussion committee. When they had finished after about thirty minutes of discussion, they had selected nine of the ten persons who had been named initially by the white group. The only difference was that a black woman, whom none of us in the group knew but who had been on the list of blacks named by the whites, was omitted. Instead, Peter Hall, who incidentally had refused to sign our earlier "statement of concern" because he said that the statement attacked the courts and it would be improper for him, an attorney, to sign such a statement, lobbied the group for the tenth spot on our discussion group. I saw the irony and found it slightly amusing. In fact, what happened was that all of the blacks suggested by the whites were present at our meeting and no one there was going to insult one of them or cause a division by leaving off one of the persons earlier named by the whites. Only the name of the woman was left off. I'm sure that if she had been at our meeting she would have been included in our discussion group. This type of behavior was typical of the black leadership. In earlier meetings we had held lengthy discussions about naming black members who might be asked to make public statements to the media on behalf of the black community. When the names of some young black professionals, such as Clarence Woods, who headed the local Urban League chapter, were suggested, there was nearly unanimous agreement that such people were "too militant" to carry out such a role. At one point A. G. Gaston responded to the suggestion of having Woods as a spokesperson by saying, "No, no, we don't want folks who might refer to the white police officers as pigs."

By March 1963 Connor's tactics had so embarrassed the city that the Chamber of Commerce and certain other white civic groups, such as the Young Men's Business Club and the Birmingham Bar Association, set in motion a successful move to hold a referendum to change the city's form of government from a city commission to a mayor-council form of government. This move was aimed largely at removing Connor, now the symbol of Birmingham's defiance against racial justice. It culminated in November 1962 with city voters deciding in a referendum to adopt the mayor-council form of government. As a result, an election for mayor and council was scheduled for March 5, 1963.

Connor and his fellow commissioners would not go away quietly, however. First Connor sought office as mayor and was narrowly defeated in the April 3, 1963, mayoral runoff by Albert Boutwell, former state lieutenant governor and a "moderate" segregationist. Connor and his fellow commissioners then refused to leave office, maintaining that they had been elected to serve four-year terms as commissioners and still had several years left. For several weeks the City of Birmingham had two city governments, both meeting weekly, on the same day, at city hall. They both adopted and approved the same agendas and actions. This continued until May 23, 1963, when the Alabama Supreme Court ruled that the mayor-council form of government was the certified government of Birmingham.

Within twenty-four hours of the April 1963 mayoral runoff election Dr. Martin Luther King Jr. and the Southern Christian Leadership Conference (SCLC) launched its planned and twice-delayed assault on Birmingham's racial segregation.[4] The planning had begun in late 1962. By May 1963 protestors filled the city jail and detention centers, and negotiations, which eventually led to a settlement, were under way. Dr. King led the March on Washington on August 25, 1963. The September 15, 1963, bombing of the 16th Street Baptist Church was a despicably horrible act, which even to this day comes to mind whenever I pass the church. When I eventually became mayor, during my first week in office I asked to review the police department's file on the investigation of the church bombing.

At the University of Oklahoma

Norman, Oklahoma, was new to me and I was not knowledgeable about its racial customs when I arrived there. This lack of knowledge led to a few unpleasant experiences for me. The first occurred on the afternoon I arrived at the university. Since the university had informed me by mail before I left Birmingham that all of its housing for married students was taken and I would have to search for private housing in the community using the university's list of approved housing, I went to the housing office to request the list. When I asked a woman at the desk in the outer office for the list and showed her my letter, she hesitated for a few seconds. Then she said to me, "I need to go speak with someone on the staff." After a few minutes she returned with another woman who explained that I could have difficulty finding private housing in Norman for my family and me. Therefore she had been authorized to assign me to the university apartment complex for married students on the old south navy base, which was now the university's property. I gladly accepted, relieved that I would not have to search for housing for my family. No sooner had we settled into our new apartment when I was greeted by one of my neighbors, George Tipton, who was black and a married graduate student in music. In our conversation I related to him how fortunate I felt I was that I would not have to go out searching for housing. He quickly explained to me that the Norman community was all white and would not rent or lease housing to blacks. I was surprised and said so. He said that the campus of the university was a "fishbowl" in which black students were given accommodations available to other students. But he told me that should I go into downtown Norman, about five or six blocks from the campus, the restaurants and bars would not admit me.

I should have suspected this but I was not familiar with Oklahoma's racial customs. Back in Alabama where racial segregation was the order of the day, I knew the rules and avoided going to public places where I would not be admitted and would only be served from a window in the back of the establishment. In new territory, I did not know the rules. Still, I found it strange in my days at Oklahoma that black foreigners, such as those from Nigeria, were accepted in the Norman community and leased private housing in the community. My guess is they at some time must have encountered the same racial discrimination I did. I later learned that university housing kept a list of private homes in Norman that would lease to black foreigners.

The thoughts about racial discrimination in Norman did not linger for long in my mind. My children were readily accepted in the public schools and on sports teams. We attended an overwhelmingly white Baptist church recommended by one of my white professors where we were always greeted warmly. So there was not my usual preoccupation with race and place. My fellow graduate students in the department were all quite friendly. My major professor, Dr. Harley P. Brown, a Mobile, Alabama, native and his wife, Kiffy, adopted my family and often had us to their home for dinner. Sometimes on the weekends they came to our apartment unannounced and invited us or our children to join them on their outings or field trips.

Most graduate students in my department spent the day in class or teaching laboratory and spent each evening doing research or making preparations for laboratory classes. My practice was to ride my bike to campus at 7:30 A.M. and back to our apartment about 5 P.M., eat dinner, and after about an hour, return to the zoology building where I remained until around 10 P.M. One evening four of us graduate students finished our nightly responsibilities early and my three fellow graduate students, who were white, suggested we go to a pub on the edge of the campus that was frequented by students. When we entered the pub it was packed with people, most of whom were partaking of the establishment's main item—beer by the pitcher. After a few moments we found an empty table, took a seat, and each ordered a pitcher of beer. The waiter returned with three pitchers of beer, one for each of my friends but none for me. "Must be tough to carry four at a time," I thought as he gave a pitcher to each of my friends. Then he looked at me and said, "Sorry, we don't serve you here." For a couple of seconds there was just embarrassed silence at our table. Then one of my friends said, "Let's get out of here." And we did. Outside they were all very apologetic and tried hard to convince me to accompany them to another establishment where they knew I'd be served. I insisted that they go on without me and I headed to my apartment.

One of my zoology professors, Dr. Carl Riggs, was a member of the Norman City Council. The next day I told him what had happened and said I planned to file a complaint about it with the Oklahoma City chapter of the NAACP. A day later he sent for me and suggested, "Get your same friends and go back to that establishment." He assured me that I'd be served but I did not go.

The southeastern area of Oklahoma is often referred to as "Little Dixie." I had never given any thought to why. But one day when one of my classes was wrapping up an all-day field trip down in the area, we decided to go to a steakhouse, which we had passed earlier in the day. We entered and seated ourselves at a corner table and began chatting away, laughing and kidding. Shortly thereafter a woman, not the waitress but perhaps the owner or manager, came over and beckoned one of the women in the group to the side. She spoke softly to her and the student came back to the table and said we would have to move into a private meeting room. We all glanced at one another, just then realizing that the restaurant did not serve blacks. I was the only black in the group. I immediately said, "Oh no, go ahead and eat, I'll just wait outside." "Oh no," pleaded several of the women in the group. "Please, Dick. Come on, let's eat together. We're sorry." Well, I did stay and order a meal. But to this day I've never gotten over the indigestion from the indignity or my acceptance of it. It's not that I was ever openly "militant" about racial prejudice in such settings; I had spent my whole life avoiding places where I knew or suspected I would not be served because of race. Somehow, after being exposed to places outside of Alabama where I encountered no open racial hostility, I had let my guard down.

BACK TO BIRMINGHAM

In May 1966 I was awarded my Ph.D. in zoology from the University of Oklahoma and headed back to Miles College to work as chairman of the Science Department and eventually as academic dean.

By 1966 Birmingham had experienced the throes of change and upheaval. By 1963 the Birmingham civil rights movement led by Dr. Martin Luther King Jr. and the Reverend Fred Shuttlesworth had forced social and political change in Birmingham, none of which had come easily. Racial bombings, the castration of a black man, and other unspeakable horrors had occurred in recent years. I remember that shortly after the 1954 federal school desegregation ruling that Shuttlesworth and his wife were severely beaten with chains by Klansmen at Phillips High School in downtown Birmingham before hundreds of onlookers as they tried to enroll their children in the school. Mrs. Shuttlesworth was stabbed and the Shuttlesworths narrowly escaped in a waiting car, which had brought them to the school.

Another incident occurred on Mother's Day, May 14, 1961, at the Birmingham Trailways Station downtown at 4th Avenue and 19th Street North. Klansmen had lain in wait for the freedom riders to arrive, and when they did, the Klansmen viciously beat them, badly injuring a young white freedom rider named James Peck. The Birmingham police, who had been forewarned of the freedom riders' arrival and had been asked to protect them, arrived at the scene fifteen minutes after the beating. The Birmingham civil rights movement became the major catalyst for the enactment of the 1964 Civil Rights Act, which desegregated schools and public places. In addition, demonstrations in Selma, "the day on the Edmund Pettus Bridge," and the Selma to Montgomery march led to the 1965 Federal Voting Act, which quickly removed the barriers to blacks' exercising their voting rights wherever those barriers still existed. The impact on Birmingham and Alabama as a whole was significant. In 1960 only 9.5 percent of blacks of voting age were registered voters. By 1966 38 percent were registered.

In May 1970 I left the faculty and administration of Miles College to become the executive director of the Alabama Center for Higher Education (ACHE), a consortium of the eight four-year historically black colleges in Alabama. The center and staff were housed in the 2121 Building in downtown Birmingham. It operated with a staff of twenty and an annual budget of $10 million, mostly from foundations and grants. The Board of Directors was made up of the presidents of the eight colleges. I had served as director of ACHE for about fourteen months when I was first approached about running for political office. The office I decided to run for was an at-large seat on the Birmingham City Council.[5]

3

THE CALL OF POLITICAL LEADERSHIP
The Council Race and First Mayoral Election
(A Revival of Hope)

It was my habit at the Alabama Center for Higher Education (ACHE) to work late into the evening. One evening in the summer of 1971, three young black men, Jesse Stewart, Al Thomas, and another man whose name escapes me, visited my office. Much to my surprise, they had come to ask me to enter the 1971 Birmingham mayoral campaign. Impressed as I was with the civic concerns of these young men, I had no desire to seek the office of mayor and told them so. In fact, I'd never given a single thought to seeking political office. In November 1968 Arthur Shores, the state's leading civil rights attorney, had been appointed to the Birmingham City Council by the council to fill a vacancy created by the death of one member. Thus he became the council's first black member and was elected to the council when his appointed term ended. If I wouldn't run for mayor, would I run for the City Council, they asked. My mind hastily searched for a "diplomatic no" to that question too. But, being sensitive to and appreciative of these men's concerns about their city, I sought to buy time to find out the best way to say no. So I said to them, "Why don't you let me think about it. Come back tomorrow and we'll talk about it." I was thinking and hoping they wouldn't come back, but by late afternoon the next day they were back in my office, committing themselves to me for more than they could reasonably be expected to do if I would enter the council race. Having no place to hide, and aware that I had as much obligation as these young men to work for our city and knowing the embarrassment I would feel if I said no to them, I consented to enter the race and did so in September. There were twenty-nine candidates seeking the five at-large council seats.

Raising campaign funds turned out to be difficult. The promises of campaign funds from Stewart and his friends did not materialize. In fact Stewart was one of the candidates and was busy in his own campaign. Another candidate was David Vann, a well-known attorney and former law clerk for U.S. Supreme Court Justice Hugo Black. I had read about Vann but knew little of him. Early in the campaign at a community candidates' forum, Vann called me aside, pulled a sizable roll of dollars from his pocket, peeled off $500, and handed it to me. He said that it was a campaign contribution from Emil Hess, a local businessman who had asked Vann to give Jesse Stewart and me $500 each. Hess was a well-known, successful local Jewish American businessman who contributed to numerous charitable causes. Hess's generosity and relatively liberal views had earned him the enmity of Birmingham's hardcore segregationists. He and his family were often the target of death threats. Still, he quietly helped fund the campaigns of two black candidates. His $500 contribution was my largest single contribution in that race. On October 12 two of the three incumbents up for reelection, Don Hawkins and Russell Yarbrough, were reelected. Three seats remained to be filled in the November runoff by the top six runner-up candidates. My making the runoff made me the focus of vicious campaign rumors.

At a luncheon for candidates sponsored by a women's civic group, one lady asked me to respond to the rumor that I was a womanizer, particularly with white women. I was caught completely off guard, as were some of the organization's other members. I had never heard that rumor and could not help but wonder if the woman was a political plant whose purpose was to hurt my political chances. Anyway, I fumbled through my response, trying to appear calm while assuring her I was a faithful husband and a good father.

Another more persistent rumor was that I had been forced to resign my position as dean at Miles College for misappropriating college funds. There was of course no truth to that rumor either. Vincent Townsend, a top official of the *Birmingham News* and a key powerbroker in Birmingham, came to my rescue. When I told A. G. Gaston, the city's leading black corporate citizen, about the damaging rumor, he sent me to see Townsend, whom he called a friend. Townsend knew I had worked as college dean when Lucious Pitts, a respected educator, was president of the college. By then Pitts had left Miles College to become president of his alma mater, Paine College in Augusta, Georgia. Townsend suggested that I ask Pitts for a strong letter of endorsement addressed to the *News*, which Townsend promised me would get prominently published in the paper. Pitts, who was highly respected among both the white and black leadership of Birmingham, wrote a fine letter that received wide reader attention. It effectively undercut the rumor, which was hurting my campaign. This was my first of several encounters with Vincent Townsend and my introduction to the influence he wielded in the community. The headline of the city's morning newspaper, the *Birmingham Post-Herald,* on November 1971 the morning after the runoff election read: "Vann, Arrington, Proctor Win: Liberals named to Council." Thus I became the second black on the Birmingham City Council, joining distinguished civil rights attorney Arthur Shores.

Birmingham's black community had mixed reactions to my election to the City Council. While blacks in general seemed pleased to see a second black in city government, many younger blacks apparently believed that I would not be an effective, militant voice for blacks' concerns. In fact, some doubted I would be vocal at all. Many callers on local black talk shows expressed the view that Arthur Shores was not militant enough as a City Council member and that I, a college professor who had never been in the forefront of Birmingham's recent civil rights movement, also lacked the major qualification that Birmingham's black elected officials must have in order to be an effective voice for the black community—militancy.

Early in my first term on the council I undertook special efforts to focus my attention on the areas of transportation and communication, minority hiring, the Birmingham Police Department's mistreatment of the city's black citizens, and police reform. In the area of transportation and communication, I played a leading role in getting state legislation passed to establish the city's first Public Transit Authority. I had come on the council at a time when privately owned public transit systems were abandoning the transportation business because it was no longer profitable. Many cities throughout the country had already made the transition from privately owned systems to publicly owned ones. This transition took place in Birmingham during my first year on the council. The history of the publicly owned transit system in Birmingham has been rather bleak, even to this day. The first Public Transit Authority had no source of funding except for fare box revenue, which of course was totally inadequate. Over the ensuing twenty-seven years the battle to provide adequate local government support for public transit has resulted in only piecemeal funding. The major local support at first came solely from the City of Birmingham. Several years later state legislation was passed as part of a political trade-off for support for the County Health Department, which required the Jefferson County

Commission and the City of Birmingham to provide annual financial support for the system from a new one-cent county sales tax. This continues to be their position despite the fact that the federal government provides an 80 percent federal match for each 20 percent of local support. While nearby cities such as Atlanta, New Orleans, and Nashville took advantage of federal assistance by providing the local 20 percent match and built fine public transportation systems consisting of bus and rail, Birmingham did not and is still saddled with an inadequate public transit system. For over three decades the overwhelming majority of suburban communities have refused to support an areawide transit system. In the area of communications I provided the leadership for developing all city legislation and policy regulations for the city's cable television franchise in 1972.

Later, into my second four-year term on the council, I brought the city's hiring practices on minorities under scrutiny by raising the issue repeatedly in council meetings, sponsoring city ordinances aimed at increasing minority and female hiring, and producing a statistical study on the city's hiring of black applicants certified to the city by the county's personnel board as "qualified" to fill various job vacancies. Despite these efforts, it would be 1982 before the city appreciably increased its hiring and promotion of blacks and women.

It was my championing the issue of police reform, especially fighting police abuse of black citizens—or, as it was generally referred to at the time, "police brutality in the black community"—that catapulted me into political prominence and earned me the unwavering political support of the overwhelming majority of black voters over my twenty-eight-year political career. It also earned me the eternal enmity of the city's police union, the Fraternal Order of Police (FOP), and most of the city's white voters.

I was elected to a second four-year term on the at-large City Council in 1975, despite the negative criticism I had from the local FOP and Birmingham's white community for my constant attacks on the administration of George Seibels and the Birmingham Police Department. The *Birmingham Post-Herald* praised my work on the council in its October 8, 1975, editorial, calling me a public official "who remembers that government is for people." I won reelection to the council without a runoff, placing second to veteran council president Don Hawkins in the number of votes received. The increasing black vote, though still a clear minority, was becoming a major political force in the city election.

The 1975 election brought other political changes. Bessie Estell, a retired black school principal, became the third black elected to the City Council, joining Arthur Shores and me to give the city government three blacks on the at-large council. David Vann, who served a four-year term on the council with me from 1971 to 1975, had thrown his hat in the ring to challenge two-term incumbent mayor George Seibels.

THE 1975 MAYORAL ELECTION

During my first council term I was constantly at odds with Mayor Seibels over the issues of minority hiring by the City of Birmingham and police brutality against black citizens. I had introduced several fair hiring practices ordinances that received majority support from the City Council and in a very pivotal vote received unanimous council support following an earlier mayoral veto by Seibels. That veto and the growing black vote in Birmingham would prove decisive in Seibels' loss to Vann in the 1975 mayoral election. For two terms as mayor, Seibels had enjoyed the strong support of the city's black voters. He had been the first city mayor to visit the black community and openly seek black political support. His reluctance to stand strong against police abuse of black citizens and his veto of my affirmative hiring ordinance, however, haunted him in the black community in the 1975 mayoral campaign. Despite dissatisfaction in the black community with Seibels over these issues, it was still not easy to pull the black vote away from him. Many black community leaders had a fondness for Seibels because of the personal attention he had given them. He was also a far cry from the fairly recent Bull Connor administration, which blacks remembered with bitterness. In two mayoral elections he had gained more than 80 percent of the black vote.

I set out with Tony Harrison, a black state legislator from Birmingham, to deny Seibels the black vote. We identified influential black community leaders, met with them, and made a strong case for black support for Vann rather than Seibels. Many of them, wanting badly to support me because of the stand I had taken for fairness for blacks in city government over the previous four years, reluctantly agreed to support Vann, but not without asking me with heartfelt concern, "Are you sure we are doing the right thing?" Harrison and I continued to rail against Seibels, using every opportunity given by black media and other forums to speak of the shortcomings of his administration. Still the battle was not won. The black weekly newspaper the *Birmingham World* endorsed Seibels for reelection, saying the blame for some of the administration's shortcomings rested with the City Council. It said nothing about his position on minority hiring and police abuse.

But the nail in the coffin for Seibels came when we located an editorial written two years earlier by the late Emory Jackson, editor of the *Birmingham World*, just after Seibels had vetoed my affirmative action ordinance. The editorial, which Jackson titled "Seibels Is Not Our Friend," was a scathing political attack on the mayor. I quickly bought space in the *Birmingham World* and ran a reprint of the Jackson editorial.

To this day I believe the editorial, which was widely circulated throughout Birmingham's black community, and the respect that the community still had for the late Emory Jackson, a major freedom fighter for black rights during his lifetime, sealed Seibels' fate with black voters. I would later say, "Emory O. Jackson reached from his grave to defeat George Seibels."

With election day approaching, Seibels sensed his loss of black support and focused on attracting Birmingham's white voters. He accused Vann of creating, with my assistance, a "bloc vote" in the city election by distorting the facts. Those tactics, he said, threatened to destroy the progress the city had made. In Birmingham the term "bloc vote" meant "black vote" and it had often been used in earlier years to defeat any white candidate who sought the support of blacks. But times were changing in 1975 and the "black vote" Seibels had ridden to victory twice was a force to be reckoned with.

Nearly 60 percent of Birmingham's 112,000 registered voters went to the polls in the November 1975 election. Vann beat Seibels by a margin of 1,300 votes. Eighty percent of Vann's support came from Birmingham's black precincts. The issue of police misconduct had helped set the stage for Seibels' defeat and Vann's victory.

The Birmingham Police Department was essentially the same department that Bull Connor had headed and whose violent disregard of the humanity of black citizens had come to public attention during the 1963 civil rights demonstrations in Birmingham. Connor's tactics and brutality were still fresh in the minds of many Birmingham citizens. Twelve years had passed since Connor had been turned out of office as the city police commander when city voters opted to change the city from a commission type of government to a city council form. As noted earlier, Connor had not left without a fight, even after voters approved the change. Connor eventually sought and won statewide elected office as a member of the Alabama Public Service Commission, which regulates utilities in Alabama.

The First Mayoral Election

One morning in early August when my wife and I were getting ready to fly to Washington, D.C., I received a call from the Reverend Elijah Jarrett asking me to meet with him and some other ministers at his church, Trinity Baptist, which was located on Graymont Avenue. At the meeting, the ministers asked me to consider running for mayor in the upcoming election scheduled for October, barely two months away. I asked them to give me time to think it over, promising that we would get together upon my return to the city in a few days. En route to Washington, Rachel and I talked only briefly about my meeting with the ministers. Her advice to me was to "do it if you want to." Then our conversation turned to our disappointment over the mayor's handling of the Bonita Carter case (see chapter 4). I had hoped to hear more from her about my running for mayor, but I did not push it. I was not sure what I wanted to do. The local media were already speculating about my candidacy for mayor. As far back as January 19, 1979, the *Birmingham News* had reported that I had said that my chances of winning the mayoral seat were good, if I chose to run.

On Monday, August 20, a couple of days after we returned from Washington, Jarrett called me to set up another meeting with the ministers the next day at his church. "The issue is still on the front burner," I said to my wife after hanging up the phone. "What are you going to do?" she asked. "Dunno," I mumbled. "I'll see what they are saying." I guess I was sounding like a candidate who wanted to be drafted.

When I walked into the church's cafeteria where the ministers had gathered, Jarrett said, "Come on and have a seat, Brother Mayor." We all laughed. Abraham Woods Jr. and Jarrett did most of the talking, explaining to me why it was time for a black mayor in Birmingham and why I was the most logical candidate. "Langford's running, but he can't win," said Jarrett. "We ought to be able to get him to drop out," he said. "Don't you think you can win?" Woods asked me. "Well . . . I think I can win—if we get black folk out to vote," I said, weighing my words. "Hell, we'll just get 'em out. They're mad. They're ready," said Jarrett. Then Jarrett said, "We've already called a press conference for noon tomorrow and we are going to draft you then, so be ready." I wasn't sure if Jarrett was bluffing, but I thought that a draft would look too contrived. So I said, "Why don't I just declare that I'm running?" "Okay. Good," several of them said almost in unison. "Let me call my wife," I said. Jarrett led me down the hallway and into his office. I picked up the phone and dialed my wife. "It's on. I'm going to announce at a news conference tomorrow. You wanna come?" "No, you go ahead," she replied. "You okay?" I inquired. "Oh, yes. Shoot, I think you can win. I think the people really want you to run, Richard. You know I'm with you." I hung up the phone. She sounded like she already knew, I thought. Then I reached over to Jarrett's desk, opened a pad of paper, and began to write my statement declaring my candidacy for mayor.

At noon on August 22 on the steps of Trinity Baptist Church, flanked by Woods, Jarrett, a number of other ministers, and the presidents of the Urban League and the NAACP, I declared my candidacy for mayor and promised a victory. Several reporters asked me if I really thought that I could win. I assured them that I did. I explained that I had been pondering running for mayor for weeks after the ministers and some neighborhood presidents had broached the subject with me.

I had hoped that the pressure for me to run for mayor would subside as some of the uproar of the black community over the Bonita Carter case died down. But the emotions over the issue still burned hotly. Nor did the earlier entrance into the mayor's race of Larry Langford, a black member of the City Council, reduce the pressure on me to run.

The day after I announced, the *Birmingham Post-Herald* reported that Langford said that my entering the race would not affect his plans to run for mayor and scoffed at rumors about his withdrawal. About a week later, I learned that some of Langford's supporters were miffed that I got into the race. I had told Langford a few weeks earlier that I was 90 to 95 percent sure that I would not enter the race for mayor.

Another person who was troubled by my decision to run for mayor was Birmingham's leading black businessman and millionaire, Dr. A. G. Gaston. A few days after announcing my candidacy I was summoned to Gaston's office. When I arrived there, Vincent Townsend was present as well. Gaston told me that I had made a mistake by entering the race. He said that I couldn't win, "but Vann surely would." He told me that I should call a news conference as soon as

I could and withdraw from the race. Townsend was in agreement and told me that if I'd withdraw, he would see that I got support for mayor when the time was right. I told them that I had a large following of citizens who wanted me to run. Unfazed by the claim, they told me the support for a black mayor was not yet there. After about thirty minutes, I left Gaston and Townsend, promising that I would think about what they had asked, but knowing all the same that I was in the race to stay. I did not speak to either of them on the subject of withdrawing again. On October 11, leading the seven-member mayoral field in the primary by a huge margin, just short of what I needed to win outright, I was summoned by Gaston to his home. He congratulated me and apologized profusely. "Richard," he said, "I just didn't think the white folks would ever let a Negro win. Boy, you just tell me what you want me to do for the runoff and you can count on it. You need any money?" I thanked him, really feeling good that this amazing man, whom I had always admired, was proud of me. I was never again without his support and counsel.

THE 1979 CAMPAIGN

By the deadline for filing for candidacy in the mayor's race, three blacks and four whites had filed. In addition to David Vann, the incumbent mayor, Larry Langford, and me, Don Black, John Katopodis, Mohammed Oliver, and Frank Parsons had also filed.

Don Black, a young white man about thirty years old, was the local Grand Dragon of the Ku Klux Klan. No doubt the Bonita Carter incident and the arrest of some Klansmen for protesting on behalf of the officers involved resulted in his decision to run. He made regular appearances at candidates' forums. A rather handsome, dark-haired, well-dressed young man who spoke well, he didn't fit my stereotype of a Klansman.

John Katopodis, an articulate and sometimes controversial member of the City Council who held a Harvard Ph.D., entered the race as had been expected. He was a Birmingham-area native who was quite liberal by local white standards. On the City Council he and Larry Langford had become very vocal political allies and were both being backed in the mayoral race by the local FOP. Katopodis's campaign manager was Steve Moon, a Birmingham police officer. I suspect that prior to my entering the race, the strategy was for Langford to draw heavily on the black vote that had helped elect Vann, while Katopodis attacked Vann as "weak" in supporting police officers, hoping that it would help Katopodis capture most of the white vote.

Frank Parsons, a local attorney from the city's heavily white and conservative eastern area, reflected the views of that area. He had not sought political office before and was considered a long shot in the race.

Mohammed Oliver, a young black laborer, was the candidate of the Socialist Workers Party. His presence in the race was solely to express the Socialist Workers platform. His party ran a candidate in each city election, alternating among black, white, and female candidates.

The issues in the campaign boiled down to crime, the economy, and race. Crime was an issue because Birmingham had experienced nearly eight years of increasing crime rates. That factor, tied to the controversy about the Bonita Carter case and my attacks on police brutality, made it ripe for the campaign. It also became the issue around which race was raised. Both Vann and Katopodis tried to subtly suggest that the election of a black as mayor would probably result in higher crime rates. In some newspaper political ads Vann had specifically cited the cities of Atlanta and New Orleans as examples of cities with both black mayors and rising crime rates. I labeled those characterizations as "racial."

At the time of the election, Birmingham's economy was in shambles. Its unemployment rate was more than 20 percent, a result of the steady decline of the city's once powerful steel industry and the large national unemployment rate, which topped 20 percent. The weak economy had forced a budget shortfall, which Vann had sought to address by not filling city vacancies, including those in the police department. His failure to hire more police officers brought him under attack by the FOP and John Katopodis. Hence, Vann, the incumbent, found himself under attack from all sides—a black community unhappy because he had not given stronger support to firing the officer who shot and killed Bonita Carter and a white community that thought him too liberal. Throw in the city's weak economy and Vann instantly became the most vulnerable of the serious candidates.

Fund-raising for my campaign was as tough as I anticipated it would be. A September 30 *Birmingham News* report, issued twelve days before the election, showed that Vann had contributions totaling $72,000. Katopodis reported $22,000; Parsons showed $41,000; Langford listed $3,000; and my campaign had raised $14,000. Black and Oliver would not divulge their campaign contributions. At that time there was no law in Alabama that required any candidate for municipal office to divulge his campaign contributions or expenses.[1]

By election day all candidates had received additional campaign contributions. The totals reported by the *Birmingham News* listed Vann at $90,000 and Katopodis at $30,000. My contributions had grown to $19,000, nearly all from volunteer groups at black churches. Of the 200 contributors to my campaign, only four gave as much as $500 each: Dora Rosen, my only publicly known white supporter; a political action committee of the city's largest bank, Am South; the black Metropolitan Democratic Women's Committee of Ensley, led by my campaign committee chairperson, Bernice Johnson; and volunteers of Trinity Baptist. Four contributors gave $200 each and the rest gave between $5 and $100.

I had been told in confidence by several *Birmingham News* reporters that the editorial staff of the paper had agreed to endorse me. I waited with anticipation for the endorsement. I thought that an outright endorsement of my campaign would help me with white voters. On Sunday, October 9, the *News* published its endorsement for mayor. But instead of an outright endorsement, the *News* co-endorsed Vann and me, saying either would make a fine choice. I called my source at the paper and asked what had happened. I was told that the top executive of the paper, who had earlier approved his editorial board's outright endorsement of me, was at home viewing the local news at 5:00, which reported that I was leading the field with 42 percent of the vote and the next candidate was a distant second. He reportedly called the news office and ordered that the endorsement editorial be revised to a co-endorsement of Vann and me.

Fifty-five percent of the city voters went to the polls on October 11. As the campaign progressed I had come to believe that I would win the election without a runoff, which required 50 percent plus at least one. It was not to be. I led the field of candidates with 44 percent of the vote, or 31,521 votes. Frank Parsons got 16.9 percent (12,135 votes), edging out Katopodis, who got 16.8 percent (12,038 votes) for second place and a position in the runoff with me. Vann received 11,450 votes (15.9 percent). Langford had 2,856 votes (4 percent), Black, 1,771 votes (2.4 percent), and Oliver, 69 votes (0.1 percent).[2] I had failed to get the endorsement of the city's major black political organization, the Progressive Democratic Council, headed by attorneys Arthur Shores and David Hood, or the endorsement of Dr. A. G. Gaston. Both endorsed Vann.

However, in the runoff, which took place three weeks later, they became strong supporters of my campaign. I also failed to attract much of the white vote, getting only 3.5 percent.

The runoff election was set for October 30. During the three-week interim the enthusiasm of the black voters did not wane. The fears and predictions that black voters would not go back to the runoff vote proved to be wrong. The scent of political victory and the frustrations from years of neglect and abuse by city police and the Bonita Carter incident inspired black voters. For the October 9 primary, 60 percent of Birmingham black voters went to the polls versus 57 percent of the white voters. Whites made up 56 percent of the voter rolls. A very well-financed and organized effort by Birmingham's corporate community to increase white voter turnout for the runoff brought the total up to 62 percent, but it was not enough. Black voter turnout increased from 60 percent in the primary to 72 percent in the runoff. Black voters would not be denied.[3]

The polls closed at 7 P.M. and excitement and apprehension were running high after a day of heavy voting throughout the City of Birmingham. Arrington campaign workers began arriving at the ballroom of the Holiday Inn on 20th Street on Birmingham's Southside shortly after the polls closed. The hotel, built a number of years earlier as the Parliament House, is adjacent to the campus of the University of Alabama at Birmingham and had been selected as the site for the Arrington campaign victory party. Many campaign volunteers came directly to the hotel from their assigned tasks for that day. By 8:00 the ballroom was overflowing with Arrington supporters, many straining to look at the voting returns on the single television screen located at the front of the room. Others talked nervously with one another about the get-out-the-vote activities of the day, no doubt anxious about the election outcome. News reporters, some with television cameras, joined the already overcrowded ballroom.

Up on the eleventh floor suite of the hotel I waited with my family and members of my campaign staff. My father and mother, Richard and Ernestine, were seated by my wife and me on the suite's largest couch. We had arrived together as a family at the hotel at about 7:30. This was my family's first post-election campaign night event. My mother, nervous and smiling, kept reaching over and rubbing my father's knee. If Daddy was excited or nervous, he hid it well. He had taken off his coat and sat quietly gazing at the television reports on the election returns. As I recalled, Dad only looked different to me because he wore a suit and tie, which he only donned on special occasions, such as church services. At all other times, whether working or relaxing, he wore his brown khaki work outfit. My brother, James, his wife, Gloria, and their children were included in the group. As I glanced around the room at those present, the gathering reminded me of a family reunion—my eight children, my brother's children, my grandchildren, and a few in-laws. Woods and Jarrett were also among the group. At about 8:00 David Vann joined us for the evening. Just minutes before 9:00, the final unofficial vote tally came on the television screen. It showed that I had 44,798 votes, or 52 percent, to Frank Parsons' 42,814 votes, or 48 percent.[4] Immediately cheers, hugs, and shouting broke out in the suite. People embraced one another and me.

Downstairs in the crowded ballroom the crowd exploded with joy. Their victorious shouts could be heard throughout the hotel as well as outside. By the time the final vote tally was reported, the entire first and second floor (mezzanine) meeting areas of the hotel were jammed, mostly with yelling, crying, and applauding black supporters. The growing crowd crushed flowerpots, chairs, and other hotel furniture accessories. Soon police and fire inspectors arrived at the hotel, stopping arriving supporters from entering the already overcrowded hotel. Hundreds stood outside, some pushing to try to get inside. Car horns could be heard blowing throughout the downtown area. Police reported to my campaign manager, Lemorie "Tony" Carter, that all streets leading to the hotel from all four directions were gridlocked for five or six blocks with cars carrying people who were trying to get to our hotel. Some drivers, caught in the gridlock, abandoned their cars in the street and headed for the hotel on foot. Fire marshals said no one else could be permitted in the hotel because of safety regulations. Tony soon came over to me, raised his arms, and hushed the crowd in the suite and announced that it was time for us to head downstairs to the second floor ballroom where our supporters were anxiously waiting. Inside the suite instructions were being given by Tony and my two security guards, whom Tony had hired for the campaign, as to how we would proceed down the elevators and to a holding area until everyone in the suite could join my family and me for our walk into the ballroom. Every single person in the suite wanted to be a part of the entourage.

Just as we had quieted the joyous group and were preparing to leave, the telephone, which had been ringing constantly for the last fifteen to twenty minutes, rang again. It was 9:15. Someone answered the phone, listened for a few seconds, and beckoned to me to come over to the phone. Holding my two-year-old son, Matthew, in my arms in preparation for the journey down to the ballroom, I pushed through the group to the phone. On the other end was the president of the United States, Jimmy Carter, calling to congratulate me on my election victory.[5] Among the things he said to me was, "Your election is a great day for Birmingham and the nation." Now somewhat excited myself, I thanked President Carter for calling and accepted his offer to visit him soon at the White House.

When we finally reached the second floor ballroom it was 9:30. The joyful crowd was so thick that it took a while for security personnel to clear a path through the crowd to the stage. As I walked through the crowd, my son in my arms, my wife at my side, and my mom, daddy, and children and the rest of the entourage from the suite following, people pushed forward, trying to shake hands or touch me. Others in the crowd climbed upon whatever they could find to catch a glimpse of me. It was a happy but somewhat scary scene. The floor shook and the wall-to-wall people reveled in victory. Finally we reached the stage. I looked out over the crowd and got choked up as they chanted with glee. I thanked and congratulated them, telling them that they were the hardest-working volunteers any candidate ever had, which I believe to this day. After a few more comments I asked the Reverend Jarrett to offer prayer. For a short time afterward we stood on the stage, reaching down to shake hands with supporters. Then we began the slow process of moving from the stage back through the crowd and toward the elevators to the suite. Once back in the suite I talked with a couple of reporters from the local newspapers. It was about 11:00 when the crowd began to thin out and my family and I headed for home with all of the family members in tow.

It was an evening I would not forget; indeed, it was historic. I had just been elected the first black mayor of the City of Birmingham. It was an election that made the front page of newspapers around the world. It seemed to many who knew about Birmingham's history that the impossible had happened. Birmingham had joined two other major cities, Atlanta and New Orleans, in electing a black mayor. The significance of my election victory was brought home to me clearly about a year later when Rachel and I visited Copenhagen as a part of an Alabama delegation on an economic development trip. Somehow a Copenhagen newspaper learned of our stop in the city and carried a short story about our being there. That same evening, the mayor of Landskrona, Sweden, a small town just across the bay from Copenhagen, sent a courier to our hotel room with an invitation for my wife and me to be his guests of honor at a luncheon at his city hall the next day. We graciously accepted his invitation and at about 11:30 A.M. the next day we boarded a small boat for a fifteen-minute ride across the bay to Landskrona. As we debarked, the mayor and other city officials welcomed us. As we walked toward city hall, about a half city block from the pier, two middle-aged Swedish women came up to me and one asked, in perfect English, if I was indeed the mayor of the City of Birmingham, Alabama. After my affirmative reply, she said, "Well, we just had to come to see it for ourselves because if Birmingham, Alabama, can elect a black for mayor, there's hope for the world." I've recounted this story to several groups I have addressed in Birmingham.

I've thought about the deeper meaning of this story during some lonely hours of my mayoral tenure, times when I faced difficult issues and some disappointments and failures. I came to realize that my election as Birmingham's first African American mayor was not just historic; for many, it was a vindication of their faith in the promise of our nation and our city, and a fulfillment of their fondest hopes. Like me, many had believed that they would not see a black mayor in Birmingham in their lifetime. Yet, unlike me, many had been the foot soldiers in the civil rights struggles in Birmingham, Selma, and Montgomery. They saw some of their dreams fulfilled in my election. Sadly for me, I had never marched with them or felt the sting of the water hoses or police batons, or the bite of vicious police dogs. My election was the fruit borne of the campaign they had so courageously waged. I saw the hope in the eyes of many as they warmly grasped the hand of "their mayor" at the victory party and the inaugural reception. I came to understand that it was about more than pride—it was about hope, hope that from this victory we would build a new Birmingham, one that fulfilled its great promise and would once again be the "magic city."

During the trying times in my tenure as mayor, such as when an initiative that was important to me failed or during the shame of the federal investigation of my administration (see chapters 7, 8, and 9), I would return to the hope and faith entrusted in me by the 1979 mayoral election. Each time I would redouble my efforts to build a stronger city. If people believed that my election was a symbol of hope for our city, I could not let it be otherwise.

It had been an interesting and exciting journey to that evening at the Holiday Inn. And it had come to a joyous end, but as the philosopher Henrietta Szold, founder of Haddash, said, "There is no ending that is not a beginning." The evening of October 30, 1979, was a milestone on a long journey ahead. How I got to that milestone and the twenty-year journey that lay ahead are the experiences I talk about in these memoirs.

INAUGURATION

My induction and inaugural ceremony was held at 10:00 A.M. on Tuesday, November 13, 1979, at the city's old municipal auditorium, which was named in honor of its first mayor under the mayor-council government, Albert Boutwell. It was a beautiful, sunny, November day, and people began arriving at Boutwell Auditorium as early as 9:00 to claim a seat in the 7,000-seat arena. Shortly before the ceremony the auditorium was filled to capacity and the city fire marshals were turning people away. The jubilation of the campaign victory in the October runoff was clearly in the air among the throng of Arrington supporters in attendance. They were joined by an equal number of Birmingham's white community who had come to witness this historic event for their city.

An impressive array of dignitaries attended the ceremonies from within and outside the State of Alabama. Among the participants seated on the platform were President Jimmy Carter's aide Jack Watson, who represented the White House; Ethel Kennedy, wife of the late senator Robert Kennedy, and their son Robert Jr.; Alabama senators Howell Heflin and Donald Stewart; and Alabama's Republican congressman John Buchanan. The list of state dignitaries was headed by Governor Fob James and Lieutenant Governor George McMillan, who was one of my strongest supporters, as well as members of the Alabama Supreme Court. Also present were Mayor David Vann, former mayor George Seibels, mayoral candidates Frank Parsons, Larry Langford, and John Katopodis, and all the members of the City Council and the Jefferson County Commission.

The two weeks between the runoff election and the inaugural ceremony had been hectic. I spent nearly every day in news conferences, greeting callers in person and via phone, and making brief appearances at various community affairs. The election of a black mayor in Birmingham was international news and quite a few members of the international media came to Birmingham in the weeks following the inauguration. My picture and the story of my election were carried in papers throughout the world, many times on the front page. Birmingham had not received such international attention since the days of the 1963 civil rights movement in the city. I asked Rachel to plan the program for the inauguration and she quickly put together a very diverse inauguration committee. She planned an important biracial ceremony that projected a theme of unity for our city. She and I were in total agreement that the events should be a step toward political and racial healing in the city. Religious leaders, black and white, Jews and Gentiles, were a part of the program. Predominantly black and white high schools and the Alabama Symphony Orchestra performed at the program. Each speaker on the program proclaimed the day a new beginning for Birmingham. Following my eight-minute inaugural address, J. V. Jenkins, a local black gospel singer, moved the crowd with his soul-stirring rendition of "Here I Am Lord, Send Me."

The theme of my inaugural address was best captured by a phrase I used near the end of my address: "I know where we are, I know where we've come from, and I know where we yet have to go as a city."[6] The two Birmingham daily newspapers used that quote for their front-page headlines the next day.

I had hoped to convey to the packed auditorium that I was fully aware of Birmingham's troubled past, its progress, and the work we still had to do as a city. I recounted my father's decision to move his family to Birmingham, and I spoke of the city's rich natural resources and the crises of the cholera epidemic, the Great Depression, and the racial strife that it had endured. But I also emphasized that the Birmingham of 1979 was quite different from the city of yesteryear. I reminded them that with all of the city's great natural resources, its greatest asset was its people. It was more than mere rhetoric. I knew from my eight years on the City Council that the city had made significant progress over the previous decade. It was also true—though not spelled out in my address—that another major crisis loomed on Birmingham's horizon: an economic crisis.

An inaugural reception open to the public was scheduled for 6:00 that evening. The fast pace leading up to the inauguration had given me little time to work on an address, although I had thought about it during my busy days. It was not until late in the evening the night before the inauguration that I sat down at home and began writing my address. I wrote the closing paragraphs the next morning after arriving at the mayor's office at about 8:30 and handed it to my longtime secretary, Jesse Huff, to type. By 9:30 I had reviewed the typewritten copy several times and released it to the media.

Among those packed from floor to balcony in the Boutwell Auditorium for the inaugural ceremony were many Birmingham police officers, including a number behind and around the beautiful red, white, and blue draped stage. As expected, several anonymous phone calls had been made to city hall that included death threats. But these calls alone were not the reason for the heavy police presence. About two weeks earlier Birmingham police chief Bill Myers had come to my office accompanied by two FBI agents. They informed me of the possibility of an assassination attempt on me by some members of the local Ku Klux Klan.[7] As they reported to me, and as my FBI files I obtained under the Freedom of Information Act twelve years later would show, on Friday, November 2, 1979, at 8:50 P.M., a young white woman in Cincinnati, Ohio, had called the Cincinnati office of the FBI and informed them of a phone conversation she had with her father, a suburban Birmingham resident, a day earlier. He reportedly said that he and several of his fellow Klan members had been approached and offered money to assassinate me. After apparently thinking about it, she decided she would relay the conversation to the FBI in Cincinnati. The FBI office there contacted the Birmingham FBI office, which then contacted city hall. While we said nothing publicly then or later about the threat, our police were advised by the FBI to provide me with heavy security. The FBI found the local Klansman, who verified the alleged offer, which he said he rejected. Nevertheless, he was kept under FBI surveillance and the city put on guard. The Birmingham Police Department's Tactical Unit and a number of other officers in civilian attire discreetly surrounded me as I mingled with the zealous crowd following the inaugural ceremony and at the reception. While a local reporter took note of and inquired about the heavy police presence, nothing was revealed about the Klan threats; only the anonymous phone calls to city hall were mentioned. There was only one brief moment of alarm, and it occurred during the evening reception in the upstairs Exhibition Hall of the Boutwell Auditorium. As we stood in the reception line surrounded by well-wishers, someone accidentally brushed against a switch that controlled the light directly over where we stood. The lights went off momentarily, leaving our area of the hall in semi-darkness. Immediately my fourteen-year-old daughter, Angela, began to scream, apparently thinking the assassination attempt was under way. Officers immediately surrounded me and the lights were quickly restored. The scream caused a stir and a fuss among the crowd, but no one really knew why she had screamed. We learned later that she had been extremely worried about the threat since being told of it earlier that evening. For the next ninety days the Tactical Unit provided around-the-clock protection for me. Each evening a detail guarded my home, and each day two detectives picked me up from home and remained with me until I returned home in the evening.[8] Anonymous phone threats were fairly common during my first year in office.

One other serious threat on my life was uncovered during my first year as mayor. I accompanied the police chief and his officers on several raids on illegal whiskey houses in the city.[9] As a result, several local whiskey house operators put up $10,000 and hired a New York City hitman to kill me. We learned of the threat from an undercover officer who had infiltrated the circle of whiskey house operators.[10] It was somewhat unsettling to sit in my office and listen to the tape of the operators discussing a hit on me and hearing several stepping forward to put up a portion of the $10,000. Our undercover officer had been wired and recorded the entire meeting.

Except for this last incident, I received only two other threats on my life during the remainder of my twenty-year tenure as mayor. I'm glad I didn't have to think about such threats too often because my days and nights as mayor were filled with trying to reshape my city and preside over it during some major transitions.

4

POLICE BRUTALITY
Terrorism in Birmingham

When I speak of "major transitions" the city had to confront, it may seem strange that I begin with a discussion of police reform. But there are two reasons for doing so. First, Birmingham is internationally known for its oppressive police department led by its infamous racist police commissioner, Eugene "Bull" Connor, during the 1960s, and though he was a decade and a half removed from city government, his legacy still tainted the department and a small but significant number of its officers. Second, Birmingham's police department, with a small minority of black officers, was viewed by blacks as a symbol of racial oppression and division. If the city was to progress socially and economically, the negative perception by blacks and much of the nation had to change. Connor's police department and tactics were largely responsible for this negative image.

The shadow of Bull Connor, as seen by the world during the 1963 civil rights movement in Birmingham, remained. The police department was still viewed by the city's black community with fear and suspicion. Some of the reasons for this are reflected in the 1977 publication of the National Police Foundation titled *Police Use of Deadly Force*. The study had been commissioned by the foundation's president, Patrick Murphy, a former police chief of New York City. The report studied police use of deadly force on citizens in American cities, focusing on seven cities. Birmingham was cited as a "most noteworthy exception" to cities its size for the use of deadly force by its officers. The number of police shootings of civilians per thousand officers or by comparative population size was far greater than that of cities twice its size.[1]

One must also remember that Birmingham's black population was soon to become the majority and its black citizens were just beginning to assume a voice in city government. The city's police department had 30–35 blacks among its 700 uniformed officers. I knew that Birmingham would never be made "whole" or have total reconciliation or a full sense of community until the city's black population believed in and supported its law enforcement officers. Blacks' fear and suspicion of law enforcement had to be replaced by trust and cooperation. If my city were to continue its progress, especially socially, there had to be a major overhaul of the police department.

It would probably be wrong to state that police abuse of blacks prior to the 1980s was unique to Birmingham. It was, to say the least, a common practice throughout most of the South and in several large urban areas above the Mason-Dixon Line. But none surpassed Birmingham in its vile hatred and violent abuse of its black citizens. Much of this is attributed to Bull Connor, who ruled the city unchallenged. Even during my growing up in Birmingham, my parents' greatest fear for my safety stemmed from rampant police abuse of blacks, males in particular.

Some have said that Connor seized Birmingham by its throat and held it captive to racial hatred, division, and fear. But I have always thought of Connor as a politician who captured the heart of most of Birmingham's white citizens with the vilest form of racial demagoguery of the mid- to late twentieth century in America. He had a special understanding of the depth to which white racial hatred of blacks went in Birmingham. Exactly how the roots of racism found such fertile soil in Birmingham, a city that did not even exist at the time of the Civil War, still remains a mystery to me, despite having read historical and sociological accounts of its causes. No local politician was more powerful than Connor in his heyday, where choosing elected officials in the South was largely the domain of the white community. White voters in Birmingham had voted for Connor in large majorities.

Jamie Moore, who had come up through the ranks of the Birmingham Police Department, was Birmingham's police chief from 1956 to 1972 and remained in that position until George Seibels appointed James Parsons as his successor in late 1972. But for a significant number of the 700 or so police officers, the practices and attitudes of the Connor years persisted. While violent acts of brutality against black citizens were carried out with frequency by only a minority of the members of the department, they enjoyed solid backing from departmental members against any disciplinary action for such behavior. Under the Seibels administration, more attention was focused on improving relations between the Birmingham Police Department and its black community. But disciplinary action for unauthorized police conduct toward blacks was sorely lacking.

One would have to have lived in Birmingham during the Connor days and the succeeding eight to ten years and perhaps be black to understand the black community's fear of and resentment toward the police department. One experience in 1972 brought home to me the continuing reality of the situation. Each year in December, the Birmingham Graduate Chapter of Alpha Phi Alpha, the oldest black college fraternity in the nation, held its major social event, the Black and Gold Ball, in the Municipal Auditorium in downtown Birmingham, just across the street from city hall. The ball was the highlight of the social season for the city's black elite. Alpha boasts among its membership many of the most distinguished black American leaders of the nation. On its roll were men like Martin Luther King Jr., Whitney Young, about three-fourths of the nationally known black leaders, and an equal percentage of the black college presidents, including men like Benjamin Mays of Morehouse College. The local graduate chapters of Alpha throughout the nation were more likely than not to include the community's leading citizens, those known for civic service and professional achievement. I can say with authority that was the case in the Birmingham Graduate Chapter of which I was a member. In fact, in my early days as a college teacher, I was especially proud to be included in that chapter. Its membership roll was a Who's Who in black Birmingham. As a young professional, I was inspired by my older brothers in the chapter, men such as James Montgomery, Arthur Shores, Peter Hall, W. Whetstone, and W. Dewy Branch. Association with them inspired me and undergirded my aspirations to work hard and become a high achiever. Alpha demanded no less, we were constantly admonished.

Clarence Mitchell, an Alpha fraternity brother who was chairman of the 1972 Black and Gold Ball, came to my office several days before the event. He wanted me to speak with the police chief, explain who our organization represented, and ask him to request that his officers not harass persons leaving the ball, which always ended at 1:00 A.M. It was commonplace for those leaving the affair to be stopped, for no ostensible reason, and questioned by police officers—and sometimes be insulted by them. I told Mitchell that I would speak to the chief about his request, but I never did. Fortunately there were no reported abusive incidents by police that evening, but I became even more determined to fight the abuse. I knew quite well that any black male driving the streets of Birmingham, especially at night, ran a high risk of being harassed by a small group of Birmingham officers. If you were black and driving at night and a police car pulled in behind you while driving or waiting at a traffic light, you became very tense. You would constantly take quick glances into your rearview mirror until you were out of the sight of the patrol car. There was good reason to feel that way. Black men had no rights that white policemen had to respect, and an interaction with an officer could be dangerous. That fear was common among black men because of the history of the Birmingham Police Department.

I decided that the most effective way to deal with this longstanding problem was to use my position as a council member to document police abuse of citizens and to focus public attention on it. Jimmie Franklin details a number of the cases I recorded in *Back to Birmingham* and made public, and I will not discuss most of them here.

I began to take affidavits from victims of police abuse, recording in detail what had happened and using their own words. Included with some of these affidavits were snapshots of the individuals to show the injuries they had sustained. I also had some victims come before the City Council while they were still swollen and bruised. Once it became public knowledge that I was documenting cases of alleged police brutality, victims readily came forward to file complaints with me. The very first person to file such a complaint with me was an Italian American resident of the western area of the city who had been convicted several times for various violations. He alleged that after he was arrested at his residence following an altercation with an officer, he was handcuffed, taken to a deserted area where he was badly beaten by the arresting officers, and then taken to the city jail. His previous arrests did not make him the ideal victim for my first public complaint. However, I filed a complaint on his behalf and made his affidavit public at the council meeting. While his criminal record gave the FOP the opportunity to portray him as "typical" of the kind of citizens I was complaining about, it did not allow them to convincingly refute that the incident had occurred. Also, the fact that the complainant was "white" in a race-conscious city drew greater public attention than it would have if he had been black.

Of the numerous complaints filed with me, only several of the alleged victims were white. In each case I publicly requested an investigation and a report on each complaint of Mayor George Seibels and Police Chief James Parsons.

After several complaints, I then sponsored city ordinances requiring police officers to take anyone arrested with the use of physical force to the local emergency room before release or incarceration. Such a policy, I maintained, would protect the city and its officers against false allegations. The City Council could hardly argue against such a policy and quickly adopted it. But the policy also gave us a medical record to document injuries a victim had sustained. Prior to that, victims who had been injured during arrest were placed in jail without any medical attention. In every case in which police used force to make an arrest, they alleged that the victim resisted arrest and assaulted the officer. But now under the new policy, every such person had to be given medical attention.

It soon became apparent that a common pattern existed in these particular arrests. Victims, according to their affidavits, were generally handcuffed by arresting officers, taken to an isolated location away from witnesses, and beaten. While all cases alleging the use of excessive force by officers were serious, some were particularly savage. The case of John Sullivan, a twenty-six-year-old black man, is one example. On July 18, 1975, Sullivan was returning home from his work on the 3:00–11:00 P.M. shift at a local plant and stopped at a service station to make a purchase. Three Birmingham police officers dressed in plainclothes questioned Sullivan and an argument between Sullivan and the officers ensued. Witnesses at the station reported that two white male officers grabbed and restrained Sullivan, while the third officer, a white female, struck him with her police baton. With his arms restrained by the male officers, the victim kicked the female officer as she attempted to strike him again, knocking her to the ground. The officers subdued Sullivan, handcuffed him, and placed him on the back floor of their car. They also arrested and handcuffed Sullivan's brother, who was accompanying him. He, too, was placed in the back of the officers' car. The officers then ordered the service station to be closed and vacated. Apparently unknown to the officers, two witnesses who left the station stayed near enough to observe what happened next. Apparently thinking that there were no other witnesses except themselves, the officers dragged Sullivan from their car onto the concrete driveway. According to the two witnesses, one of the male officers placed his foot on Sullivan's head and pressed it to the concrete. The other male officer took his baton and smashed it into Sullivan's left eye, resulting in the loss of that eye. The officers later maintained that Sullivan's eye was injured in the scuffle to subdue him. But the report of the attending physician at the emergency room, where the officers took Sullivan, indicated that the injury resulted from a direct blow from the end of the baton into Sullivan's eye, "literally smashing his eyeball like a splattered egg."[2] No disciplinary action was taken against the officers.

The use of deadly force or the shooting of victims under the most questionable circumstances never prompted disciplinary action against the officers involved. Disciplinary action for police who repeatedly abused citizens was a rarity, despite all of the publicity and documentation. This would only change after I became mayor and had final authority in city hall on the issue of disciplining city employees. (I will discuss this later with regard to hiring a new police chief.) Despite the failure of the police department and mayor to discipline officers, the constant publicity brought pressure to bear on the department and helped decrease the number of such incidents. It also led the Internal Affairs Division of the police department, which was charged with investigating complaints against officers, to become more attentive and professional in their investigations. I also assumed that some of the officers did not like seeing their names being associated with alleged abuse in the news media. Yet a small number of Birmingham police officers were repeatedly accused of using excessive force against citizens. The fact that new city policy required that records be maintained and made a part of monthly reports to the council's Public Safety Committee helped identify a number of the problem officers and the extent and frequency of citizens' complaints about them.

A pivotal case of alleged police abuse occurred a few years later in 1979 under the administration of Mayor David Vann, who appointed Bill Myers, a highly regarded Birmingham police captain, to the position of chief of police on October 13, 1978, when Parsons resigned to become police chief of New Orleans. It was the case of the murder, by Birmingham police, of a young black woman named Bonita Carter.

THE BONITA CARTER CASE

By the summer of 1979 David Vann, my political ally during my first term on the City Council (1971–75), was nearing the end of his first term as mayor of Birmingham. He and I had continued to be strong political allies throughout his tenure as mayor. I had grown fond of Vann during our time together as council members. He was certainly, by all southern standards, a moderate liberal, although most blacks would probably have labeled him as a "moderate." He had returned to the city to practice law in 1954 after clerking for Supreme Court Justice Hugo Black. When the 1954 Supreme Court decision on school desegregation, *Brown v. Board of Education,* was handed down, Vann was Black's clerk and, by his own account, a close observer of the Court and its deliberations in that case. But he made it clear that he was a clerk and was not privy to any of the Court's ongoing deliberations. Vann had also run for the U.S. Congress in 1964. During that race, he had railed against the 1964 civil rights bill, calling it "fraud" and urging its defeat.[3]

Working with Vann during our first term on the City Council was a great learning experience for me. I was impressed by his keen intellect and vast knowledge of municipal law in Alabama. Even though service on the City Council was considered part-time and we were paid accordingly, Vann spent as much time at city hall working on municipal matters as a full-time mayor. He became the leader of the council's five-member moderate majority while also serving as the chair of the council's Finance and Administration Committee. As chair of the committee, he redefined the power of the chair, and observers quickly recognized him as the council's most influential member. He became my political mentor at city hall and we spent many hours in my office at the Alabama Center for Higher Education, located in the 2121 Building downtown, or in my home, working on city policy issues. As noted earlier, I played an important role in Vann's successful run for mayor in 1975, especially in helping him win an overwhelming majority of the city's black vote, the key to his mayoral victory.

Vann's tendency to tinker incessantly with solutions for any problem he was pondering resulted in his approaching problems from every angle and proposing several ways to address a municipal policy issue. This practice and his fascination with the public policy process were sometimes seen as negatives in terms of his mayoral style. Some council members and a few of his staff complained about the mayor's reluctance to delegate responsibility. "No matter how good any proposal may be, David has to change something in it; he wants at least to dot the I's and cross the T's," his chief of staff said to me on several occasions. Soon, the word around city hall and out in the neighborhoods was that Vann was very bright, but a sloppy administrator. In four years as mayor, however, Vann streamlined city government and amassed large sums of city funds to implement new programs in housing and other community development areas. Being very meticulous in his planning, he was slow to actually implement his new programs. Perhaps he thought that he would use his second term as mayor to put his planned programs into effect. However, he would never get that second term. The issue of police brutality continued to crop up during his tenure as mayor, but little if anything was done to address the behavior of abusive officers. This was an issue over which Vann and I often disagreed.

"The tragic shooting of a 20-year-old black woman named Bonita Carter by a Birmingham police officer near the end of David's term spelled his political downfall," writes Jimmie Franklin in *Back to Birmingham*.[4] Franklin's account of the Bonita Carter case and its impact on Birmingham's political fortunes is spelled out in great detail and thoroughly documented by city hall reports.

In introducing the Bonita Carter case, Franklin notes,

> As a result of this young woman's death, the city would undergo a political transformation of profound consequences. As is often true in history, an event that triggers historic change is unplanned and can appear when people least expect it. Whether such an event becomes a tool for social or political action is determined by the readiness of a people to act concertedly, and the quality of leadership. Because of the history of police brutality and Arrington's work, black Birmingham had developed the resolve to stop police abuse of blacks. Ironically, Vann, who had done so much to shape the city's history, would find himself in the midst of a volatile current of social action that politically pushed him aside, but eventually swept in a new day in the history of Birmingham. Richard Arrington's political career and political change in Birmingham were inextricably tied to the untimely death of this young woman.[5]

The death of Bonita Carter at the hands of Birmingham police on June 22, 1979, brought Birmingham to its bitterest racial crisis since the heyday of the civil rights movement. The incident occurred in the community where Carter resided, an area of the city known as Kingston, a working-class community with a large housing project. The incident took place at a small convenience store or "quick stop" business called Jerry's 7-Eleven. It began when a black man of the community, Alger Pickett, accompanied by his wife, Helen, drove into Jerry's to purchase gasoline. Pickett was soon embroiled in an argument with Michael James Avery, a white employee, about the store's policy of paying for gasoline before pumping it. Tempers flared and soon the two men exchanged punches. Wayne Crusoe, a black employee, stepped between them to halt the fight. Pickett hurriedly left the store and drove away. Soon Pickett returned to the store with a rifle and began firing into the store, striking Avery in the left shoulder.

The store manager, a white man named Ray Jenkins, was awakened from his sleep in the back room of the store by the shooting. He reported later that he assumed that the store was being robbed and rushed to sound the store's robbery alarm. Seconds later, Jenkins and Crusoe, who had taken cover from the shooting, heard a voice outside of the store yell, "He is getting away in the car!" Jenkins rushed toward the door to peer outside. As Jenkins reached the door, Bonita Carter and a young female friend named Louise arrived at the store on bicycles. Sitting in the store's parking lot was Pickett's automobile, which he had left there as he fled across the street on foot after firing into the store. From across the street, Pickett yelled for someone to bring him his car. According to Louise, Bonita said, "I am going to get his car and take it home because they will pull it in." She got into the car and began to drive it off the store lot onto the street. At that moment, two Birmingham policemen in civilian clothes pulled up to the station. Jenkins yelled to Bonita to halt the car. She immediately stopped the vehicle and remained quietly in the front seat on the driver's side. The car stood motionless in the right-hand lane of the street, just in front of the store. The two officers, Richard Hollingsworth and George Sands, were responding to the robbery signal that had gone out about fifteen minutes earlier. They jumped from the car with their pistols drawn. Jenkins yelled to them, "There they go," pointing to the standing car containing Bonita Carter. The officers walked toward the car, Hollingsworth on the driver's side and Sands on the passenger side. Several witnesses of record began to yell to the officers, "The dude with the rifle has gone across the street! That's a girl in the car!" Officer Hollingsworth reported that he and Sands called out, "Police officers! Y'all hold it, come on out." Witnesses disputed this claim.

As the officers moved alongside the car, Bonita raised up from the front seat where she had been lying. Sands, standing slightly to the rear of the passenger side, quickly fired four shots in her direction. Three of the shots struck Bonita in the back, killing her. Hollingsworth, who was standing by the front door on the driver's side, never fired his weapon.

Shortly after the shooting, anger spread through the Kingston community as rumors spread about what had happened. Some people claimed that the police had callously murdered the young woman. Soon several hundred angry black protestors were at the scene and began shouting and throwing rocks at passing automobiles containing whites.

Early that evening Police Chief Bill Myers reached me by phone at home. He told me about the ongoing disturbance in Kingston and expressed his desire to bring the situation under control without having to use police force, which could further inflame the situation. He asked if I would be willing to ride out to Kingston with him and appeal to the protestors to avoid violence. I said yes and we agreed to meet at city hall and ride together to Kingston.

When we arrived at Jerry's, I became concerned about the large number of protestors and the hostility they were expressing. On the side of the street where the store was located, police officers stood guard, many in riot control gear. Across the street the protesting crowd hurled insults at the officers and occasional missiles. As soon as Myers and I got out of the car, many of the protestors recognized me and began to rush toward me, bringing part of the hostile crowd dangerously close to the officers. I talked with the protestors, trying to quiet them and persuade them to disperse, but the situation was becoming more intense as more of the protestors crossed the street to where I was standing. One of the group members, the Reverend Tony Cooper, a vocal police critic at recent City Council meetings, apparently sensed the growing danger of the situation. He leaned toward me and in a low tone of voice suggested that I move across the street in order to move the protestors away from the police officers. As he and I walked across the street the protestors followed, moving away from the officers. For the next half hour or so, I moved among the protestors appealing them to "cool it" and disperse. Someone handed me a bullhorn to use in addressing the protestors. Still, only a few would disperse. But they began to quiet down and stopped throwing rocks and bottles. The situation was very tense as Myers and I rode back to city hall.

Back at city hall, we went to Mayor Vann's office to discuss the situation. At one point in the discussion, I asked Myers if he knew the name of the officer who had done the shooting. He did. It was Officer George Sands. "Uh-oh," I groaned as I looked at the mayor. In the past year or two I had filed several citizens' complaints with the police department accusing Sands of physical and verbal abuse. Those complaints had led me to speak to Vann and get his commitment to have Sands reassigned from the heavily black north police precinct to the east or south precinct, where the population included only a small number of blacks. Vann had agreed to do so. Now, about four months later, I was learning that Vann had done nothing about keeping that commitment.

In his eight years on the Birmingham police force, Sands had more than a dozen citizen complaints, all but one from blacks, alleging that he had physically abused them. The police department had investigated the complaints and found that he acted improperly in only one of the cases. In that case, he received a verbal reprimand. A review of Sands's file revealed a person whose two psychological evaluations showed him to be a troubled individual with "feelings of inadequacy." Public revelation that Sands was the officer responsible for the death of Bonita Carter added fuel to the fire. Blacks began to demand Sands's dismissal from the police force. The hostility of the Kingston protestors continued. Soon, the Ku Klux Klan staged demonstrations in Kingston in support of Sands. The Klan was met with direct threats of physical confrontations from black protestors. Only the action of the police Tactical Unit, now assigned full-time to the Kingston area, prevented violence between the two groups. Eventually, the officers arrested eight Klansmen.

The killing of Bonita Carter enraged Birmingham's black community to the extent that black community leaders began to call for Mayor Vann to fire Sands. Soon the Southern Christian Leadership Conference (SCLC), led by the Reverend Abraham Woods Jr., became the coordinator of the protest to have Sands fired. Having Woods and the SCLC at the helm of the protest was an important development for the city. Woods spoke for the grievances of the black community more than any other single person at the time, especially for blacks at the bottom of the city's socioeconomic scale. No person had greater credibility with the black masses on racial justice issues than Woods. For years, Birmingham's black working class had taken its complaints against racial injustices to Woods and he had never failed to raise their issues and demand justice. Seen by most of the city's white community and a few of its middle-class blacks as "an agitator," he brought a deep civil rights commitment, a keen intellect, and an articulate "black ministerial style" to his advocacy. Aside from his leadership of SCLC, he was the pastor of St. Joseph Baptist Church and a professor of history at Miles College in Birmingham. I had first come to know Reverend Woods during my time as dean at Miles College. But my friendship with him really developed after I was elected to the City Council. On the council I turned to Woods regularly for advice and counsel. I knew he could be counted on to tell me exactly what he thought about any human rights matter, as well as speak honestly to me as to whether he agreed with how I handled civil rights issues. But equally important to me was the unwavering support he always gave me, even during my most difficult times. Eventually Woods, along with another black Baptist minister, Elijah Jarrett, became my close political allies and my ambassadors to Birmingham's influential black ministerial alliance.

When Martin Luther King and Fred Shuttlesworth led the Birmingham civil rights movement in the 1960s, Woods was one of their chief lieutenants. Steeped in the philosophy of nonviolent protest, Woods became a key influence for "keeping the lid" on the growing anger of blacks in Birmingham over the killing of Bonita Carter. He held meetings with other ministers and other black community leaders to shape the black community's response to the murder.

With Woods as the leading spokesperson, black ministers increased their pressure on Mayor Vann and the council to establish a citizens' review board to investigate complaints of police brutality and the Bonita Carter killing. With bitterness toward city hall moving toward rage in the black community, Vann made a bold and perhaps somewhat calculated move. He announced that he would appoint a special "blue-ribbon" citizens' panel empowered with subpoena powers to look into the Bonita Carter incident. Vann appointed an eight-member panel of four blacks and four whites on June 28, 1979.

The four blacks were Dr. James Montgomery, the city's leading black physician, an outspoken civil rights advocate, and civic leader; the Reverend Edward Gardner, president of the Alabama Christian Movement for Human Rights (ACMHR) who led numerous nonviolent protests on behalf of the city's black community before and leading up to the Martin Luther King–led protests in Birmingham; the Reverend Sam Davis, pastor of the St. Paul AME Church; and Emmett Lockett, president of the Kingston Neighborhood Association.

The white members were Rabbi Milton Grafman of Temple Emanuel and a member of the clergy group whose criticism had led to Dr. King's 1963 "Letter from a Birmingham Jail"; Dr. Wilmer Cody, superintendent of Birmingham's public schools; Dr. Blaine Brownell, administrator at the University of Alabama at Birmingham; and Julia Anderson, president of the Thomas Neighborhood, whose rapport with blacks and the Birmingham Police Department was exceptionally good. Vann's move infuriated the FOP and its supporters.

On July 7 the committee completed its difficult and controversial investigation and reported its findings. It concluded by a 7–0–1 vote that Officer Sands did not have sufficient justification for the shooting. Julia Anderson was the abstaining member of the committee.

With hopes for Sands's dismissal now high and strengthened by the committee's report, the black community waited for Mayor Vann's decision. On July 9, a group of one hundred citizens ran a half-page ad in the *Birmingham News* and the *Birmingham Post-Herald* titled "A Statement from Birmingham's Black Community; We Only Ask for Justice." The ad called on Birmingham's citizens to support the efforts to bring about justice in the Bonita Carter case and to halt longstanding injustices in law enforcement practices in the city. It defended Vann's citizens' committee findings and thanked Vann, the police chief, and the Community Affairs Committee (CAC) of Operation New Birmingham for supporting the investigation into the Bonita Carter incident. The FOP was criticized for its opposition to the investigation. Finally, the ad said that the citizens would work in the days ahead for the removal of officers who were guilty of abusing citizens. It called upon the city's black community to continue to show restraint and to use peaceful means to gain justice. Leading the list of signatories to the ad were Abraham Woods, A. G. Gaston, Arthur Shores, and all local black elected officials. I was one of the signatories. I was also the sole author of the ad, which Woods had asked me to write.

On the morning of July 17, Mayor Vann held a 9:00 meeting in his office with a committee of the city's black ministers at which time he informed them of the decision he had reached in the Bonita Carter case and would announce publicly in a news conference he had scheduled for 10:00. I was present when he told the committee that he had come to the conclusion that Sands's action was a "mistake" borne of inadequate police department training. He would therefore place Sands on desk duty and prohibit him from having contact with the public as an officer. He would also direct the police department to immediately begin to strengthen its training program for officers. Immediately the ministers, led by Woods, protested that the decision was unjust and inadequate. At first the discussion between them was civil. But when Vann would not change his decision and stood up to say that he needed to leave for the scheduled news conference, the frustrations of the ministers rose to near fever pitch, with several of them talking at the same time, imploring the mayor to reconsider and to "at least withhold" a public statement of his decision so as to allow them to confer further with him. In the midst of that confusion, the mayor, who was now standing, reached down to his desk, picked up his written statement for the news conference, and politely walked from the room. Some of the ministers walked closely behind him, pleading with him not to make his planned statement. Vann walked through his office door and down the hall to the council chambers, where the news media were waiting. He read his statement and distributed copies to the reporters.

Within a few hours, the ministers held a news conference, denouncing Vann, Sands, and the decision. On July 20, the SCLC led a protest march of an estimated 3,000 persons from Kelly Ingram Park to city hall. The protestors walked the five blocks to city hall in the rain while chanting slogans and calling for the ouster of Vann and Sands. I waited with Vann at the 19th Street entrance to city hall, where a speaker's podium and microphone had been placed for the protestors. As the protestors came within a block of city hall, Vann walked down the steps and up the street to meet them. Shaking hands with leaders of the protest, he walked shoulder to shoulder with them to city hall and stood quietly near the podium, listening as speaker after speaker castigated him and called for a black boycott of city businesses. All in all it had been a tough day for my friend David Vann. But peaceful protest had prevailed over the bridled anger of the protestors. I was filled with mixed emotions, disappointed and angry with Vann, but hurting to watch the mayor's relationship with the black community disintegrate. It had all come to a head almost four years to the day that Birmingham's black voters had boosted Vann to a mayoral victory. I was publicly critical of the mayor's actions, but restrained. In the following month, criticism of Vann continued in the black community and the ministers continued their strategy sessions, which resulted in their move to draft me for mayor.

After I defeated my runoff opponent, Frank Parsons, on October 30, 1979, it was time to implement the platform I had run on. There was no shortage of problems or promises, and I set out to prioritize my plan of action.

5

Police Reform
A First Priority

When I assumed office in November 1979 the City of Birmingham was in the midst of economic stagnation, and the nation as a whole was in the throes of a deepening economic recession. The steel industry, which had served Birmingham well for nearly a century, had fallen upon hard times and the number of jobs in the steel industry in the Birmingham area had declined to approximately 3,000, down considerably from its heyday of the late 1940s when there were more than 30,000 steel jobs. By 1881, when the City of Birmingham had been incorporated for ten years, it was known as a place rich in natural resources. Coal, iron ore, and limestone, the basic raw ingredients needed for making iron and steel, were found in great abundance in the hills and valleys of the Birmingham area. The Tennessee Coal, Iron and Railroad Company (TCI) began making steel in the city in 1889. People flocked to Birmingham from rural Alabama farms to seek their fortunes in the city's steel mills. The city grew so fast that it was dubbed the "Magic City." By 1907 TCI had sold its mills to U.S. Steel, which began manufacturing vast quantities of steel for export from the city, creating thousands of new jobs. By 1948, Birmingham's population of more than 340,000 made it the second largest city in the southeastern United States. It also enjoyed one of the best economies in the region. Only New Orleans had a larger population in the Southeast.[1] But the faltering steel industry in 1979 led to the complete shutdown of the U.S. Steel operation in Birmingham within about a year. In the midst of a national economic recession with a 24 percent unemployment rate, Birmingham's unemployment rate reached 20 percent. The high unemployment rate coupled with the high suburban migration and the political transition created an atmosphere of uncertainty about Birmingham's future.

Despite the serious economic crisis Birmingham faced as I entered office, the issue that claimed just as much public attention was the relationship between the new mayor and the city's police department. My eight-year fight for police reform as councilman left most of the city's white residents skeptical about my support of law enforcement and my commitment to reduce the city's crime rate, which had been rising for the past eight years. None was more skeptical about me as the new mayor than the local FOP. There were 62 black police officers among the city's 700 officers. Only two of those blacks were affiliated with the FOP. My initial focus within the police department was on ending police brutality and increasing the number of blacks on the force; black employment across city departments was minimal. In fact, in nearly every department except that of streets and sanitation, the number and percentage of blacks in the labor force were smaller than those in the police department. Pressure from the city's black community with its increasing number of voters since the passage of the 1965 Federal Voting Rights Act resulted in greater efforts to increase the number of black officers. Overall, blacks made up about 12 percent of the city's labor force, most of whom were in menial positions. The single black department head was city attorney James K. Baker, who had been appointed to his position by David Vann.

The success of the city in increasing the number of blacks in its labor force was outstanding over the next two decades. By the end of my tenure, black city employees made up 50 percent of the total labor force. By 1995, 60 percent of the city's black employees had some supervisory responsibilities. The number of black department heads during my tenure as mayor increased from one to twelve out of twenty-four department heads. The hiring and promotion of women also increased significantly. By 1999 the City of Birmingham had the most diverse labor force, both in terms of gender and race, of any government in the State of Alabama.

During my first year as mayor I led an aggressive program to shut down illegal whiskey houses in the city's black community. One legacy of racial discrimination that persisted in the city's black areas after government-sanctioned racial discrimination was dismantled was the operation of these whiskey houses, called "shot houses." Shot houses were social gathering places for many working-class blacks, who were denied service in the city's white social gathering places. There, one could buy alcoholic beverages by the shot or in large quantities. They also bred other crimes such as selling stolen goods taken in burglaries and payoffs to police officers who permitted the houses to operate. On many occasions during my growing up in Birmingham, I saw police officers pay regular social visits to known shot houses where they collected payoffs. It was my crusade against shot houses that led shot house operators to raise $10,000 to pay a hit man to kill me (see chapter 3).

A New Police Shooting Policy

A citywide street lighting program and volunteer citizen neighborhood patrols coordinated by the police department were established to assist in the fight against crime. All of these efforts combined with increased policing would eventually lead to a steady decline in city crime in eighteen of my twenty years as mayor. In spite of these early efforts to fight crime, the perception of me as a black mayor "soft" on crime persisted among most whites. I think their perception remained essentially unchanged because at the same time I was demanding that our police conduct themselves in a professional manner. I underscored that demand by instituting a new firearms or shooting policy in June 1980 for the police department. The new policy was developed by a biracial, forty-member "blue-ribbon" panel of police officers, corporate leaders, and community leaders. At the time that the policy was put in place by mayoral executive order, the "fleeing felon" law was still in effect throughout the state. Under this law, an officer could legally use deadly force against any person fleeing the scene of a crime or suspected crime if the officer believed that a felony had occurred and the fleeing suspect ignored police commands to stop. The "fleeing felon" victims of deadly force by police officers throughout Alabama were almost 100 percent black. In many instances in Birmingham and elsewhere in Alabama "fleeing felon" shootings by officers resulted in considerable unrest among blacks.

The new Birmingham Police Department shooting policy prohibited officers from using deadly force except in cases in which an officer believed his life or the life of another was in jeopardy. Several years later the U.S. Supreme Court would in effect outlaw the fleeing felon law, but Birmingham was some years ahead of the Court. On July 7, 1980, Myers issued a new department firearms policy based on the work of the committee. The FOP reacted immediately. Its president, Jimmy Williams, who had served on the committee, informed the public that the new policy was a threat to the safety and property of Birmingham citizens.

I overruled the chief's recommendation of a written reprimand for an officer who had justifiably killed a woman while he was on duty but lied about his alcohol consumption just prior to his reporting to duty. I ordered a thirty-day suspension for the officer. The criticism of me became angry and heated. In each case the County Personnel Board upheld my decision when it was appealed. Still, the citizens' complaints of police brutality continued to crop up— a citizen's arm was broken during an arrest, a teenager's jaw was broken when struck with a gun butt after his arrest, and so forth.[2] I stated clearly that my policy would continue to be that officers who clearly acted within the written policies of the department would have full city support as well as my personal support. Even in cases where the evidence suggested doubt as to whether an officer had acted within policy, the benefit of the doubt would be given to the officer. But where the evidence clearly showed a serious policy violation, appropriate disciplinary action would be taken. Jimmy Williams continued to blast the policy and me at a press conference on July 9, 1980. On July 11, I notified Williams that he was being charged with violations of personnel board rules and that he would be given a hearing in my office at 10:00 A.M. on July 14. On July 16, following a hearing, I suspended Williams for four days. Any suspension of fewer than five days was not subject to appeal to the County Personnel Board under the merit system law. Williams appealed unsuccessfully to federal court in an attempt to overturn his suspension.

The *Birmingham Post-Herald,* a biracial group of ministers, the black police Guardian Association, and black citizens' groups publicly supported the new firearms policy, but the Chamber of Commerce expressed reservations about it.

In early September the FOP succeeded in getting state attorney general Charles Graddick to issue an advisory opinion that the new firearms policy violated the Alabama fleeing felon law. Despite Graddick's opinion, I stated that the new policy remained in effect. Chief Myers surveyed one hundred cities on their firearm policies. Our new policy was consistent with those of 68 percent of those cities. Patrick Murphy, president of the National Police Foundation, sent a letter supporting the new policy. The opinion created greater confusion and led to editorials in the *Birmingham News* and *Birmingham Post-Herald* criticizing Graddick's position. The furor over my actions regarding the police department and the bitter criticism leveled at me by the FOP placed Police Chief Bill Myers in the middle of a controversy over authority within the police department.

THE RESIGNATION OF BILL MYERS

When Bill Myers had been appointed police chief, the 6′3″ redhead had built himself a fine reputation as a smart, tough, no-nonsense, professional lawman who had been on the force on for nearly thirty years. He took the difficult task of police chief seriously and exhibited good managerial skills. His commitment to working with and showing loyalty to the mayor was something I never questioned. This is not to indicate that Myers meekly agreed to every position I took. The Bonita Carter case, which had set in motion the incidents leading to my running for mayor, was one source of friction between Myers and me. In August 1979, George Sands had been declared by several city physicians as physically unable and psychologically unfit to continue as a police officer. The physicians' report stated that Sands was "totally incompetent for performance of duty and is likely to be incapacitated permanently." Mayor David Vann had offered to transfer Sands to the fire department, where he had once worked, with a salary comparable to his police pay. Sands refused the offer and asked for assignment to the Tactical Unit. His request was denied and Sands took sick leave on August 25, 1979.

On August 3, 1979, Sands had applied to the city's personnel board via the Jefferson County Personnel Board (an unusual position) for an extraordinary disability pension, which is granted to a city employee who is disabled in the line of duty. Sands, who did not meet the criteria of length of service to be eligible for an ordinary pension, could receive the higher extraordinary pension pay if he were disabled while performing his duties. This was his claim. The county personnel board sought an opinion from the state attorney general, Charles Graddick, as to whether Sands met the criteria for extraordinary disability. The attorney general said he could not determine Sands's state.

In October, Sands provided the county personnel board with a statement from a University of Alabama at Birmingham psychiatrist stating that Sands's disability was not "total" or "permanent." He, along with another psychiatrist, reported that Sands would recover with proper therapy. Sands's attorney, Curtis Gordon, continued to press the board for action on Sands's disability application. On January 4, 1980, two months after I became mayor and chairman of the city's pension board, the board denied Sands's application for an $875 monthly pension.

On February 20, 1980, Myers announced that Sands had applied for reinstatement as a police officer and that he intended to grant it. Sands had physicians' statements saying he was now fit to resume his police duties. The chief's statement caught me by surprise. I attempted to block it by offering Sands a position in the fire department at the same pay grade. But with Myers' approval the county personnel board ordered Sands reinstated. I then ordered that he be restricted to desk duty. Even with controversy raging around Myers about the mayor's usurping his authority, Myers adhered to professional standards. He spoke to me about his full respect for the chain of command in which the elected mayor was the head. But he pointed out that my overriding his decisions on discipline placed him in the difficult position of appearing to be a chief without authority or the backing of the mayor for whom he worked. I then instructed Myers to confer with me on disciplinary matters before making his recommendations public. Although he stated his objection to this policy, he adhered to it. On several occasions he offered to resign, and rumors were circulating that I wanted to bring in a black chief. I asked him to stay on and to work with me in building a thoroughly professional department, and he consented to do so. In April the Birmingham City Council gave Myers its full vote of confidence. But Myers was also under increasing pressure from the FOP to take a strong stance against my "interference" in the department. The Guardians, headed by Kenneth Glover, one of my security staff, also entered the fray, saying the department was full of racists and alcoholics. Eventually the pressure on Myers reached a point where he asked for a meeting with the FOP president and me on April 18, 1980. During that meeting Myers spoke openly about his concerns about his officers' perception that he was not being permitted to manage the department and stated that he would not become just a "pencil pusher" or "paper shuffler." Following our meeting Myers made the same statement to the media. Looking back over these events years later, I realized that my running feud with the FOP via the media only added fuel to the fire. It was a mistake on my part.

After several months of trying to appease the FOP and me, Bill Myers resigned as chief, effective January 16, 1981.[3] With the vacation time Myers had accumulated this meant he would leave in December. Soon after learning that Myers could no longer be persuaded to remain as chief, I set the process in motion for selecting a new police chief with a January 16, 1981, letter to the personnel board, in which I proposed qualifications for the new chief. It was a process that would lead to further public controversy and conflict.

SELECTING A POLICE CHIEF

In 1981 Birmingham remained one of about a dozen cities in the nation of its size or larger that required that all department heads be hired through the merit system.[4] While the outdated countywide merit system under which Birmingham fell had some strengths, having to hire department heads under the rules of the Jefferson County Personnel Board's merit system was problematic in two ways. First, a new administration inherited the existing department heads, who were tenured under the system. A new mayor had no opportunity to choose his own department heads or "cabinet" unless a vacancy occurred. Even then the search for potential candidates to fill the vacancy was the sole domain of the personnel board, which had the authority and responsibility for coming up with a list of candidates the board deemed qualified to fill the job. From that list, which was oftentimes the product of poor recruitment and very limited background checks, the mayor would be given the names of the three top-ranked applicants to interview and from which to make a selection. The policy of giving the mayor the three highest-ranking candidates was known under state law as the "rule of three." The law provided that the mayor had the right to have three candidates willing to accept the job submitted to him by the board. If one of the three candidates under consideration withdrew for any reason, the board could be required to provide the mayor with the name of the next qualified candidate on the list. If the mayor wished to reject any candidate he had to submit his reason for rejection to the board for its review and approval.

A second problem was that "tenured" department heads of whatever quality could sabotage the initiatives of a mayor and avoid appearing to be insubordinate. The process of getting rid of an unproductive department head except in the most extenuating case was lengthy, cumbersome, and subject to the final approval of the board. Hence, department heads who became "tenured" after a twelve-month probationary period that began on the date of hire enjoyed the kind of job security that gave them wide latitude in terms of how they performed their duties. If a department head disliked a new policy initiated by an incoming mayor, he might undermine the mayor's program by merely dragging his feet.

Although the merit system was established to avoid political cronyism, it was far from an apolitical system. No one understood this better than employee organizations like the FOP and firefighters. Both groups had accumulated considerable influence with the three board members and the personnel director appointed by the board. These four individuals oversaw the workings of the system. The FOP and firefighters were rarely hesitant to use their influence in matters of employee discipline. Mayors of the seventeen cities within the county that were under the county merit system sometimes saw the board overturn their actions on employee discipline and other decisions regarding their employer when employees appealed to the board. For example, it was not uncommon for a tenured police officer fired for cause to appeal to the board and have the mayor's action overturned after a hearing. The board or its designated hearing officer might decide on a less severe punishment for the violation. The lesser punishment could range from suspension to completely overturning the mayor's action.

Once Myers announced his resignation, I had several meetings with Joseph Curtin, the personnel board director, to discuss guidelines for selecting a new chief and the role the mayor would be given in the process. We agreed that a national search for a new police chief would be held. I was permitted to outline the qualifications I sought in a chief for the board's review and approval. The board had the final say, but it did adopt my recommendations including waiving a requirement for a college degree in lieu of sufficient experience. The board also conducted the search and specified the examination process for applicants. Nineteen applicants were accepted and tested. The board informed me that eleven were placed on the "eligible list" for chief. Of the eight who did not make the list, one had failed the written test, three had failed the oral test, and four had failed to appear for the oral interview.[5]

Although the board refused at first to share with me more than the names of the top three eligible candidates, I subsequently learned during the protracted fight with the board over this appointment that the board had ranked the eligible candidates as follows:

1. James Parsons$\Rightarrow$ 86.88, former chief of police in Birmingham

2. Tommy Rouse$\Rightarrow$ 85.88, deputy chief, City of Birmingham

3. Arthur Deutsch$\Rightarrow$ 83.20, captain, New York City

4. Michael O'Mara$\Rightarrow$ 81.61, captain, City of Chicago

5. Richard Townes$\Rightarrow$ 79.59, captain, City of Birmingham

6. George Howze$\Rightarrow$ 76.44, assistant chief, City of Birmingham

7. Howard Rogers$\Rightarrow$ 76.20, assistant chief, City of Cincinnati

8. Herbert Straley$\Rightarrow$ 72.47, former chief, Lakeland, Florida

9. Corrin McGarth$\Rightarrow$ 70.94, deputy and sheriff, El Paso, Texas

10. Jack Warren$\Rightarrow$ 70.12, acting chief, City of Birmingham

On May 27, 1981, the board sent me the names of its three top-ranked candidates—James Parsons, Tommy Rouse, and Arthur Deutsch. For reasons unknown to me, the board gave me ten days to select one of these applicants. I requested background information on the candidates and learned that the board had done only a partial background check on them. Joe Curtin and I met several times to discuss my concerns about the three candidates and to discuss my desire to reject two of them: Parsons and Rouse. Curtin insisted that I had to give the board "valid reasons" for any rejection. I told him I would need more time to do my own background checks on the candidates. I turned my attention first to Parsons, who had resigned as Birmingham police chief in the fall of 1978 to become chief of New Orleans and then resigned in 1980. I had come to know Parsons while I served on the Birmingham City Council. My persistent complaints about brutality had resulted in many discussions between Parsons and me. In none of our discussions was Parsons ever anything but professional. During his time as Birmingham's chief he had shown fine abilities and had taken some progressive steps to upgrade the department. He was well liked, especially among the city's corporate community. In reorganizing the Birmingham Police Department Parsons established an Internal Affairs Division, which had the responsibility of investigating complaints and other problems within the department. The department investigated every citizen complaint, and it made its findings available to me when I requested them. But in the overwhelming majority of the cases, the department found insufficient reason to take action to discipline the officers in question.[6] So I knew Parsons at that time as an able and accessible chief. When he applied for the New Orleans job, I had given a favorable recommendation to New Orleans mayor Dutch Morial, who was a longtime friend and acquaintance.[7]

During Parsons' thirty-month stint as New Orleans police chief I was kept abreast of his work by Morial, who eventually came to have mixed emotions about Parsons' performance. Parsons' service as chief in New Orleans ended on a sour note as a result of white police shootings in a black neighborhood.

Gregory Newpert, a New Orleans police officer, was found murdered near a black housing project. Three days later a suspect in the death of Officer Newpert, Raymond Ferdinand, was shot and killed. Two days later a special police squad, suspiciously of all-white officers, allegedly acting on information from an "informer," carried out an early morning raid at the housing project. During the raid the squad killed two more suspects, James Billy and Reginald Miles. Officers also killed Sherry Singleton, the girlfriend of one of the suspects, during the raid. She was reportedly taking a bath at the time. Parsons later told the *Birmingham Post-Herald* that he was sitting in a restaurant drinking coffee with Dave Kent, the police officer assigned by Parsons to handle the investigation of the housing project incident, when the police raid took place. He admitted knowing of the warrants for the raid and that the raid was taking place, but he said he had left the matter in Kent's hands. He told the reporter that he thought the shootings could have been prevented "if cooler heads had prevailed." The killings led to an angry outcry and protests from the New Orleans black community. A few days later in the midst of a racial uproar, Parsons resigned and returned to Birmingham to try to get back his old job as Birmingham police chief.

I dispatched one of the city's personnel officers to New Orleans to complete a background check on Parsons. As soon as I read the report on Parsons, I wrote the board that I was rejecting Parsons' name and asking the board to provide me with another candidate, the next on the list, to replace Parsons. In my letter to the board I wrote, "Unfortunately many questions remain about the recent police killing of blacks in New Orleans while Parsons was Chief. This cloud of suspicion has followed Mr. Parsons to Birmingham and would serve to seriously undermine his effectiveness as Chief in Birmingham, which has a long history of strained relationships between the city's majority black population and police department." On July 14, 1981, Jim Field, deputy director of personnel for the board, wrote to inform me that "under these circumstances, the Board is removing Mr. Parsons' name from the certification list."[8]

Parsons reacted angrily, filing an unsuccessful suit to have his name placed back on the certification list and telling the Birmingham Young Men's Business Club at a luncheon of his "strong dislike for me."[9] A few months later, a federal grand jury in New Orleans indicted seven white police officers on civil rights charges of beating blacks while carrying out the investigation of the New Orleans housing project raid.

Candidates Richard Townes, Michael O'Mara, Howard Rogers, and Herbert Straley withdrew from the competition at my request. Noting what I believed were deficiencies in the qualifications of Tommy Rouse and George Howze that had turned up in background checks, I rejected them and asked the board to remove their names from the certified list. The board refused, saying my reasons were not adequate.

I rejected Rouse's name seven times, but the board maintained that my reasons for rejection were "not valid" and kept his name on the list. I then asked the board to permit me to select a chief from the entire list of remaining eligible candidates, but it refused, citing the "rule of three." The list eventually dwindled down to six candidates: Rouse, Deutsch, Howze, Rogers, McGarth, and Warren.

During this time Joe Curtin and I were embroiled in discussions about my failure to comply with the board's request to make a selection within ten days. Curtin finally asked me one day, "Is there anyone on the list you would appoint?" I replied, "At this time there is only one I know for sure I'd appoint and that is Jack Warren." On that point further discussions between Curtin and me ceased. The board sent me a letter setting an August 14, 1981, deadline for me to select a chief. The deadline passed without my making a selection. The board filed suit in circuit court asking Judge Jack Carl to order me to make a selection from the three names certified to me—Rouse, Howze, and Deutsch.

In court my attorney, David Vann, argued that the board had "rigged" its evaluation of candidates by deciding that no candidate could get more than twenty evaluation points for experience.[10] Warren, the candidate I favored, had forty years of experience and according to Vann's argument was entitled to

38.5 points for experience rather than 20 points. The board had given heavier weight to education; Warren had less education than all of the other candidates. The board alleged that my failure to make a selection from its certified list was an illegal act. On November 3, 1981, Judge Jack Carl ruled that I had ten days to appoint one of the three applicants once the board gave me full background checks on them. Failure to do so would lead to a contempt citation. I appealed to the federal court for an injunction on Carl's order but my plea was denied.

The court case and jockeying between the board and me continued for nearly two months before Judge Carl again ordered me to make an appointment from the list of three by November 12 or face the consequences. This ruling came after the board filed a new motion on October 13 asking the judge to order me to make a selection.[11]

The clash with the board over the appointment of a new chief laid the groundwork for me to begin to lobby our delegation to the state legislature to amend the county's Merit System Act to permit mayors of the county to have more authority in choosing their department heads. Finally in May 1984, about three years after my losing fight with the county personnel board over the selection process for a police chief, the legislature moved to amend the act. Senator Jim Bennett introduced legislation to permit a mayor to choose a department head from the entire list of eligible applicants approved by the personnel board, effectively ending the "rule of three" in department head appointments. The amendment met with strong opposition from the FOP, which lobbied for its defeat. But the sixteen-member personnel board supervisory committee of local college presidents and presidents of the leading county civic leagues, which also appoint the three members of the Jefferson County Personnel Board, supported the amendment. In the 1985 Alabama legislative session after delaying tactics were beat back, the bill became law.

This was the first of many cases I would lose before Jack Carl, who became well-known for his numerous rulings against the City of Birmingham during my tenure as mayor. Carl prevailed in the chief selection case, but in nearly every other future ruling against the city, the Alabama Supreme Court reversed him. Facing the judge's mandate, I moved to complete the background check on Police Captain Arthur Deutsch of Brooklyn, New York, who was forty-nine years old. After background checks, which were somewhat mixed, I appointed Deutsch as Birmingham police chief, effective January 2, 1982.

Above: Fairfield home of Mayor Arrington's family (left side of duplex), 1940. Courtesy of City of Birmingham Public Library Archives.

Left: Dr. Arrington speaks at Elyton Mini-Park picnic during the 1979 election campaign. Photo by Emmette Smith.

Mayor Arrington on election night, 1979. (Left to right): Pam Arrington (daughter-in-law), Kenya Arrington (granddaughter), Kenneth Arrington (son, holding Kenya), Richard Arrington, Rachel (wife), Erica Arrington (daughter). Photo by Lucious Washington.

Above: Mayor Arrington relaxes with his parents and brother on election night, 1979. (Left to right): Ernestine Arrington (mother), Richard Arrington, James Arrington (brother), and Richard Arrington Sr. (father). Photo by Lucious Washington.

Left: Arrington reads his inaugural speech in the mayor's office before the inaugural ceremony, November 1979. Photo by Don Sharpe.

Above: Mayor Arrington being sworn in as mayor of Birmingham, 1979, by Justice Janie Shores, as George Seibels, David Vann, and Arrington's wife Rachel look on. Courtesy of the City of Birmingham Public Information Office.

Opposite:
Mayor Arrington meets with President Jimmy Carter at the White House, November 1979.

At televised campaign debate with Dr. John Katopodis during the 1984 mayoral campaign. Courtesy of the City of Birmingham Office of Public Information.

Above: The mayor and family members greet the crowd on election night, 1987. (Left to right): Jennifer Rose (daughter), Richard Arrington, Matthew (son), wife Rachel. Courtesy of the City of Birmingham Public Information Office.

Opposite:
Mayor Arrington being sworn in for third term, 1987, by Justice Oscar Adams; wife Rachel with Bible. Photo by Eddie Hand, employee of the City of Birmingham.

Mayor Arrington with Larry Striplin of the Alabama Hall of Fame (right) and SEC commissioner Roy Kramer (left) at the September 30, 1991, opening of the Southeastern Conference Office. Courtesy of City of Birmingham Office of Public Information.

Willie Mays at Historic Rickwood Field, 1986 (serving as ambassador for U.S. Youth Games hosted by the City of Birmingham). Courtesy of City of Birmingham Office of Public Information.

6

The Controversial Reign of Chief Artie Deutsch

Arthur Deutsch, who preferred to be called Artie, began his service as Birmingham chief on January 2, 1982.[1] Shortly after he was on the job I held a news conference to introduce him to the media and the public. He was accompanied by his lovely, statuesque blond wife, Elaine, his two teenage daughters, and his eight-year-old son. They were a strikingly good-looking family, including Artie himself, who was quite handsome and athletic. The news conference went quite well and for the next several months Artie, who spoke with a distinct Brooklyn accent, received wide, positive local news coverage.[2] But it was not to last long, for soon Artie Deutsch would become a controversial figure and the subject of repeated negative media coverage.[3]

The controversy surrounding Deutsch's tenure as police chief would nearly overshadow that of the selection process leading to his appointment. As I mentioned earlier, I had thought that hiring a chief from outside the Birmingham Police Department was the right course of action if I could not hire Jack Warren, who was serving as acting chief between Myers' resignation and Deutsch's hiring. Warren was a forty-year veteran of the Birmingham Police Department and had done a good job as acting chief. He knew the department well and was well liked by the department until the FOP learned that he was my choice for chief. Some of the officers set about to criticize Warren by bringing up his alcoholism of earlier years and his lack of any college training. Some even went as far as mocking Warren's southern accent, making him appear to be barely literate. To see the FOP turn on Warren simply affirmed my belief that the organization had no credibility. Warren wanted the job and I very much wanted him to have it. But the FOP enjoyed considerable clout with the Jefferson County Personnel Board and its executive director, Joe Curtin. Once I admitted to Curtin—in what I thought was confidence—that Jack Warren was my choice, he was doomed. There was simply no way that the board would certify his name for chief.[4]

So Jack Warren was out and Deutsch was in. The FOP, many of the members of the City Council, and soon many others were not pleased. But before talking about some of the specifics of the controversy, let me speak briefly about the two police officers I first selected to serve as my personal bodyguards or security—Gwen and Billy Webb. Both would soon earn Deutsch's enmity.

THE MAYOR'S PERSONAL SECURITY

My eight-year history on the City Council as a vocal critic of police misconduct made me the FOP's number one enemy. This was not good: the FOP, which dated back to the infamous days of Eugene "Bull" Connor and his dogs and water hoses, was a powerful political force in Birmingham.

For the first month or two after I took office, Chief Bill Myers had assigned the department's highly trained SWAT team to provide security for me because of the large number of death threats I had received as well as warnings from the FBI that I was in danger of being harmed. So for twenty-four hours a day members of the special police team were always with me. But soon things quieted down and Myers was ready to relieve the SWAT team of the security responsibility and name several individual officers as security for me. Myers told me that he had several good officers to recommend and that I could choose from among them. However, I told Myers that I wanted to choose my security without reviewing his recommendations. I now know that I offended him, but at the time my paranoia made me suspicious that any officers he suggested would be spies for him and the FOP. I must admit that during the time Myers served as chief under me, he was never to my knowledge disloyal, hostile, or unprofessional, but my paranoia blinded me and probably offended Myers, though he never showed it.

I had no officers in mind for the security assignment. In fact I knew very few of the department's eight hundred or so officers. After thinking about the matter for several days, I recalled that I had had some pleasant encounters with a young white lieutenant named Billy Webb when he served as head of the police department's Internal Affairs Division, which investigated complaints and allegations of police misconduct during my tenure on the City Council. I remember Webb mainly because of the professional manner in which he conducted investigations into my complaints about police misconduct. I also noted that unlike other officers assigned to internal affairs I knew, he was never hostile toward me and at times seemed sympathetic to my crusade against police misconduct.

I asked Webb to come to my office, and I offered him the responsibility of heading my security team. He said he was willing to do so but could not accept the responsibility because he wanted to be on duty with his wife, whom he needed to protect. I then learned that Webb had recently married a young black female officer. He indicated that he and his wife, Gwen, were targets of insults in the department because they were an interracial couple. The Webbs were working the "graveyard shift" at the city jail. Despite his seniority, which had given him more desirable department assignments, Billy Webb had requested the assignment at the jail in order to be with his wife. After we finished our conference, I recalled that a couple of years earlier during my tenure on the City Council, a county constable and friend of mine, the Reverend W. W. Wheeler, had mentioned to me that there was a "serious interracial romance" in the police department between a black female officer and a white male officer. It was all mentioned during a conversation he and I were having about my ongoing efforts to halt police abuse—mainly on some of Birmingham's black citizens. I don't recall that he ever named the officers. In fact he mentioned it only as a side issue in our conversation. I recall that we both chuckled about his remark and parted. Now after having talked with Billy Webb I assumed that this was the couple that Reverend Wheeler had referred to and they now were married. I had said to Webb before he left my office that I would consider some other assignment for his wife that would remove her from the jail environment to one where he felt she could work in a pleasant surrounding.

After conferring with the city attorney, Jim Baker, about his interest in having an officer assigned to his staff to assist with his department's investigations and getting a positive response from Baker to my suggesting Gwen Webb for the job, I decided to offer the job to her. That assignment would bring her to city hall, where her husband would be most of the time. When I later mentioned this to Billy Webb, he thought it would work but he wanted to discuss it with his wife first. The next day he came to my office accompanied by his wife to discuss my proposed assignment for them. I then recognized Gwen Webb as the attractive, dark-skinned young woman who had come by my office a couple of years earlier while I was on the council. I recalled that she had showed up and asked to see me. When my secretary, Jessie Huff, brought her into my office she said that she simply wanted me to know that some of the police officers supported my efforts to halt police misconduct. She added that I could be certain that one of the officers, a lieutenant named Bill Webb who was leading internal affairs, was a fair-minded individual and could be trusted to treat everyone fairly. I thanked her, she left, and I never saw her again until she walked into my office with her husband. Now, two years later, Gwen's visit to my office and her comments about Lieutenant Webb began to come together.

The Webbs accepted their new assignments. Gwen went to the law department on the sixth floor of city hall, and Billy came to my office on the third floor to head up my security. He brought with him a young black officer named Kenneth Glover, who was president of the police department's Guardians Association. At this time, in 1979, only two of Birmingham's black officers were affiliated with the FOP. Black officers had apparently not felt welcome in the FOP. There was also the undeniable fact that the few officers most often accused of police misconduct toward blacks were active in the FOP. So the black officers had formed their own chapter of the Guardians.

For the first couple of months the Webbs' assignment worked well. Gwen was often seen in the mayor's office chatting with her husband. She also began to ride with Billy and me to evening events. But soon Gwen and the city attorney disagreed about the manner in which she was performing her job. He wanted her removed from his staff. When I spoke with her about the city attorney's concern about her work, she became agitated and upset. In a few days I reassigned Gwen to my security staff to work with Billy and Ken Glover. Soon the Webbs were featured in the local and some national print media as the interracial wife-husband team protecting Birmingham's first black mayor. The Webbs seemed to enjoy the work and the publicity. They were very attentive to their responsibilities and my security. It was not long before the Webbs were constant companions to my wife and me at city and social functions. We even visited the Webbs at their home. The relationship between the Webbs and the Arringtons grew to be a strong one. Billy and Gwen became increasingly protective of me, even taking on verbal battles with persons who were politically critical of me. They told the media that they were totally dedicated to me, even to the point of laying their lives on the line to see that no harm came to me and I had no reason to doubt them. It was a fine relationship for five years and I had grown quite fond of the Webbs.

However, our relationship took a negative and bitter turn after Gwen developed a growing interest in city and political affairs and even began to speak of her interest in elected office. She ran for the office of president of her neighborhood association and won. She was as aggressive in speaking out for her neighborhood as she was in defending me. When I successfully lobbied members of the City Council to support my proposal to expand our Airport Industrial Park, Gwen's neighborhood association opposed the plan because they said that the expansion of the park would encroach on their residential area. After several discussions about the issue, the Webbs and I agreed to disagree. When the matter came before the council for their approval, Gwen appeared before the council in opposition and criticized council members who voted against her position. Shortly after that meeting several of the council members came to my office and expressed their anger at me for lobbying them to support the controversial issue and then permitting a very visible member of my staff, Gwen, to attack them at a public council meeting. I promised them that I would rein in the feisty Gwen.

When I had the Webbs in my office to tell them as members of my staff they could not publicly oppose a position that I had taken, the Webbs strongly disagreed with me. Billy angrily told me that his wife's position as a police officer did not take away her constitutional right as a citizen to oppose my stance on political issues. He made it clear that any punitive action such as reassigning her would result in her filing a complaint with the personnel board. The discussion ended on a hostile note and our relationship became somewhat strained. I thought seriously about reassigning the Webbs but decided not to do so.

In the Democratic presidential primary in August 1980 I supported Walter Mondale and the Webbs strongly supported Jesse Jackson. In August, I left for the Democratic National Convention in San Francisco, where I chaired the platform committee. Before leaving for San Francisco, Billy had come to me and recommended that Gwen accompany my wife and me to San Francisco to provide security for me. I told him I wouldn't need security at the convention. However, Gwen showed up at the convention and used her position as my security to gain admission to the convention floor, which was reserved for delegates. I was upset when I learned about this. When I returned to Birmingham I informed the Webbs that I was reassigning them and asked what other position in the police department they preferred. They moved to their new assignments but were soon telling people that I was corrupt and had taken financial payoffs. When the fifth person came to me to tell me what the Webbs were saying I sought the advice of Jim Baker about what action I might take. He suggested that I ask the person who had come to me with the Webbs' information to give sworn affidavits about it. With my permission Baker gave the affidavits to Chief Deutsch.

The relationship between Deutsch and the Webbs was a hostile one. Deutsch had apparently been unhappy when he learned that the Webbs were a part of the background investigation on him while I was considering him for chief. Gwen Webb's report to me on Deutsch at the time was not particularly favorable. The Webbs had also been very critical of Deutsch after his appointment as chief, even suggesting to me on several occasions that Deutsch should be dismissed. Deutsch, apparently knowing about the Webbs' criticism of him, had approached me several times to ask me to allow him to remove the Webbs as security guards. He tried to convince me that they were not my friends and were not doing a professional job as my security. He said he could provide me with much better security personnel. I told him, "No." "Alright, Boss," he said, "but they are not your friends." Now with my having removed the Webbs as security personnel, Deutsch was asked to investigate their allegations relayed to us by the five persons who had provided sworn affidavits and demanded that they give him the information about any violation of law by me that they had knowledge of. When they refused he filed disciplinary charges against them for claiming to have knowledge of illegal actions committed by me but refusing to cooperate with the department in investigating the allegations. At their hearing the Webbs refused to respond to inquiries and the chief, undoubtedly with glee, fired them. The Webbs angrily told the media that I had "turned the chief loose on them" to get even with them for differing with me on political matters. They then appealed their dismissal to the Jefferson County Personnel Board but their retaliation did not stop there. I later learned from federal documents (through the Freedom of Information Act) that Billy Webb had gone to the FBI with allegations of my taking political payoffs. The FBI was unable to substantiate the allegations—they had never occurred.

The personnel board held a public hearing on the Webbs' appeal on their dismissal. At the hearing, which took two weeks, the Webbs testified that they had learned of alleged payoffs to me on two separate occasions. Gwen Webb testified that a local contractor had come to my office when I was away and requested to see me. When she told him I was not in, he took cash from his pockets, placed it in an envelope, and asked her to give it to me and to tell me thanks for helping him get some building permits. It was a story that was easily called into question when investigators could not find any city permits given to the contractor. Billy Webb testified that he had seen some checks from a black Tuskegee, Alabama, contracting firm on my desk. The check made out to me had only the signature of the company's executive with the amounts left blank, he said. The board subpoenaed the firm's canceled checks and found no checks made out to me. In preparation for the board's hearing, the attorney for the Webbs had subpoenaed records and canceled checks from the Tuskegee firm. When the attorney received the checks it was apparently noted that several of the firm's numbered series of checks were not included. When the firm's accountant answered the board's subpoena he was unable to explain why several checks were missing. The attorney for the Webbs left the board with the impression that the missing checks in the numbered series could be those that Billy had allegedly seen on my desk. It was a convincing ploy. But it backfired a few days later when the accountant rushed back to Birmingham from Tuskegee to again appear at the hearing. He came back because he had discovered the missing checks, which he brought with him. It turned out that the checks had not been used because of a printer's error. They had been returned to the printer, who retained them. A few weeks later on February 27, 1985, five minutes before midnight as I returned to Birmingham from a ten-day trip to Israel, I learned that the board upheld Billy's firing by a 2–1 vote and upheld Gwen's firing by a 3–0 vote.[5] The board said it found no evidence of wrongdoing by me. In a rare written statement the board explained its decision to uphold the dismissal of the Webbs. "No evidence was presented to the board that implicated the Mayor of any wrongdoing," it wrote. The Webbs appealed to the federal court but lost there also. They never regained their jobs as police officers.[6]

THE DEUTSCH ESCAPADES

A few months into Deutsch's tenure as Birmingham's chief several controversies surrounding him surfaced, along with his heated disagreements with the FOP. During his first week Deutsch came to my office to discuss any particular concerns I had about the police department. I spoke to him about my concern about developing a more professional police department and shared the details of my eight-year battle with the department about police brutality against blacks. I also warned him that he could expect to encounter great opposition from the FOP. About the latter matter he said, "Boss, don't worry about them. I can handle them. They won't be in your hair."

It was clear to me as I read and viewed media reports of discussions with some members of the FOP that they vehemently disliked Deutsch and intended to see that he failed as chief. Working with reporters on the police beats, they leaked one negative story after another about the chief. They first complained bitterly about Deutsch's order that officers in uniform meet certain dress standards, including wearing their caps while on duty and saluting superiors. The cap requirement really riled many officers. They faced command discipline by their superiors for noncompliance.

Soon there was a front-page story in the city's largest daily about an incident in which the chief had reportedly seen a car illegally careening across one of the city's snow-covered golf courses as he drove past it. The report said that Deutsch pursued the car, stopped the car, and dragged the driver and the passenger, both of whom turned out to be paraplegics, from the car onto the ground, roughing them up. Deutsch denied the allegation. In municipal court the paraplegics entered a guilty plea to a reduced charge in exchange for agreeing not to sue the city.

Then came the bitter public dispute between Deutsch and Russell Yarbrough, chairman of the council's public safety committee and the owner of a used-car lot, who said Deutsch had tried to borrow one of his vehicles to move some of his belongings to Birmingham from New York. It all began at a meeting of the council when Yarbrough questioned some of the moving expenses that Deutsch had submitted to the city for reimbursement. Deutsch denied that the expenses were inflated, leading Yarbrough to make the charge about Deutsch trying to borrow one of his vehicles. As soon as Yarbrough made the statement, Deutsch yelled, "Councilman, that's not true. Why, your cars wouldn't make it across the county line." Yarbrough and several other council members bristled with anger. I interceded to quiet the chief, who continued his exchange with Yarbrough.

The *Birmingham News* would soon report that Deutsch had accepted the Birmingham position after leaving two other smaller cities, thinking that he had been on his way to becoming their police chief. Deutsch denied the stories, which included quotes attributed to the mayors of the two cities that backed the story. Before long a female reporter for the *Birmingham News* claimed that she had pursued the chief into a city hall elevator, attempting to get him to respond to some of her inquiries. She claimed that he jabbed her with his elbow as he left the elevator. The *News* carried the story and its publisher, Victor Hanson, called my office to complain about the alleged treatment of its reporter. Deutsch immediately denied that the incident had occurred.

Around this time John Katopodis, a city councilman and Deutsch critic, told the City Council that Deutsch had punched him very hard in his stomach while the two were at a social event at a private residence. According to Katopodis, he was also maliciously punched by Deutsch in the chief's office following a meeting between Katopodis, Betty Collins, and me to voice their complaints about Deutsch's conduct. When I questioned Deutsch about the allegations, he said that what had happened was nothing more than kidding between the two men. Katopodis was greatly exaggerating the incident, according to Deutsch. I found it strange that Deutsch and Katopodis were on friendly enough terms to involve each other in horseplay. John Katopodis, like Councilman Yarbrough, was a strong FOP ally who repeatedly criticized Deutsch at meetings and in the media. Deutsch was not the first police chief Katopodis had publicly attacked. Jack Warren had been repeatedly attacked by Katopodis, especially after the FOP came out in opposition to Warren's selection as chief. In one heated incident before the council on April 28, 1981, Katopodis accused Warren of lying about the transfer of a police officer. Warren called Katopodis a liar. The two had a heated exchange and I had to lead Warren out of the conference meeting room. As he left he said, "Twenty-five years ago I would have whupped him," referring to Katopodis.

The City Council balked at paying Deutsch's $3,600 moving bill, and when the council learned a year later that a group of businessmen were raising money to pay for the expense, they voted to investigate "the improper conduct" of the chief and whether he was violating city policy by accepting moving expenses and a housewarming gift from people in the business community. They also wanted to know whether a local bank had given him a favorable mortgage rate on the home he purchased in Birmingham. The ethics commission found no violations. This council action was followed by a number of incidents of bickering between the chief and council. On February 23, 1982, Deutsch did not attend an 8:00 A.M. meeting with the council to respond to some concerns of a citizens' group; instead, he sent two deputy chiefs. The council was livid. I would later learn that Deutsch's absence from the meeting was due to an honest miscommunication.

On January 13, 1984, over two hundred citizens met at the headquarters of the FOP to support the police officers and to criticize Deutsch and the mayor for suspending two officers for an unauthorized taping of conversations with the chief. At the same meeting a Birmingham police officer, R. C. Taylor, told the citizens that the chief had asked someone to trump up charges against an officer who had recently been cleared of selling drugs in a federal court case.

In February 1985 the council learned that the chief was mailing a monthly departmental newsletter to some members of the business community. Since it was being done at the city's expense, the council demanded that the chief turn over his mailing list for their inspection. When he hesitated to do so, the council threatened to use its subpoena power to obtain the list. I ordered the chief to make the list available and to make a public apology to the council. He complied.

The chief had also been the subject of a July 21, 1982, *Birmingham News* article that alleged he charged the city $588.42 for calls to his New York home. There is no doubt in my mind that a city employee had tipped off the media about the calls. Deutsch pleaded ignorant to the unwritten policy that prohibits such calls and paid the city $588.42.[7] He also took the occasion to say that in the future he would hold regular news conferences to permit open communication between the media and him. Still four months into his job as chief and despite controversies, the Birmingham corporate community gave Deutsch favorable reviews in the *Birmingham News* on July 25, 1982.

On June 8, 1985, a young black man named James Lowe was arrested and charged with murdering a nineteen-year-old white waitress, a coworker of his at a local restaurant. According to a police homicide sergeant, Lowe was left alone in an interrogation room with the chief. Soon after hearing a scuffle in the room, the sergeant said Lowe burst from the room saying the chief struck him and threatened to kill him. The chief denied it and the U.S. Justice Department investigated and dropped the claim on insufficient evidence during Lowe's trial for murder. Lowe later said that some officers offered to drop weapons charges against him if he'd tell what Deutsch had done to him. Lowe refused to file a complaint with internal affairs. Deutsch was also accused by unnamed officers of spitting on a prisoner in a patrol car, leading to an internal affairs investigation that did not substantiate the allegation.

Even with all of the controversy surrounding him, Deutsch did have some significant achievements in his first year. Among these were a complete and more professional reorganization of the department, a 9 percent decrease in major crime, new policy upgrades, special in-service training programs/modules for officers, and an overall professional upgrading of the police department. His leadership eventually led the department to become one of only about sixty accredited police departments in the nation. One early change the chief implemented was a complete reorganization and upgrading of the department's property room. I mention the property room because I want to cite it as an example of one of the administrative deficiencies of the police department and other city departments.

Shortly after becoming mayor I learned that a number of city departments that collected revenue for the city on a regular basis were never audited. While the city completed an audit by a CPA firm each year, the audit only looked at the city's finance office and how it handled its collected funds. There were a half dozen or more city departments that collected city revenue and turned it over daily or periodically to the city's finance office. Since there was no audit of the departments or the funds they handled, there was no way to know if the amounts turned over to the finance department were accurate. As far as I could determine this had always been the practice at city hall. Soon after learning of this practice I established the city's first internal auditing program, overseen by a special committee. The committee also made decisions about which city departments would be audited; the department would be notified a week or so prior to the beginning of the audit. The internal auditing program revealed that six city departments had failed to report all revenue collected by them to the finance office. The shortage of funds ranged from a few thousand dollars in some departments to about $80,000 in the police property room, which led to investigations, suspensions, firings, indictments, and imprisonment of some city employees. The audit found that the largest amount of missing money was affiliated with the police department's property room.[8]

The property room was located in the basement of city hall and contained all property, including cash, confiscated by law officers during arrests. For example, when an individual was arrested for selling drugs, any money found on his person was taken by the investigating officers, placed in a large envelope, and filed and kept in the police property room. There were many other items, such as TVs, guns, bicycles, and appliances, placed in the property room. I came to learn that many of the properties, including cash, were never reclaimed by the owners or accounted for by any other manner, except for occasional destruction of guns as required by state law and public auction for some items. The situation was ripe for corruption. I'll never forget my first visit to the property room. It came after an August 1984 audit of the property room, which showed that a significant amount of cash that was supposedly in the property room was missing. What I found in the property room, in addition to the types of items I've mentioned, was a system of handwritten records on filing cards that were catalogued and placed on the shelves of the room. No items were under lock. I saw large, unsealed manila envelopes, labeled by the property staff and often containing cash, on the shelves. A month into the audit we had discovered that $70,500 in cash was missing and the amount was growing. We soon needed to discontinue the audit, knowing the audits could never determine all the cash missing. I thought the media would see the new internal auditing division and subsequent revelation of corruption as a positive development. Instead the *Birmingham News* headline about the property room ran as an example of corruption in the Arrington administration.[9]

The Downfall of Artie Deutsch

Deutsch waged a bitter fight with the FOP during his first two months as police chief. Despite numerous efforts, most led by the FOP, to discredit him, Deutsch succeeded in reshaping the department, trumping the FOP and avoiding every effort to oust him. But he sealed his downfall on July 5, 1990, following the arrest of my daughter Erica (see next section). His actions on that day placed him in the clutches of his worst enemies—the FOP and the local media. This time they would not let Artie escape.

Erica was arrested by a Birmingham police officer, Jerry Bahakel, in the entertainment district called Five Points South and jailed on charges of disorderly conduct, inciting to riot, and failure to disperse—all of which she would be acquitted of later in municipal court. Learning of her arrest early on the morning of July 5, I called Deutsch at his home and asked him if he could tell me what had led to her arrest. Deutsch knew nothing of the arrest, which had occurred about six hours earlier. He asked me to let him get some information on the matter and get right back to me. At about 10:00 Deutsch was in my office at city hall apologizing about the arrest and telling me that he would personally look into the incident. "Just let me handle it, Boss," he said as he got up to leave.

Whenever someone is arrested and placed in Birmingham city jail his or her name is entered on an arrest log, a police document that reporters on the jail beat review daily. Apparently a reporter for the *Birmingham News* had seen Erica's name on the log on the morning of July 5. Whether the reporter had discovered her name through an early morning routine inspection of the docket or had been tipped off about the arrest by an officer was never known. But later in the day when the reporter came back to the jail to look at the docket he discovered that her name had been removed from it. In fact, the entire page of the docket had been removed and replaced with a new sheet. How much of this information had been discovered by the reporter on his own and his reasons for coming back to the jail to review the docket again are left to conjecture. My guess is that one of Deutsch's enemies in the police department, of which there were many, was aware of what had occurred and had alerted the *News*. I learned about the docket change from the evening edition of the *News*. I was never concerned for myself since I had known nothing of the tampering until it was reported by the media. I was concerned, however, for Deutsch and any of his accomplices who may have changed the log.[10] Deutsch told me that he had no knowledge of the tampering, but I had a deep suspicion that the chief had instructed someone to alter the log.

As the heat was turned up on the incident by the media, someone on the jail staff apparently replaced the substitute sheet with the original docket bearing Erica's name. But the damage had been done. The media, which already had a very rocky relationship with Deutsch, focused public attention on the incident in featured stories day after day. Soon the *News* printed its predictable editorial, calling for the district attorney to investigate the "tampering with public records," which was a violation of state law. The district attorney was David Barber, who before his election for district attorney was the chief attorney for the FOP. Barber announced he would convene a grand jury to look into this allegation.

Interestingly enough, in the midst of the furor over the record tampering, another allegation of tampering with public records arose. This was in the office of the Jefferson County Commission. An aide to County Commissioner Betty Collins had reportedly erased a portion of the tape of a County Commission meeting in order to delete an unfavorable statement by Collins to some complaining citizens at the meeting. When some of these citizens requested a copy of the tape, apparently to have a documented record of the commissioner's response to them at the meeting, they discovered that one of the commissioner's staff had erased that portion of the tape. By law, the tape is a public document. This alleged record tampering story drew scant attention and died within hours. I made a public suggestion that the district attorney, who had the Birmingham jail records case before a grand jury, should also have the jury look into the county tape case. But there was no media outcry about the alleged county record tampering and no action on it by the district attorney.

There was no question in my mind that Barber would have the grand jury indict Deutsch. I thought that the media, especially the two local daily newspapers, had already indicted him. The Alabama Bureau of Investigation had also investigated the allegation. On December 11, 1990, Deutsch and three officers on the jail staff were indicted by Barber's grand jury and charged with tampering with government records.[11] All were given separate trials. Each, including the chief, was placed on paid administrative leave pending the outcome of the trial. The three officers were found innocent or got a hung jury.

Arthur Deutsch's trial was before Judge Joe Jasper, whose hostility toward my administration and Deutsch was well-known. One needed only follow his handling of Deutsch's case, which started on April 1, 1991.[12] The jury eventually returned a guilty verdict against Deutsch. He was convicted of knowingly making a false entry or altering a government record. Judge Jasper threw the book at him. He gave Deutsch the maximum sentence of twelve months of hard labor in the county jail and a $2,000 fine. Deutsch immediately appealed the conviction. But in a surprisingly strange handling of the case by Jasper, the appeal hearing was delayed. Jasper, despite the protest from Deutsch's attorney, delayed making the transcript of the trial available, which was needed as part of the appeal record. Eventually the appeal reached the Alabama Supreme Court, which overturned Deutsch's conviction on July 24, 1992, on the grounds of Judge Jasper's failure to clarify for the jury what Deutsch's legal and criminal liability was for the acts of others—the major issue affecting the jury's decision. The case went back to Jasper for a new trial but that trial never occurred.

One afternoon Deutsch was found lying at the foot of a first-floor stairway in city hall, dazed and unconscious. He would later recall that he tripped over a piece of indoor-outdoor carpet runner at the head of the stairs. Apparently the fall down six or seven steps led to his injury. Even though Deutsch's critics, particularly the FOP, continued to push for another Deutsch trial, the chief was unfit to stand trial, according to court-appointed physicians. He would never be tried again in this matter or return to the position of chief.

In 1991 Deutsch was required to face charges in federal court, along with two of his staff and me. Velinda Oladeinde, a black female officer who brought the charges, alleged that she had had her constitutional rights violated by the chief and the officers in an investigation over her admitted misuse of city funds given to her for use in undercover drug cases. She also claimed that she had been wrongly denied a promotion to lieutenant, even though she admitted in sworn testimony that she had misused the city funds and that she ranked several steps below the officers who had been promoted to lieutenant. The case had been filed before Deutsch's indictment. The federal jury returned a verdict clearing the accused officers and the city. Even after the jury's findings, Federal Judge William Acker, whose attitude was similar to that of Judges Carl and Jasper, went through all kinds of machinations to make the city liable for not promoting the female officer and liable for paying her legal fees. The officer appealed the jury ruling to the Federal Circuit three-judge appeals court. While he waited for the federal appeals court decision, Judge Acker took the highly unusual action of calling members of the Birmingham City Council to his chambers to urge them to go ahead and settle the case by agreeing to have the city pay $750,000 in legal fees to Officer Oladeinde's attorneys. The council did not cave in to Judge Acker's pressure. In late 1999 the Federal Appeals Court upheld the jury's decision. Deutsch's enemies never gave up. Deutsch filed for and received a handsome federal payment for injury in the line of duty despite the opposition from the FOP.

The Abuse of Erica Arrington

On the evening of July 4, 1990, Erica and a friend named Marquita Kirkland went to Five Points South, a popular restaurant area near the campus of the University of Alabama, to eat dinner. People enjoy the area's restaurants and bars, the camaraderie of crowds milling around, and the fountain with the *Storyteller* sculpture by Frank Fleming. Five Points South is a festive and crowded place on July 4. Special entertainment begins around noon on a stage constructed near the fountain. Local artists perform until about midnight, and the crowd lingers around into the wee hours of the next morning. After trying to find accommodations at several restaurants and waiting in the long line of would-be diners at one, Erica and her friend decided to abandon their plan of dinner in Five Points South and go elsewhere. It was now about 10:00. From here I pick up the account from the City of Birmingham police files.

As the two girls walked from the restaurant and onto the crowded streets, Erica spotted another friend, Jan Ashford, in the crowd and walked over to speak with her, separating herself from Marquita. Finished with her busy chat with Jan, Erica began looking for Marquita. Suddenly in the area of the fountain a fight broke out and the crowd began to scatter. Erica moved about fifty feet away from the fountain area and stood on the sidewalk scanning the excited crowd for Marquita. A female Birmingham police officer used a bullhorn to order the crowd to disperse. At about that time, a dozen or so witnesses claim that they saw Officer Jerry Bahakel walking over to a black man who was seated in the window of his car and began beating him with a baton. Bahakel arrested the man, who was later identified as William Gregory. Later Gregory filed a complaint accusing Bahakel of attacking him without provocation.

Officer Bahakel then turned his attention to the crowd standing on the sidewalks, shouting out, "Clear the streets!" As Erica turned to leave, still not having sighted Marquita, she was grabbed by Officer Bahakel, who twisted her arm behind her back, forced her against a police patrol car, and tightly handcuffed her hands behind her. He then pushed her into the back seat of the patrol car, striking her face against the top inside door facing of the patrol unit. By that time Erica's friends, Jan and Marquita, were yelling out to the officers, "That's the mayor's daughter!" After about ten minutes, Bahakel transferred Erica to a police paddy wagon where he left her for approximately thirty minutes while he conferred with a group of Birmingham police officers nearby.

The paddy wagon then left the scene and transported Erica to the city jail. At the booking area police records show that Erica immediately complained to Lieutenant Joseph Rucker about the pain she suffered from the handcuffs and the other force Bahakel had used during her arrest. David Agee, a city magistrate assigned to the city jail, reported observing the scene when Erica was brought into the booking area. He reported that Bahakel, whom he knew by sight, came to the booking area but left without filing an arrest report on Erica, as department procedures required. He returned fifteen minutes later with an arrest report, which he filed with the magistrate charging Erica with disorderly conduct, inciting to riot, and failure to disperse. Magistrate Lonnie Washington, who was beginning his shift at the city jail at the time, refused to sign Bahakel's arrest warrant. At that point Agee claimed that he observed bruises on Erica's face, upper arm, and wrists.

After Erica had spent several hours in city jail, Marquita Kirkland signed a bond for her release. Erica complained of having back and shoulder pain and was treated at the emergency room of a local hospital that morning before returning home.

After I had talked to Erica on the phone early in the morning on July 5 and inquired about her condition, I asked her to go with her brother to the Office of Internal Affairs of the Birmingham Police Department to file a complaint on Jerry Bahakel. At around 9:00 A.M. on July 5 I called Chief Arthur Deutsch and eventually reached him at his home. When I asked him if he could tell me what he knew about my daughter's arrest, there was silence for a few seconds. Then in a surprised and somewhat disappointed voice, he explained that he knew nothing about it but would immediately find out what happened and call me back. No one had informed the chief about the arrest. In about an hour an apologetic Chief Deutsch met me at my city hall office. He said he would personally handle the matter and get a full report to me.

Jerry Bahakel

Bahakel had been a member of the Birmingham Police Department for several years. I had never met him but I did know his father, Izas Bahakel, and his brother Alfred, both of whom were local attorneys. In 1983 when I ran for reelection as mayor a friend of mine, Joe Nasef Rookis, had recruited Izas and Alfred Bahakel to be on my reelection team. During the 1983 campaign, my campaign literature featured a picture of my advisory committee that included a picture of the Bahakels as well as their names. The Bahakels, who are Lebanese Americans, resided in the city's Southside and worked to get their Lebanese American friends to support my reelection. They walked me door to door in their community, introducing me to their neighbors and asking them to vote for me. To give me such public support in Birmingham in 1984 was a courageous act for any white. Yet somehow in 1990, six years after the Bahakels befriended me, I never thought about the support they had given me, not even after I learned several weeks after the arrest of my daughter that the arresting officer was Izas Bahakel's son. Angered by my daughter's abuse at the hands of Jerry Bahakel, I was blinded to the good deed of the Bahakels six years earlier. In fact, I am ashamed to admit that I never regretted not sitting down with Izas Bahakel at the time and trying to resolve the matter. He of course was concerned about his son's career and I about my daughter's plight. Years later I felt that my failure to talk with Izas Bahakel was an act of total ingratitude on my part, one that I regret even today.

As I always did in high-profile cases of alleged police brutality, I inquired about whether the accused officer had any other citizen complaints filed against him and the nature of those complaints. It turned out that Bahakel had a number of complaints filed against him, alleging the use of undue force and authority. The records showed six excessive force complaints and seven conduct and abuse of authority complaints, none of which the police department's internal affairs sustained. In one excessive force case in 1988 a young white physician and two of his female friends filed excessive force complaints against Bahakel in an arrest and later filed a court case over their alleged treatment by Bahakel. The city settled the matter out of court by paying $20,000 to the complainants in September 1991. While the investigation of my daughter's arrest was under way, Bahakel was facing complaints from three citizens in connection with the July 4 incident in which he arrested my daughter. On August 14, 1990, a committee of three officers selected to hear the complaints against Bahakel sustained the complaint and he was suspended for twenty-five days and ordered to undergo psychological examination. While on suspension Bahakel refused to go for the psychological examination, which the police department had arranged with a University of Alabama psychiatrist. In fact the police department had difficulty locating Bahakel to serve him with the order from the chief for the examination. Efforts to reach him at his residence went unanswered. Finally, two Birmingham Police Department officers staked out his residence and served him as he was leaving his residence. Days went by and Bahakel refused to take the examination. The police chief then fired him. But the matter was not yet over. Bahakel appealed his dismissal to the County Civil Service Board and lost. He then filed suit in federal court in 1991 naming Chief Arthur Deutsch, Lieutenant R. L. Webb of Internal Affairs, and me as defendants. On February 25, 1992, after a year or so of depositions and other litigation, Federal Judge Robert Propst ruled against Jerry Bahakel and dismissed charges against all three defendants.

Nothing else was heard of Bahakel until I learned about a year later that Jefferson County sheriff Mel Bailey had hired him as a deputy sheriff. Upon learning of his hiring I filed a complaint with the County Civil Service Board, noting that the board had violated its longstanding policy of not certifying a fired law enforcement officer for a law enforcement job anywhere else in the county system. At a brief hearing before two of the three civil service board members with the Bahakels present, the board executive admitted that she had certified Bahakel to the sheriff position. She tearfully claimed that she had done so by mistake. The board took no further action and Bahakel remained with the sheriff's department.

Erica's Trial

Erica was set to go to municipal court in July on the three charges against her. I learned that four of the city's judges excused themselves from hearing the case. Apparently the judges felt caught between presiding over a case in which the mayor's daughter was charged with violation and running the risk of angering the Birmingham police if Erica was not convicted. There was one exception, however. Judge Carol Smitherman, a young black woman, volunteered to hear the case. At the trial, which took thirteen hours and lasted two days, the judge denied the request of Erica's attorney, Clyde Jones, to enter Bahakel's record of citizens' complaints into the record. She also refused to admit evidence of altered record tampering, declaring them not relevant to the case before her. After several hours of testimony and varying accounts from citizens called by the city prosecutor, she dismissed two of three complaints against Erica, noting that the department's arrest warrants were dated July 17 and stated that the incidents had occurred on May 4 on one warrant and June 4 in another warrant.

The trial continued on the remaining count of disorderly conduct. The city prosecutor placed several police officers on the witness stand who were at the scene of the July 4 incident. Included were Sergeant Ann Ballard and Officer Charles Bently, both of whom backed Bahakel's earlier testimony that Erica had been disorderly that night and had threatened to have her father fire him for messing with her. Each officer gave identical versions of what occurred. However, the civilians called to testify on behalf of Bahakel gave different and often contradictory testimony.

When the trial resumed the next day, the judge granted Clyde Jones's motion for a verdict of "not guilty" on the last charge. Jones never called any of the twelve defense witnesses he had listed to testify on Erica's behalf. A few days later Jones filed a claim against the city on Erica's behalf for false arrest, physical abuse, and attorney fees.

Although the city's legal department usually handled such claims and any recommendation for settling the claim in an unpublicized manner, Erica's claim was handled quite differently. The practice of the department was to recommend a settlement amount, if any, to the mayor and council members. If the mayor and five councilmen concurred and signed the settlement agreement, the matter was closed without any public announcement.

In Erica's case I excused myself from the settlement matter. The law department sought to get the signatures of six councilmen to settle the case for $21,000. However, only five councilmen, all black, agreed to the settlement. The three white councilmen, David Herring, Bill Myers (former Birmingham police chief), and Pat Sewell, refused to support the settlement, stating that they had not read the record on the investigation of the case. They were joined in their position by one black councilman, William Bell.

The record on the investigation was available to all council members, though some chose not to read them. In fact, in the more than one hundred cases the city had settled over the previous eighteen months for a total amount of $3.7 million, no council member had asked for files on those cases before approving them. But this was a much more sensitive matter.

Finally, in March 1991, the law department again placed the proposed $21,000 settlement on the council agenda. By a 6–3 vote with Bell switching his vote, the settlement was approved.

On March 21, 1991, I made my first public comment about Erica's arrest. I wrote in my weekly column for the *Birmingham Times,* a black weekly, about the hurt and sorrow I had endured. I tried to answer the many criticisms about my daughter's filing a complaint against the city. I in no way was apologetic about that action by my daughter. I felt she should not be treated any differently than anyone else. I wrote, "I do not believe as many apparently do, that she has fewer (or more) constitutional rights than any other citizen." To those who predicted that my daughter's case would hurt me politically, I wrote, "If her case hurts me politically, then so be it. Should this happen, it would probably be more accurate commentary on where we are as a city that believes in social justice than it would be on her or me. She didn't ask to be my daughter and I'm not going to ask her to endure her situation in silence just to help me politically."[13]

Perhaps the most galling thing I endured during my daughter's ordeal was the absolute silence of some of the city's leading citizens with whom I met monthly to discuss city affairs. Despite all of the publicity about my daughter's case, not a single one said to me, "I'm sorry to hear about the incident involving your daughter." I felt then as I do now that if my dog had been subjected to such alleged abuse and received similar publicity, most of those people would have expressed their concern about the incident. But despite my public statement to that effect, no one to this day has mentioned the incident. Indeed, I lost a bit of faith in what I thought was their humanity.[14]

But I should not end this discussion of my daughter's ordeal without mentioning the political ordeal Judge Carol Smitherman had to endure. She was appointed by the governor to fill a circuit judgeship vacancy in Birmingham just months after hearing my daughter's case. About a year later she ran for re-election and was narrowly defeated by Alfred Bahakel. The theme during that political contest was one of attacks on Judge Smitherman for her ruling in the Bahakel case. Much of metro Birmingham's white community, which makes up two-thirds of the electorate and which until 2002 had never given substantial support to any black political candidate who ran countywide, handed her a political defeat for a ruling that favored my daughter. When I spoke with Judge Smitherman a few days after the loss and following her public expression that she believed race was a factor in her defeat, she told me that Judge Marvin Cherner, a longtime Jefferson County Circuit Court judge, had come to her and recommended that she not make such a statement again. He reportedly told her that her defeat had nothing to do with race but had occurred because of her association or identification with me and my political organization, both of which he called "racist." (I say more about this incident in chapter 12.) Later Alfred Bahakel's sister Gloria ran for a judgeship. The theme of her campaign was an attack on my political organization and me and it succeeded.

In the 2000 election, two other Bahakel family members, one of whom was Jerry Bahakel, sought political office and lost. Their campaigns also focused on attacking my political organization and me.

STING OPERATION—MY SON

When one enters politics, every aspect of one's life is considered fair game by the media, including one's wife and children. Soon after becoming mayor I learned to take media criticism of me as par for the course in the political game. However, I could never quite insulate myself from the pain I felt when negative media reports targeted my children.

Two of my children experimented with illegal drugs and ran afoul of the law. Seeing their problem reported by the media was always painful. In the case of my son, he was arrested for purchasing an ounce and a half of cocaine in a Birmingham Police Department sting operation about two years after he had been in several drug rehabilitation centers.[15] Although he seemed to be doing well during the first year and a half of his rehab, he then began to experiment with crack cocaine and the downward spiral of drug addiction in his life rapidly accelerated. His arrest by Birmingham police was marked by curious circumstances, which I want to share.

I have no clear evidence that Chief Arthur Deutsch orchestrated my son's arrest; it's only a suspicion. One afternoon in late 1984 two Birmingham police officers made an urgent request to see me in my office. They had come to ask me how they should handle a complaint they had just received from the principal of the school attended by one of Deutsch's daughters. The principal had alleged that Deutsch's daughter had come to school that day, complaining to him about physical abuse from her father. In turn, the principal reported the allegation to police. The two officers wanted to know from me how they should handle the complaint.

I inquired as to how the department had handled such complaints previously and said they should handle it in their usual fashion. This meant that the officers went to the principal's office and spoke with the student. When the student declined to press her complaint, the matter was dropped. When Deutsch later learned about the incident he was reportedly furious with the officers involved and with me. He never spoke to me about the incident.

Shortly afterward, a Birmingham police sergeant, Charles Jordan, apparently through drug informants, introduced himself to my son while posing as a drug user and using the fictitious name of Steve Holland. Jordan, according to my son, cultivated a friendship with him, visiting my son's home on several occasions and bringing along a young child who was supposedly his daughter. His daughter and my son's daughter visited while Jordan and my son used drugs. Soon the police department set its well-planned trap to arrest my son.

Late one evening, Jordan appeared at my son's home claiming to have come into a handsome amount of money. Would my son purchase $1,950 worth of cocaine for him and let him pick it up at a given time the next day at my son's home? My son took the bait; he had been set up to buy enough cocaine to make him guilty of a felony. While Jordan waited in a car with my son the next day for the drug supplier to arrive at my son's home, undercover police in vans and other vehicles waited on the street near the house. When the supplier arrived, the officers in the van taped the transaction. My son went to the supplier's car, got in, and purchased an ounce and a half of cocaine. He got out of the car and delivered the cocaine to Jordan. Jordan gave him $50 for the deed. At that moment police sprang from their cover and arrested my son and the supplier.

Later that evening a high-ranking officer, Captain Charles Newfield, who had been in charge of the sting operation, called my home protesting to my wife that he did not know it was my son he had arrested. Of course he was lying. In February 1985 my son entered a plea bargain, testified against his supplier, and was placed on five years of probation.[16]

No such operation could have occurred without the police chief's knowledge. In this case, I believe that Deutsch was behind the entire operation. Deutsch and I did not speak about my son's arrest until nearly a year later. While riding with him from the police firing range to city hall one afternoon, I said, "Chief, I didn't uphold my son in any wrongdoing. But tell me, why did you set him up for a felony arrest instead of a misdemeanor?" Deutsch immediately claimed to have no knowledge of what I was talking about. I dropped the matter, believing he was flat-out lying. Deutsch promoted Jordan to lieutenant during the next promotion period.

I had seen Deutsch's treacherous behavior on an earlier occasion. Shortly after becoming chief, Deutsch and City Councilman John Katopodis got into a running public feud in which they hurled public insults toward each other. Some months later on a Sunday afternoon, Deutsch called me at my home and asked if he could come over. I said yes and in less than thirty minutes Deutsch, accompanied by two attorneys, was at my door. One attorney said that Katopodis had harassed one of his clients and the other attorney over a period of months. They were seeking some relief by complaining to the chief, and the chief wanted me to be aware of their request and the confidential manner in which they wanted the matter handled. About a month later Deutsch came to my office and asked me to accompany him to a meeting with FBI agents on the Katopodis matter. As we approached the FBI building three FBI agents in a car met us in the alley behind the building. Deutsch and I were asked to get in. We did and the driver headed for the interstate. As we drove up and down the interstate for about twenty minutes the FBI agents explained to me that they had been investigating the Katopodis matter but had no concrete evidence of criminal activity. At that point it was clear to me that Deutsch had gone to the FBI in the Katopodis matter and given them the impression that I, not he, wanted Katopodis investigated. As soon as we got out of the FBI car, I asked Deutsch if he had told the agents that I requested the investigation. "Oh no," he said. He just wanted me to know that he had looked into the matter. Again, I was sure he was lying.

7

The Beginning of the Federal Investigation

The most embarrassing and frightening period of my twenty years as mayor occurred in 1991 when the office of the U.S. Attorney for the Northern District of Alabama launched what he labeled as a "Federal Grand Jury investigation of corruption" at Birmingham City Hall. U.S. Attorney Frank Donaldson stated at the outset that the investigation was not aimed at me personally but at allegations of city hall corruption. From the very outset no one familiar with the political machinations of an investigation into political corruption at city hall could seriously doubt that it was an investigation aimed at me. As I came to realize later, such a statement from the U.S. attorney is simply the setting of the stage for the U.S. attorney's office to later announce, as it does in nearly every investigation, that it had conducted an investigation that simply followed the evidence and of course that evidence naturally led them to an investigation of me—eventually leading the U.S. attorney to name me as the target of the federal grand jury investigation in the very year I was up for reelection as mayor (in November 1991). I concluded that it was an attempt by the U.S. attorney to drive me from political office and, if need be, to indict me for federal crimes.

At first I was naïve enough to believe that the investigation was not aimed at me. I immediately sought an audience with Frank Donaldson in his office when I heard about it to discuss the rumors about the investigation and to offer my full cooperation. He greeted me in his office with a friendly slap on the back, asked me to give him my suit coat, which he hung on a hanger, and proceeded to say, "Sit down, Mayor, and make yourself comfortable."

Donaldson, in his most friendly manner, was quick to reassure me that the investigation was not aimed at me, and for the next thirty minutes we engaged in a very cordial conversation on topics ranging from the bullet hole in a window of his office to a few light comments about allegations and rumors that invariably crop up from time to time about government operations. It was a very convincing performance and I left Donaldson's office feeling that I'd just made a wonderful friend. As I left, I gladly accepted his invitation to be his guest at a seminar he was sponsoring at the Sheraton Perimeter Hotel in a couple of weeks. He also gave me his office number and that of his secretary and assured me that he would be quickly accessible if I called. If he was not in when I called, he said, his secretary would know to immediately find him and have him return my call. Donaldson was true to his promise. He immediately responded to my several calls to him, whether he was in or out of the city "until the stuff hit the fan."

Little did I know as I left Donaldson's office that he had already conducted several lengthy investigations of me, some dating back ten years.[1] I would only learn of these in late 1988, when I requested and eventually received my Freedom of Information file (FOIPA) from the U.S. Department of Justice.[2] Perhaps Donaldson was so reassuring to me because he knew and had reported to the Department of Justice that his office had been unable to find any violation of federal law by me. It would be months later that I learned of these investigations and read Donaldson's letter to the Washington office included in my FOIPA file. I came to realize that I had been totally naïve in my early dealings with Frank Donaldson.

Early Rumors of Federal Investigations

It was probably late in my second term as mayor, which would be about 1985, when someone mentioned to me that federal investigators were quietly probing the operations of my administration. This information was given to me in my office one day by Lieutenant Billy Webb, the head of my security detail. Webb said he had picked up information from a Birmingham police officer who often worked with the local FBI that their agents were seeking information about alleged corruption in my administration. There was nothing specific according to Webb, just inquiries as to whether any officers knew of illegal acts within my administration. I had little concern about the rumors and soon forgot about them. Webb and his wife, Gwen, would later play a major role in an FBI investigation of me. But indeed, as I was to learn later, the investigation was under way. Several incidents would underscore this fact. At one point an outside consultant retained by the city to develop a plan to upgrade the communications system of city hall discovered that all sixteen phones in the mayor's complex had been bugged. I received that information in a letter the consultant sent to my office. I was shown the phones that had been bugged and that the consultant had moved those phones to the basement of city hall.[3] He and I speculated that the bugging was probably the work of someone in the Birmingham Police Department and not the FBI office; the consultant indicated that had it been FBI work, the bugging would have been more sophisticated. It was easy for me to believe that the police were responsible since I was engaged in a full-scale, hostile, and public battle with the local FOP over alleged police misconduct against blacks.

Some time later this same consultant found a "bug" in my city-issued automobile.[4] He had been asked to inspect the vehicles after a friend of mine suggested that such an inspection was a good idea in light of the earlier reports of the bugging of my office phones. The bug beneath the vehicle's dashboard was wired into the radio system and transmitted on a radio frequency. Still, I discounted the idea that the FBI might be behind the bugging. The bug is on file in my archives at the Birmingham Library, along with the consultant's letter.

A few days following a Republican political fund-raiser for then-governor Guy Hunt at the house of a local leading corporate and civic leader, a Republican legislator from Jefferson County came to visit me in my office. He was concerned about a conversation between several well-known and powerful Republican businessmen of the Birmingham area that he had overheard at the Hunt fund-raiser. One participant, a well-known leading Alabama Republican conservative and one of Alabama's leading philanthropists, had reportedly asked members of his small informal conversation group why Frank Donaldson had not moved to "bring Arrington down." I was corrupt, he was alleged to have said, and he speculated that "Donaldson probably didn't have the backbone to take me on." My Republican friend was concerned about the conversation he had overheard and thought that I should be aware of it. I thanked him for his concern and his courage, promising not to divulge that he had given me the information. I did nothing with the information and knew nothing that I could do except to be aware of their perception of me. The chief spokesperson in that conversation at the fund-raiser was widely known as a "racist" and one who readily admitted it. He had told me over martinis at a banquet at the Birmingham Museum of Southern Flight one evening that he was racist when it came to blacks. But he assured me that his children, all young business professionals, did not share his views on race. As we both walked away from the bar after finishing our martinis, he turned to me and asked, "Dick, why don't you consider becoming a Republican?" We both smiled and went our separate ways. So I was not shocked to hear of his comments to a few friends at the Hunt fund-raiser.

Still, information about the federal investigation continued to come to me and I continued to believe that any such investigation had little or nothing to do with me. One Tuesday morning following a City Council meeting Robert Yarbrough, whose concession company held the city contract for the city's 85,000-seat Legion Field and the city zoo, came to my office to tell me that he, his brother, and mother had been subpoenaed to appear before the federal grand jury the day before and had been questioned about alleged requests for payoffs or extortion attempts by city officials in exchange for the concession contracts. Yarbrough's attorney had advised him that he could share the information with me if he wished and he had chosen to do so. He said he had also been asked about a city consultant named Marjorie Peters as to whether she had approached either of them for a bribe on behalf of any city official. The information did not alarm me, as I felt certain I'd never be implicated of wrongdoing in any investigation. I later learned from the FBI files obtained in 1992 through the FOIPA file that the FBI had begun investigating me in 1972 and reopened its investigation, which lasted from 1984 to 1992.[5] Assistant U.S. Attorney Herbert "Bud" Henry had written the Washington office of the Justice Department in 1990 saying the investigation found no violations by me.

Soon it was public knowledge that Marjorie Peters was the target of a full-blown federal grand jury investigation on corruption charges related to Birmingham city government contracts and alleged tax evasion. The *Birmingham News* reported on the federal investigation on Peters.[6] I had first been introduced to Marjorie Peters in my office by Willie Davis, a member of my staff. He would also later introduce me to Peters' business partner and friend, Tarlee Brown, an architect from Atlanta.

The Pursuit of Marjorie Peters

Peters was trying to establish an office in the City of Birmingham and was looking forward to being an integral part of my administration's all-out push to increase opportunities for minority businesses in Birmingham. I could not have known then that she would later—perhaps a year or so—become labeled by the local U.S. attorney's office as a "bag lady" for me and my administration. Brown would become the U.S. attorney's key witness in the conviction of Peters and the feds' efforts to indict me for corruption. Before her trouble with the feds, Peters would weave herself well into Birmingham's circle of minority businesspeople, all of whom were actively seeking business from the public and private sectors of our city. She was quite knowledgeable about construction and engineering and capable of holding her own with the best in the city.

She secured several contracts for work on city projects from my office. Her work and that of her firm were, except for one project, completely satisfactory. She also secured several contracts from the Birmingham Airport Authority and the University of Alabama at Birmingham, neither of which was awarded through the mayor's office. She was also asked to sit on the board of the Junior Chamber of Commerce—a respected position in the city's business community. Exactly what led to her becoming a person of interest to the U.S. attorney's office is not known to me. But I strongly suspect that it was her active role in my administration and its strong and often bitter battles with Birmingham's business community—especially the city's Associated General Contractors—to force minority participation in city contracts. But her fate was sealed when I decided to push forward with constructing the controversial Civil Rights Institute and turned to her to help me find the most reputable minority architectural firm in the country—a task she carried out successfully and in what appeared to me to be the utmost professional manner.

The grand jury investigation was headed by Bill Barnett. It was not too long before there were rampant rumors that the grand jury was really investigating me. Two local attorneys who were representing Marjorie Peters in her tax troubles reportedly told attorney Donald Watkins that Barnett had described me to them as a "crook."[7] It was also around this time that a friend of mine in Atlanta called to tell me that he had just been questioned about me in his office by an assistant U.S. attorney named Barnett.

Within an hour of receiving that call I was in Donaldson's office asking what was going on. He assured me that there was nothing for me to worry about, and he denied my accusation that Barnett was on that very day, in Atlanta, investigating me. He told me what a fine attorney Barnett was and expressed the utmost confidence in him. I left Donaldson's office in an uncertain and nervous state. But I reminded myself that I had been involved in some bitter legal battles over minority participation in city contracts. Perhaps, I thought, this was why Barnett had asked questions about me. But I also wondered whether Donaldson truly did not know that Barnett was questioning people about me or was lying to me.

When city resources were in place late in 1985 for the construction of the Civil Rights Institute, I turned to Marjorie Peters, who said she would consult with Tarlee Brown. Both had been involved in several special Atlanta projects, including the Martin Luther King Center in Atlanta. Late in October or early November, Peters and Brown had met with me and recommended that I consider the firm of Bond, Ryder, and James (BRJ), headed by and named after three black professors on the faculty of the Columbia University School of Architecture in New York. The firm had also been architects for the King Center in Atlanta and the Schaumburg Museum in Harlem, New York, and had been a part of designing several other notable structures in New York, including the Guggenheim Museum.[8] I was impressed by their credentials.

Peters and Brown told me that they had arranged to be partners with BRJ in submitting a proposal to the City of Birmingham for design of the proposed Civil Rights Institute. The team submitted its initial proposal to me in December 1985. The following March I visited Atlanta and New York with Peters and members of my staff to view some of the properties designed by BRJ. On April 7, 1986, I chose BRJ to design the Civil Rights Institute. Peters was authorized in writing by BRJ to serve as its local liaison project coordinator with the authority to submit periodic billings to the city for the firm consistent with the agreement with the City of Birmingham. The project proceeded smoothly.

After Phase I of the project was completed in January 1987, Peters submitted a BRJ invoice for $121,917, which the city paid, only to have the check returned to the city a week or so later from the firm saying it had not authorized the invoice and was not in total agreement with the latest report submitted to the city for the Civil Rights Institute by Peters. At this point Peters and BRJ disagreed on what portions of the funds were due Peters' firm, Marjorie Peters Enterprises. After a protracted dispute over the payment, Peters ended her firm's relationship with BRJ and by mutual consent was replaced by another firm that would settle the account with Peters. The project proceeded on schedule but the dispute between BRJ and Peters would later become pivotal in the federal prosecution of Peters. By 1991 the *Birmingham News* was reporting that Peters was under federal grand jury investigation. During this time the City of Birmingham and the U.S. attorney's office, led by Bill Barnett, were engaged in bitter public charges and countercharges. The acrimony had little to do with the grand jury investigation, Peters, or the BCRI as far as those of us in city government were concerned. But our fury was being fueled by revelations about federal investigations of me that had gone on for years without my knowledge. On May 21, 1991, Assistant Attorney General Bill Barnett called the city attorney and requested a meeting, which was granted. He came to city hall that afternoon and informed my attorneys that the Peters investigation had ended and that they had found no wrongdoing on my part. "Perhaps the mayor should be a little careful about whom he associates with," he said, in an obvious reference to Marjorie Peters, "but I want to make it clear the mayor is not a target." City attorneys wrote Barnett on June 11 thanking him for meeting with them on May 21 and responding to his request at the time that he would like to meet with me in the next six weeks to make clear that I was not the target of the investigation and to take a statement from me. They reported my willingness to meet. When attorneys reported to me on the Barnett meeting I was greatly relieved. I thought to myself that the long acrimonious battle with the U.S. attorney was ending. I was wrong; it was just the beginning.

In August 1991 the federal grand jury indicted Peters and set her trial to begin in September—exactly two weeks before the mayoral election. Peters was indicted on twenty-six counts. Aside from charges of tax evasion, the indictment dealt with Peters' actions between May 1986 and April 1987, the time that she was involved in work on the BCRI. It alleged that she had conspired with many people to defraud the City of Birmingham and BRJ of $220,000 in connection with the design and construction of the BCRI. It charged that the invoices submitted to the City of Birmingham by Peters on behalf of BRJ were "forged, altered and false" and that a $50,000 payment to Peters by a management firm that replaced her firm was unlawful and a payoff. The indictment said there were only two other "unnamed, un-indicted co-conspirators." But a week later, after Barnett told city attorneys there had been no wrongdoing on my part, he became involved in an argument with Peters' attorney, J. L. Chestnut, over Peters' rights to a "bill of particulars" giving more specific statements from the government about the charges against her. Clearly Peters was entitled to such a bill of particulars. But Barnett did not want to provide it. When

Chestnut said he would file a motion with the court to get the information, Barnett threatened to name me as an "un-indicted co-conspirator" with Peters if Chestnut filed his motion.

Chestnut walked into my office with my attorneys to tell me about Barnett's threat. I encouraged Chestnut to proceed with the motion and he filed it the next day. Hours later Barnett amended the Peters grand jury indictment to name me as one of the unindicted co-conspirators. Others also named on the amended indictment were Tarlee Brown, Art Clement, manager of Diversified Project Management (DPM), the firm that replaced Peters' firm on the BCRI development team, and Leonard Adams, a member of the city's finance office staff. It was a despicably low blow indicative of the level to which the U.S. attorney's office had sunk in its fight with the city. Months later the court would grant our motion to strike any mention of me as an unindicted conspirator from the records.

The city took issue with the indictment, stating that it had not been defrauded on the BCRI project and noting that the city had received all of the services for which it had contracted and at the price agreed upon by the contracting parties. This simple fact, the city argued, precluded any finding of fraud.

The Peters trial got under way in September 1991 despite protests from Peters' attorney that they had not been given enough time to prepare its defense. The trial dominated the local news through its conclusion. The trial was before federal judge James Hancock, who was often called "the prosecutor's judge." On October 17, 1991, a jury of three women and nine men returned a guilty verdict against Peters on all counts. After deliberating for nineteen hours, the jury foreman, James Byrd of Parrish, said all jurors were convinced of her guilt, according to the *Birmingham News*.[9] But a few weeks later an elderly white female juror told the *Birmingham News* that she felt that she had been coerced into voting "guilty." She did not think Peters was guilty, she said.

Shortly after the guilty verdict Peters' attorney appealed the decision to the U.S. 11th Circuit Court of Appeals. In February 1992 it returned the case to the district court, ruling that Peters' lawyers should have been granted more time to prepare their case and to get beyond the 1991 Birmingham mayoral election. It ordered the district court to grant her another trial.

On June 16, 1993, instead of facing retrial and expenses, Peters entered a plea agreement with the feds, pleading guilty to a single count of conspiracy to commit mail and wire fraud and one count of tax evasion. In exchange Assistant U.S. Attorney Michael Nicrosi recommended that Peters receive a three-and-a-half-year sentence for conspiracy and a "low-end" sentence on tax charges. Sentencing was set for July 12, 1993. Birmingham city attorney Donald Watkins told the *Birmingham News* that Peters pleaded guilty as a way to bring an end to her long ordeal: "She just ran out of gas emotionally and physically," he said.[10] The U.S. attorney was apparently pleased to settle for a reduced single-count plea. Its original intent, I believe, was to convict me. Having failed in that effort, having milked the Peters ordeal for all of its negative publicity against me, and having failed to defeat my reelection effort, it was not interested in a new Peters trial. But much of the bitter controversy between the U.S. attorney's office and the city during the grand jury investigation stemmed from our discovery early on that the three U.S. district attorneys in Alabama had compiled a federal "hit list" of Alabama's black elected officials (BEOs). Immediately BEOs began accusing the feds of orchestrating a harassment campaign aimed at them.

THE PROBLEMS OF THE HARASSMENT OF BLACK ELECTED OFFICIALS AND REVERSE DISCRIMINATION

I had no black political role models growing up in Birmingham. Indeed, black elected officials (BEOs) were practically nonexistent until the late 1950s. When I was reelected to office in 1983, the attitude of the federal administration toward cities had taken a huge negative swing under President Reagan's first term. "Reagan's Revolution" of less government made him a popular president, but his popularity in black America remained low. He was viewed by blacks as anti–civil rights. His administration abandoned key federal programs for city assistance, especially those that inner cities like Birmingham found helpful. Two of Reagan's positions angered the Birmingham black community.

The first was his position on affirmative action. In 1981 the Justice Department took the initiative in recommending the settlement of several lawsuits filed in federal court alleging that Birmingham and neighboring cities practiced racial discrimination against blacks and women in their hiring and promotion procedures. The cases had lingered, unsettled, in the federal court system for nearly a decade when the Justice Department recommended to the City of Birmingham that the suits be settled by having city government enter into a consent decree that set goals for hiring and promoting women and minorities. I applauded that action and the city readily signed on to the decree drafts from the Justice Department. The city abided by the decree religiously, enabling the city to significantly increase employment opportunities for minorities despite accusations from the city's white employees—police officers and firefighters in particular—that the city was practicing "reverse discrimination." To counter these charges the city instituted a court-approved policy of having a local federal judge review each promotion of a minority before it became effective to ensure that the employee in question was qualified and met the promotion criteria of the consent decree. Still, the white firefighters filed suits in the same court accusing the city of racial bias and reverse discrimination. The district court under Judge Sam Pointer continued to hold the city's action as legal.

But at the same time, the Justice Department that had committed itself to legally defend the consent decree against attacks reneged on its own consent decree program and began an abrupt about-face. Such a decree, it said, represented reverse discrimination and the Justice Department abandoned the city and joined Birmingham's white firefighters to charge the city with reverse discrimination for carrying out the Reagan consent decree. Unable to prevail in Federal District Court, Alabama Republicans succeeded in getting Reagan to appoint a member of the staff of the Alabama attorney general to the appeals court in Atlanta. When a three-judge appeals court found Birmingham guilty of reverse discrimination for its hiring practices under the consent decree, that sad decision was penned by the judge who had recently been appointed to the appeals court from the Alabama attorney general's staff. The U.S. Supreme Court narrowly upheld the decision. Birmingham, a city that had been the worst in the nation in terms of fair employment practices for blacks, was now guilty of discrimination against whites and liable for the settlements to white firefighters and other white employees. (They were still reaping the benefits of those settlements when I left office in 1999.)

Second, the Reagan administration's U.S. attorneys began a campaign of harassment of black elected officials (BEOs) nationwide. In Alabama alone during the 1980s, twenty BEOs were indicted: two pleaded guilty; three were found guilty; and fifteen others were cleared of all government charges by juries. These actions came on the heels of the Alabama Black Belt voter fraud trials, in which elderly rural blacks were targeted for alleged voter fraud. Only a national outcry about this despicable practice by southern Republican U.S. attorney, now Senator Jeff Sessions, halted the injustice.

It was in this atmosphere that BEOs in Alabama moved to fight the rapidly growing harassment of BEOs. In May 1989 Joe Reed, president of the Black Democratic Conference in Alabama, was quoted in the *Birmingham News* as saying that the time had come for blacks to organize and fight the harassment of BEOs by Republican attorney generals in Alabama. On May 30, 1989, I wrote a letter to Reed, State Senator Hank Sanders, State Senator Michael Figures, State Senator Earl Hilliard, and attorney J. L. Chestnut suggesting that we lead an effort to form an organization to fight this type of harassment. Senator Sanders also called for united action, noting that 50 percent of all Alabama BEOs were under investigation.[11] We all agreed and asked BEOs from all over Alabama to meet with us in Montgomery at the Dexter Avenue Baptist Church (once pastored by Dr. Martin Luther King) on June 7, 1989, to form a united effort against this harassment. The church's basement overflowed with BEOs on June 7, 1989, and there were no doubt several black FBI informants there as well. At the news conference, over which I presided, I was quickly attacked by two "news reporters," both of whom were soon identified as FBI agents acting as reporters. They attempted to embarrass me by asking questions about why I had permitted a black man named Henry Johnson, who was in the Birmingham jail for Department of Human Relations (DHR) violations at his daycare facility, to be illegally freed from the Birmingham jail the previous week. This was a reference to a commutation given by the city's pardon and parole board to a group of inmates, one of whom was Johnson. This of course was a standard action by the pardon and parole board; a dozen or so inmates were periodically paroled to ease overcrowding in the city jail under a federal court mandate. The housing of a felon at a city jail was rare and this, I believed, was a mistake. Nevertheless, it served the purpose intended by the feds, which was to temporarily distract attention from our goal. The *Birmingham News* reported on the Johnson parole, criticizing the act by the city in an editorial.

Despite this effort at sabotage, one of many the feds would attempt, we succeeded in forming the Alabama Organization for Legal Defense of Elected and Appointed Officials[12] and set to work documenting federal abuse of BEOs and calling on the Justice Department to correct this injustice. Our reports and carefully planned media program drew national attention to the problem for the next year. In addition to meeting with Senator Joe Biden, chairman of the Senate Judiciary Committee, and his staff I met with several other members of Congress to discuss the issue and our reports. Several national groups, including the Regional Convention of the NAACP, which met in Washington, D.C., had me as the keynote speaker to address the issue of harassment of BEOs. We succeeded in making the issue a hot topic of national discussion. Foremost among those who would resent and not forget our efforts were members of the FBI and the U.S. attorney's office in the three Alabama federal districts.

On June 8, 1989, the *Birmingham News* reported on our Dexter Avenue Baptist Church meeting in an article titled "Arrington Wants Probe of Federal Prosecutors," noting that many Alabama BEOs were in attendance. The good attendance was in response to a joint memo from several well-known BEOs publicizing the meeting. But two other factors no doubt worked to swell participation: first, the lingering anger among many black political observers of the Black Belt voter fraud trials in which Jeff Sessions had conducted a lengthy investigation, and second, harassment of elderly blacks in the rural Black Belt (the feds alleged that federal voting laws were being violated in the absentee balloting process that is common in Alabama's rural Black Belt areas). The tactics of intimidation, including late-night FBI visits and blacks being taken by bus from the Black Belt to Mobile for questioning, angered black Democrats across the nation and led to a national campaign against such harassment.

The Alabama Black Elected and Appointed Official Legal Defense Fund retained the pro bono services of Montgomery civil rights attorney Donald Watkins, who secured the services of a half dozen attorneys to investigate and document the harassment of BEOs by Republican federal agents and the FBI. Several lengthy reports were published documenting the investigative techniques used by the feds. Those reports were circulated widely throughout the country and especially in Washington, D.C.[13] The Alabama organization immediately affiliated with the National Organization against Harassment of BEOs. The reports gained national attention and soon Richard Thornburg, Reagan's U.S. attorney, issued a public denial about the conduct of the federal agents. We continued to turn up the heat, filing complaints with every federal legislative and judicial body we could identify. Soon the federal Office of Professional Responsibility (OPR) had to launch a formal investigation of our charges. In March 1990, Senator Howell Heflin entered one of our reports into the congressional records. It became impossible for the news media, including Alabama's, to ignore our complaints.[14]

The July 3, 1990, edition of *Newsweek* carried a story on the brewing controversy under the heading "Backtracking in Birmingham," leading U.S. Attorney Frank Donaldson to issue a letter to the editor of *Newsweek* denying our allegations. Across the nation the harassment of BEOs was spotlighted. The heat was on for the feds. But they were not sitting quietly by doing nothing. Instead they were working on their own response and secretly identifying their targets. In late July State Senator Earl Hilliard, later Alabama's first black congressman since Reconstruction, dropped by my office. He reported that he had been asked to attend a meeting at the office of a prominent Birmingham white attorney who had once held high state office. According to Hilliard, this attorney warned him that Alabama federal officers meeting in the Mobile office of the U.S. attorney had compiled "a hit list" of BEOs. The attorney provided Hilliard with the list, which he had obtained from a friend who worked on the staff of the Mobile U.S. attorney. My name, of course, led the list, which also included Hilliard, State Representative John Rodgers, and City Councilmen William Bell and Jeff Germany. Our attorneys immediately made the list public, a strategy we would follow on every move the feds made. We were determined that they would not scurry about in secrecy and darkness and carry out their entrapment plans. Time after time, as I will detail later, we released entrapment plans by the feds to the news media, sometimes leaving the feds speechless and no doubt wondering where the leaks were coming from and at other times swearing the charges were false. But the more information we made public the more information we got from other sources—defense attorneys representing other clients, staff in the offices of the U.S. attorneys, former and current FBI agents, and FBI informants, the latter of whom we learned existed in large numbers.

Three Decades of Federal Investigation

When I stood in historic Dexter Avenue Baptist Church on June 7, 1989, and called for a united front against the Republican-led harassment of America's BEOs, I knew that I had been a target of such harassment in the form of FBI

investigations dating back to 1972, one year after I had been elected to Birmingham's City Council. That revelation first came to me in 1988. At the time
we were in the midst of the federal investigation of the alleged corruption surrounding the development of the Birmingham Civil Rights Institute.

In the midst of the campaign I was leading against the harassment of BEOs,
Joe Whatley, one of the attorneys working with the Alabama Black Elected
and Appointed Officials Legal Defense Fund, suggested that I request a copy of
the files that the federal investigative agencies might have on me. That request
was possible because of the federal Freedom of Information Act that permits
any citizen to request such information. So on October 29, 1986, I submitted
my request. For the first couple of months a few sheets of information from
various federal agencies drifted in via mail. Then one day the Postal Service
delivered a cardboard box crammed with files from the Justice Department,
mainly the FBI. The box contained 500 pages of material. I stared at the stacks
of files after opening the box, wondering to myself, "Could this possibly all be
on me?" It was. That box opened my eyes to what harassment could be like and
inspired me to stand up and fight.

Before me were the files that told me that I had been labeled by my government as "a national security risk" and placed on a watch list of those whom
the FBI should undermine. For days I wondered what I had done to earn such
dubious distinction from my government. After all, I had never been in any
trouble. I had never run afoul of our laws. And by no means had I ever been
thought of as militant. Quite the contrary: those who knew me thought me to
be "a soft moderate" without a fiber of militancy in me. Having been alive during a period of civil rights demonstrations and sufferings and fights against
vile racial oppression in the midst of America's Johannesburg, I had never participated in a civil rights demonstration of any kind. I had watched courageous men, women, and children challenge America's worst forms of racial
oppression and remained on the sidelines. My feelings of guilt surfaced at
times. Even at my election in 1971 as the second black in city government,
some wondered aloud what I brought to the freedom struggle of generations of
my people and those who stood with them. Did I deserve such an important
position in a city where black people had struggled so long to have a voice in its
government? My FOIPA packet made it clear to me that the FBI's picture of me
was that of an official prone to corruption and, for some reason, a danger to the
security of our nation.[15]

The 1972 Cointelpro Label

During my second year on the Birmingham City Council, the local offices of the U.S. attorney launched an investigation of me based on what the FBI files said was a "suspicion" that I had a relationship with the Alabama Black Panther Party, a supposedly militant activist group that became notorious for its fight against the federal government. The names of Huey Newton, Eldridge Cleaver, and others were commonly reported on as Panthers during the 1960s. The conclusion that the FBI intended to destroy the Black Panther Party and its leaders is inescapable for anyone who reviews the voluminous record on government investigation of the Black Panthers and militants like Birmingham native Angela Davis. The slaughter of Chicago black militant Fred Hampton by government agents and informers in his sleep at his residence following lengthy federal surveillance activities is but one example of the extremes the Hoover-led FBI took against the Panthers and other suspected black militants. Kenneth O'Reilly in his book *Racial Matters: The FBI's Secret File on Black America, 1960–1972* details the federal actions leading to the killing of Hampton. It also reveals the FBI's horrifying assaults on black American leadership, beginning in the 1960s, a period during which the FBI inundated America's black community with black government informers and spies reminiscent of what America was being told took place only under Communist regimes such as the Soviet Union. The truth is, however, that then—and in my opinion now—the black community of America is a continuing target of surveillance by the FBI, often using black informants who are paid and/or caught committing crimes. In exchange for money and/or avoiding prosecution for running afoul of the law, many black Americans of every social class become spies for the FBI. In many cases the informants are caught for some "minor" federal violation involving a relatively small amount of money or illegal drugs. (Below I cite a specific case of this type involving the FBI investigation of me.) I hasten to point out, however, that as the mayor of Birmingham for twenty years I am fully aware of law enforcement's use of informers and "citizen information" to solve crimes. Without such activities many crimes would go unpunished. But what is so shocking about the FBI's spying on America's black community is the large number of blacks working as FBI informants and the assault on the civil liberties of FBI targets by the agency's activities.

During the Johnson administration, FBI director J. Edgar Hoover carried out a pervasive surveillance system aimed at America's black leadership—a counterintelligence program (Cointelpro). Hoover mobilized the FBI to smash black civil rights, often targeting everyday people who lived in the black community, and to ouster black political activists. O'Reilly reports that in August 1967, with America's cities facing race riots and civil rights demonstrations, the FBI launched a new counterintelligence program called BLACPRO patterned after the Communist Party and Ku Klux Klan operations that targeted civil rights leaders and Black Power advocates. At the same time the FBI targeted black America under a series of community surveillance programs. Volumes of now unclassified government records and records of a congressional investigation into the practice attest to the FBI's activities.

In one part of the spy program the FBI compiled a "watch list" of 1,600 black leaders who were to be targeted and spied on by FBI field offices. According to congressional hearings records, Hoover sent written orders to FBI field offices throughout the country, directing agents to take actions to destroy the credibility and character of the black leaders on the FBI list.

I was not surprised that prominent civil rights leaders like Dr. Martin Luther King Jr. were included on the list. Media stories publicized the FBI's spying on King, reporting on King's alleged sexual liaisons. King, after all, was "big fish." But when I learned in 1986 that I was also included on the FBI list of 1,600 blacks, I was surprised. The Birmingham field office of the FBI had been instructed to spy on me and to destroy my good name and credibility. Putting me on that list was straining at "little fish or minnows." But that was how the FBI program worked.

I also assume that I was included on the list because of my outspoken criticism of the well-documented brutality of many Birmingham police officers against blacks. After a few months on the City Council I was pushing for new policies and programs to halt such brutality. It was not long before I was viewed by most of Birmingham's white community as "anti-police," "a coddler of black criminals," and one who "tied the hands" of police officers. The criticism I received was frequent and public. But police abuse of Birmingham's black citizens was so well-known in the black community that its leadership rallied to my support. Every black man wondered whether he might be the next victim. For the first time there was a voice at city hall focusing the public spotlight on police abuse. All of a sudden the perception that many blacks had of me as not having won my civil rights badge changed. I was the new black political voice and power of Birmingham. Even two of my white fellow council members called me aside on several occasions to kindly tell me that my campaign against police abuse was justified, but they cautioned me about both the political risk and personal danger I was encountering. What made me the city's preeminent black political leader for a decade and a half made me enemy number one in the Birmingham Police Department and apparently among some local FBI agents.

There is probably one other fact that gave me the dubious distinction of being affiliated with the Alabama Black Libertarian Front (the name given to the Black Panther Party in Alabama). It was my longtime defense of a young black man and ex-convict named William Lake, or Mafundi. Mafundi was about 5'6" and had a dark complexion. He had a deep-seated hatred of Birmingham police: he claimed that he had been the target of their brutality on many occasions. He regularly called my attention to cases of alleged police abuse of blacks. He never showed any fear of or respect for Birmingham police and wore his hostility toward them on his sleeve. Mafundi observed police officers arresting citizens and often investigated the arrest of blacks by the police. If he had any information that suggested police misbehavior, he called this to my attention. Many police officers despised Mafundi for what they perceived to be his "interference." I was called to circuit court to testify on his behalf following one of his encounters with police. For many that was simply further proof of my hatred of police.[16] It was becoming clear that the jaws of a corruption probe were slowly closing around me.

8

In the Eye of a Corruption Probe
FBI Surveillance

By May 1985, following what FBI files claim were numerous complaints of corruption at city hall, Cecil Moses, director of Birmingham's FBI office, received authorization from the national FBI office and U.S. Attorney Frank Donaldson to initiate FBI entrapment activities targeting me to determine whether I was corrupt or "prone to corruption."[1] I would not learn of these activities until nearly two years later. The list of alleged complaints ran the gamut from accepting bribes for city hall favors to entrapment activities perpetrated by the FBI. Every negative local news story of any sort found its way to the FBI and into my files.

In 1987 the new local FBI field office director, Allen P. Whitaker, had received authority from Frank Donaldson and Bill Barnett to use electronic devices, phone taps, videotapes, hidden microphones, closed circuit television, photographs, and a host of other devices to monitor my conversations and other activities. FBI files show that Whitaker compiled several hundred tapes of my phone conversations from taps and hidden microphones and nearly an equal number of photos and videotapes. My files also show that as late as August 1988 Donaldson or one of his assistants, Bud Henry, wrote the national FBI office informing them that their undercover investigations of me had been completed and that they found no violations. So after hundreds and hundreds of hours of secret FBI surveillance, they found no wrongdoing on my part. One would think that surveillance would be halted. Not so. Instead, three months later Donaldson, Barnett, the local IRS office, and FBI agents launched a new effort of extensive "sting operations" to try to entrap me into violating some law or to show that I was "predisposed" to commit a crime. During the course of the entrapment activities, six agents would receive special training in Atlanta to investigate me. Following their six-week training period, they

were assigned twenty-four-hour surveillance of me.[2] On at least four occasions they showed up in my office masquerading as businessmen representing
firms from Atlanta, Huntsville, New Orleans, or New York. Using fictitious
names and business cards, they attempted to lure me into some corrupt activities. They offered attractive development deals to the city and sought to get me
to write incriminating letters to them in response to their offers. Week after
week they sprang new entrapment programs on me. One week a young black
FBI agent, posing as a wealthy Atlanta businessman, came to see me. The suspicious young man claimed to have considerable business wealth and to have
just purchased the downtown Birmingham Bank for Savings building. What
assistance could I offer him, he wanted to know, to help with the renovation of
the building. He was set on me, I perceived, because of my strong push to assist minority businesses. He pursued his entrapment efforts off and on for six
months.

At one point six FBI operatives, saying they were a large development firm,
came to my office with a grandiose multimillion dollar plan to revitalize a
half dozen dilapidated downtown properties and to build a downtown mono-
rail system. Their plan was so preposterous that I asked them to go out and get
written options to purchase the properties in question and bring them back to
me along with some architectural plans. Sure enough, a month later they were
back with alleged written options and a member of a local architectural firm.
They were getting nowhere but they didn't stop trying.

The Undercover Black Minister, July 1989

I was particularly upset with the feds on one occasion when I thought a young
black minister who visited me on several occasions was really an FBI agent
posing as a minister to get an appointment with me. I was wrong.

In July 1989, Caroline Knowles, who handled all my appointments, placed a
written request on my desk from a Reverend Clyde Beverly, pastor of a Baptist
church in an area of the city called Sherman Heights. I did not recognize the
name but I jotted "O.K." on the request for appointment form, which meant
she should proceed with setting an early appointment for the person making the request. There were literally dozens of requests daily for appointments
to see me. It was never possible to see all who requested an appointment. My
policy was to refer those I couldn't see to one of my staff. But there were people

with certain positions of influence such as neighborhood presidents, corporate executives, and ministers whose requests were given priority. So this young man who identified himself as a minister was given an appointment and came to see me. He said his reason for coming to see me was that his church owned a vacant piece of real estate that he wanted to develop with some type of assistance from the city. Once he identified the location of the alleged property I immediately knew it was outside of the city's corporate limits and told him so. He would have to annex the property to the city, I said, and then I would see how the city might assist with its development, perhaps by helping provide a portion of the cost for infrastructure, such as sewers, water, sidewalks, or curbs. He appeared to have no understanding of the development process and I viewed him as a young minister trying to expand his church's mission. We finished our first meeting but he came back to request a second meeting a couple of weeks later. I gave Caroline my "O.K." to set up the appointment, thinking that maybe he had some definitive plans now to share with me. But the second meeting was much like the first—almost idle talk about his desire to develop the property. By now I'd concluded that this young minister was simply naïve. Weeks later he called, again seeking an appointment. In fact he made two other attempts to set up another appointment with me, but I told Caroline I didn't want to waste any more time with him. If he had something I needed to see, I asked her to tell him to please put it in writing and leave it. I said that I would see him later.

Several months later the real estate firm of Barnes, Pitts and White, then located at Third Avenue North and Ninth Street, called my office one morning. Could I possibly give them thirty minutes that afternoon in their office to introduce me to a developer and show me a proposed project he was backing? My security head, Lieutenant Eugene Thomas, drove me to the real estate office in the midafternoon for the meeting. I was introduced to a young black businessman, who, as he told it, had put down $125,000 in earnest money on a large tract of land that I knew was a former Boy Scouts camp area. The dilemma that he was facing, he said, was that he only had about five days left to come up with the purchase price of the property or lose his earnest money. He wanted to know whether the city could help him secure the needed funds and, if so, under what conditions. Tacked on the wall of the office was a large map showing the boundaries of the property.

All the while he was talking to me and the real estate agents, thoughts were running through my mind: "I've seen this guy somewhere before." I noticed that he was extremely nervous and perspiring profusely. I explained that the city had looked at the property years ago and determined that the city had no interest in it. It was also located outside of the city. Then, as I stood to leave, it struck me: this young developer was the minister who had come to my office six months earlier with a piece of property his church wanted to develop. With some effort, I stopped short of divulging the fact that I now recognized him and knew he was running a "game"—probably for the FBI. In fact, as I got back into the car with Lieutenant Thomas, I blurted out to him, "You know, it's a damn shame that the FBI has a black agent walking around here masquerading as a minister." As soon as I reached my office I picked up the phone and called the real estate agent. "How well do you know that developer?" I asked. "Oh, I know him well," the agent replied. "His mother lives in my neighborhood and I've known him for years." "But do you know," I asked, "that several months ago he introduced himself to me as a minister?" "Oh, he is a minister," the agent said to me. "He pastors a church in Sherman Heights." I was silent for a moment, and then said, "Well, okay, I thought he was running some kind of game," and I hung up the phone. I never said anything else about the incident and my suspicion although I was somewhat mystified by the whole affair. I thought that I had become paranoid because of the federal entrapment efforts. When the same young minister and a portion of his congregation showed up at my church one Sunday afternoon for a worship service where he delivered the message, I felt a little embarrassed about my earlier suspicion about him, but I didn't mention it and left at the end of the service without speaking to him.

But a couple of months later—quite by chance—I was talking with an old friend who was also a political junkie. His name was Dewy Woods and he lived in the adjacent county of Walker. He worked on everybody's political campaign in the state—from governor on down—and there was hardly a Democratic politician in the state who didn't know old Dewy.

Riding to a meeting with Dewy one day we were discussing the ongoing federal investigation of me when I mentioned how I had thought this young minister had been an FBI operative. Immediately Dewy asked, "What did you say his name was?" I repeated the name. "Oh, that's the guy the feds arrested a few months back for allegedly taking money from the treasury of the local coal miners' union." Dewy said the minister had been the union's treasurer and was unable to account for some of the funds. A federal investigation led to his being charged with theft as well as possession of illegal drugs. Now the pieces came together. The feds had not taken him to trial but put him to work as one of their "undercover spies" under one of the federal programs that permit the U.S. attorneys to place some first-time offenders in undercover information programs for up to fifteen months. If the offender serves satisfactorily, his record is sealed or purged and few people ever know of it. Part of this offender's assignment was to help entrap me.

I would have a somewhat similar experience later. The *Birmingham News* carried a story of the arrest of three young local IRS agents who had been caught using illegal drugs. They were charged and dismissed, but not tried and sentenced. Later Frank Donaldson's office worked through the county's personnel board to get one of the agents hired in the city's finance office to fill a position as a revenue agent. When he was hired by the city there was no record of his problem as an IRS agent. We learned of his problem and how he ended up in the finance office quite by accident. A paralegal working with my attorney, Donald Watkins, during our fight with the feds, overheard a conversation in the city cafeteria between this former IRS officer, now a city revenue officer, and a couple of friends who were kidding him about being an undercover IRS agent. The paralegal immediately came to my office and wanted to know if I knew a former IRS agent was on my finance staff. Of course I didn't. But my attorney smelled the rat right away. "Hell, he's a damn FBI plant," he said. Then he called the police lieutenant in and asked him to check the National Crimes Programs database for the name. As soon as the agent's name was entered, the following information popped up: "Do not detain, contact FBI agent." Now we were sure. "Let's call him up here now," my attorney said, and we did. When he walked into my office I immediately recognized him as a young fraternity brother of mine who reminded me of that fact whenever I bumped into him. I also remembered that my wife had directed his marriage to a young lady who lived directly across the street from us.

The young man readily admitted that he was working undercover for the FBI and had been doing so for several months. "I only have about three months left in the program and I'm clear of the U.S. attorney's office," he said. "Just let me keep my job," he pleaded. We asked him a few other questions and learned that in the short period of time—about thirty minutes—between when we pulled his name up on the crime file and called him to come to my office, his

FBI handler had called him, telling him the city had gotten a "hit" on him. "What do they want?" he said his handler had asked. "I don't know," he reportedly said. "I've just been asked to come to the mayor's office." "OK," his handler said, "go see what they want and call me back." So within the hour the FBI undercover operative became a double agent.

It was not uncommon for staff in our finance office to come to my office to inform my chief of staff that some FBI agent had walked into the finance office, chatted briefly with them, and then tried to get them to go across the street to the park to meet with them on their lunch break. How many met with the agents and maybe later worked with them, we didn't know. But some did and we knew they did because they were also cooperating with us.

Twenty-Four-Hour Surveillance

My files obtained from the FBI under FOIPA clearly showed that six specially trained agents followed me around the clock, recording my activities, my contacts, and my whereabouts. One file even included a description of individuals (and their license plates) who showed up at one of my campaign fund-raisers at a local downtown club.

This year-long, around-the-clock surveillance was unknown to me until I read my FBI files. It helped explain one incident that occurred at about 8:00 one evening after I left my office. These special agents, while keeping tabs on me, carefully stayed out of my sight. There was one exception, however—an intentional effort by the agents to let me know I was being followed. Exactly what their point was in revealing their presence to me I don't know. I had made a phone call to a young woman who lived on the city's Southside who had helped me with a campaign fund-raiser. In the course of the conversation, during which she said she was alone for the evening, she invited me to her home for a drink. I had never been to her home and was uncertain about the directions to her home that she gave me. So I asked her if she would meet me at the Highland Racquet Club parking lot in her car and let me follow her to her home. She agreed. As I got within a block of the parking lot two vehicles with Shelby County license plates, each containing two white men, took turns pulling up alongside my car and staring at me in a fashion I could not help but notice. I pulled into the parking lot where my friend was waiting. I pulled up alongside her car and told her I was being followed and that she had better go on. She then drove away. I sat in my car for a few seconds and then pulled over into a space near a phone booth, got out of my car, and pretended to be talking on the pay phone. They pulled into the parking spaces on either side of my car, got out, and stood watching me, never saying a word. I got back into my car, backed out, and drove off. They stood beside their cars staring at me as I drove off.

THE TRAGIC DEATH OF ROBERT MOUSALLEM

According to my FBI FOIPA files, Frank Donaldson, Assistant U.S. Attorney Bud Henry, and FBI agents met and reviewed evidence gathered by undercover FBI operatives about me. They concluded that there was no evidence of wrongdoing on my part and reported to the Justice Department that the investigation of me would be closed on August 4, 1988. This was approximately fifteen months after the FBI formally launched its investigation of alleged city hall corruption. Interestingly this appeared to be the time that the U.S. attorney was cranking up its investigation of Marjorie Peters' alleged defrauding of the City of Birmingham.

Two months later, Bill Barnett and FBI and IRS agents launched a new investigation targeting me. This time they chose to use one of the undercover operatives who had been key to the successful prosecution of an organized group of tax dodgers, including some of the so-called Posse Comitatus. This operative was named Robert Mousallem. Mousallem had been in trouble with the feds for tax evasion and attempted bribery, and apparently became an undercover operative for the local U.S. attorney's office, helping entrap several key tax dodgers. In exchange for his role in the entrapment and successful prosecution of these violators, Mousallem said he was promised probation. Mousallem's dream of federal probation became a nightmare, ending with his death under highly suspicious circumstances. As he left a downtown building Mousallem was surprised to be stopped by his FBI and IRS handlers and Bill Barnett and asked to get into their car. According to his sworn affidavit, he was told Barnett had "one more assignment" for him to complete.[3] He was driven to an office building occupied by the IRS, placed in a room, and left sitting there alone. Plastered on several file cabinets and other places around the room were several huge signs reading "corruption" and a large picture of me.

I had come to know Mousallem, a Lebanese American building contractor, when I was running for reelection for mayor in 1983. My campaign manager, Lemorie "Tony" Carter, came to the downtown campaign office to tell me that he had met Mousallem near the campaign office. He told Tony that he was an Arrington supporter and would be glad to help me in the election out in the eastern area of the city. Tony and I were very pleased with the new volunteer, especially coming from the city's largely white eastern area where there was great white voter hostility toward me, to put it mildly. Tony later introduced me to Bob Mousallem, who offered to provide a free campaign office for me in a shopping area in Roebuck. Tony and I debated the idea of a campaign office in Roebuck, right in the midst of my political enemies. Would it be a mistake to have an Arrington campaign office there as a daily reminder to them to get out and defeat me, or would it be seen as an overture from me to white eastern area voters? We decided on the latter. Mousallem not only provided us an office in a vacant commercial building but he recruited several white women to staff the office. Oddly enough, we moved into the wrong building and set up our campaign office. Weeks later Mousallem told us we were in the wrong office but that he had arranged for us to stay where we were.

On several occasions Mousallem pulled together a dozen or so older white men to eat dinner with me at the local Denny's restaurant and to hold several small fund-raisers for me. We soon developed a camaraderie and I was quite comfortable meeting with them and discussing election strategies. Several members of the group would remain political allies until I left the mayor's office in July 1999. There was one noticeable exception: a member of the group named Jay Kelly, who lived in Tarrant City. When we held our second meeting at Denny's with the gang, he didn't show but sent word to me via Mousallem that while he wished me well he didn't want to participate in the group because he was a "racist." Other members of the group said to me, "Let's just forget him. He's got old KKK ties and can't get it out of his system." I never saw him again. But a few years later he would provide me with important information about the U.S. attorney's effort to get him to "create evidence" to incriminate me.[4]

As for Mousallem, I saw him infrequently after the election. When the city was attempting to build a water theme park, he came to see me, expressing his interest in competing for the construction of the project using a Canadian-based firm. He supplied me with a large feasibility study on a theme park that bore the name of a Canadian firm. He also helped me identify several potential sites for the park. He went so far as to get a state legislator from North Jefferson County, near Gardendale, to pass a bill in the legislature de-annexing several hundred acres of vacant land from Fultondale and annexing it to Birmingham. The bill required Birmingham to develop the property in seven years or have it revert into Fultondale, which it eventually did when the city chose another park site and two members of Birmingham City Council—John Katopodis and Betty Collins—filed suit to halt the park development. The idea of a theme park in Birmingham died with that action. On October 25, 1988, IRS undercover agents who had helped entrap Mousallem in the tax evasion case were given a written statement by Mousallem for the FBI files in which he noted that he had never offered me a bribe because he thought I would not accept one.

When Mousallem had been "swooped up" (federal term) and taken to an IRS facility (in the IRS room plastered with my picture and the words "corruption" beneath it), the feds told him that his new assignment was to entrap me and several other local black officials into illegal activities. He was permitted to use $115,000 in federal funds he had used in an earlier federal tax entrapment scheme to carry out his assignment.[5]

On November 23, 1988, he was given a letter signed by U.S. Attorney Frank Donaldson acknowledging his participation in the entrapment scheme and promising him leniency for his assistance. Months later, Mousallem called my office for an appointment to see me. When he came in I was pleased to see him and wanted to know how he had been doing since I had last seen him. We made small talk and after about ten or fifteen minutes I stood and said, "Bob, I have another meeting to get to," which I did. He stood and shook my hand and said, "Let's get together sometime for dinner." I said yes and he left.

About two weeks later Bob called again for an appointment to see me. On this visit he seemed a bit uneasy but wanted to know if I'd ever been to Cancun. I had not and he wanted me to accompany him on his next visit to Cancun. I asked him to let me know when he might be going and we parted. I was to learn later that on both of those visits Mousallem was wired by the FBI and the agents were in a car outside city hall listening to our conversation.

Mousallem Reveals Entrapment

On the evening of April 25, 1989, at around 8:30, I was playing with my daughter Jennifer Rose in our den when the doorbell rang. Jennifer went to the door and returned to tell me there was a man in the living room who wanted to see me. I walked into the living room and there stood Bob Mousallem. He began to tell me a hair-raising tale of his long entanglement (three years) with the FBI, including his arrangement to entrap me. He said he had endured considerable pressure from Bill Barnett for his failure to frame me. He felt he was also in danger from the FBI and related to me how his three FBI handlers had followed him and his family to Tennessee for their church's picnic. He was clearly troubled and seemed frightened. He had decided to reveal his involvement in federal entrapment activities and was sure it would be in the media in a day or so. So he wanted me to know the facts before hearing about or reading of them in the media.

But on the next night at about 9:30, he showed up at my home unannounced again, this time asking me to call A. G. Gaston, a local black millionaire and banker, on his behalf. He said he was attempting to make a $100,000 loan from Gaston's bank in order to hire attorneys to represent him in his upcoming showdown with the feds. He said he needed $75,000 to $100,000 and mentioned the name of a local attorney he said he had spoken with about retaining, as well as the names of two out-of-state attorneys. Early the next morning I contacted Donald Watkins and gave him an affidavit of the Mousallem conversations. Mousallem would later give Watkins his own. A few days later he was taken before a federal grand jury and indicted on tax evasion and bribery of an IRS official. Having never had any type of illegal activities with me, he was hard put to spring any entrapment plan. He was placed under increasing pressure and was unable to deliver. Finally Barnett told him the deal was off and Mousallem's sentencing was set to come up soon. At this time, I believe that Mousallem learned that he would have to do some time despite his earlier cooperation in cracking several major tax evasion groups. He had been led to believe that he would get probation for his tax evasion acts that led him to become an FBI stooge. When he couldn't entrap me he felt Barnett had reneged on his earlier promise of probation. So he struck back by revealing the entire plot, including several tapes of conversations he had had with FBI agents discussing the entrapment plans aimed at me and other black elected officials. Mousallem had become so upset at learning that he faced imprisonment that he made one last attempt to entrap me just prior to coming to my house on April 25. I learned of the desperate attempt a week after the Mousallem story broke. State legislator John Rogers, who lived one street away from me, said

Mousallem had come to his house one evening and placed several thousand dollars on his coffee table as an offer to get Rogers to help him entrap me. Several days after the Mousallem story broke locally, he was taken to court and convicted of tax evasion and bribery of IRS agents. His sentencing date was set for October 30, 1989.

I can only surmise what had transpired that led Mousallem to reveal the entrapment efforts. My theory is based on the September 28, 1989, Associated Press story in the *Montgomery Advertiser* that was similar to the stories carried by the *Birmingham News* and *Birmingham Post-Herald* on September 28, 1989, on the killing of Mousallem. The most succinct summary was by the *Montgomery Advertiser*. Its story, titled "Developer's Shooting Called Accident," included the following:

> A checkered past developer who claimed the FBI tried to frame Birmingham's black Mayor was meeting with a gubernatorial candidate in a dilapidated (Birmingham) house when a shotgun blast to his face took his life.
>
> "That's a pretty bizarre ending to a bizarre story," said Washington attorney Mark Lane, the man who unsuccessfully defended [Mousallem] in two trials last week. "A lot of people didn't want Mousallem to talk anymore," Mr. Lane said after Mousallem's death Tuesday. They knew Mousallem worked for the FBI— which was trying to destroy Mayor Arrington.

The forty-one-year-old Mousallem was with Jim Watley of Hamilton, a Republican candidate for governor of Alabama in the following year's election, and three other men, including Hoyett Goggans, a bail bondsman in whose residence the killing occurred. Goggans, who did the shooting, was a shady character who was often seen hanging out at Birmingham City Hall passing out his bail bondsman business cards and telling some elected officials that he worked for the CIA and had contacts "all the way up to the White House."

According to the statement Watley gave to the police, the five men were seated at a table in the Woodlawn house planning a fund-raising barbeque for Watley's campaign. Goggans offered to show the group a buffalo gun he had placed in a corner of the room in a scabbard. As he pulled it from its scabbard, "it exploded like dynamite," said Watley. The shot from the gun blew away the bottom half of Mousallem's face and splattered his flesh on the wall and ceiling of the room.

A next-door neighbor heard the blast at the house and called the Birmingham police. Minutes later when the police arrived at the scene, FBI agents had taken over and prevented Birmingham officers from entering the house for about thirty minutes. How the FBI knew of the killing and was able to arrive first remains one of the unanswered questions in the killing. Mousallem's death was ruled "accidental" and the inconsistencies in the statements of people present at the scene at the time of the killing have never been explained or reconciled.[6]

The Death Scene

On the morning after the killing, I asked Chief Arthur Deutsch to come to my office that afternoon and brief me on the investigation. Deutsch arrived at my office accompanied by a police officer he identified as Detective Fred Clanton, who was in charge of the investigation. Deutsch told Clanton to "tell the boss what you know" and remained strangely quiet thereafter. Clanton seemed to know little. He could not tell me why FBI agents were on the scene before our police or even why they were there. He confirmed that the FBI controlled the scene and delayed the entrance of police to the house—an unusual development given the fact that police officers of Birmingham are usually in charge of such a scene within the city.

The only substantial information I got from Clanton was a copy of the taped interview he had had with Goggans, who was unable to explain just how he had killed Mousallem, and the gruesome photos of Mousallem. The pictures show Mousallem, bloody, sprawled on the floor near a chair, on his right side, in a pool of blood, clenching a pen between his index and middle fingers. He was dressed in a blue pullover shirt, light-colored pants, and tennis shoes. On the table in front of where he had been sitting was a notepad with a list of items about a fund-raiser, apparently written by Mousallem, and a copy of *Newsweek* from July 3, 1989, open to the story of the confrontation between Donaldson and me. It also contained head shots of each of us and Joe Reed, chairman of the Black Democratic Conference.[7]

THE PAT DAVIS CASE

As noted earlier, several black legislators from Jefferson County were indicted for corruption in 1989. One was Patricia Davis, a representative from one of the state legislative districts in Birmingham. I had come to know Pat as one of the members of my political organization, the Citizens Coalition. She had run unsuccessfully for the Birmingham City Council with coalition support. She would later run successfully for state legislator with coalition backing.

Like most other black legislators from Birmingham who were elected with coalition backing, she at first worked closely with my office, especially on legislation affecting Birmingham. She soon grew somewhat distant with me, and the city was often unsure as to whether we could expect to have her vote on important issues. Generally speaking, Pat was becoming "more independent" of the coalition group. Shortly before her reelection campaign in 1987, I debated with one of my staff advisors as to whether I should support Pat or her opponent, since her loyalty to my administration was in question. Despite my uncertainty I decided it would be politically wise for me to respond to her invitations to attend her fund-raiser at the Birmingham Tutwiler Hotel. I wrote a $250 personal check to her campaign and left my office at 5:30 P.M. to walk across the park from city hall to the fund-raiser. My intention was to show my face to Pat, make my contribution, and leave right away for "another engagement." But as I walked over to Pat to explain that I was leaving for another engagement she asked me to walk over to another part of the room and let her introduce me to a friend of hers who was working a business plan in Birmingham.

I was introduced to a white man of about forty years of age who warmly greeted me, thanked me for supporting Pat, and said how thrilled he was to meet me. As I started to walk from the room, Pat and the man called out to me, asking if I would have my picture taken with them. We took the picture and I left. The picture became part of the FBI file later used in the federal prosecution of Pat.

What I—and no doubt Pat—did not know at the time was that her friend with whom she was working to secure a site for business in Birmingham was an undercover FBI agent posing as a businessman wanting to find a site in Birmingham for a garbage disposal project. Months later at Pat's trial (in December 1990) it would be disclosed that he was bribing Pat, who in turn had him believing that she was sharing bribe money with me and several other black elected officials. Pat never hinted anything to me about a bribe. Before Pat's cover and that of her undercover FBI agent were blown, I learned that the agent, whom I believe was the same one introduced to me by Pat, had testified in another federal case against an accused federal violator. I was told by a person in attendance that the defense attorney for the person on trial asked the FBI agent on the witness stand if he were participating in any other corruption investigations. He revealed that he was working in the Pat Davis case, paying her bribes that she told him were being shared with me and other black elected officials. I was surprised to hear about his testimony, but I said nothing about it to Pat until many months later after her conviction.

Pat's bribery by the FBI apparently continued for an extended period of time and involved sizable payoffs. A part of the entrapment plan apparently called for Pat to pay me to help find a site for the garbage disposal business. She apparently kept her FBI undercover agent believing that I was an integral part of the ongoing plan. After a while, and shortly before Pat was indicted by the feds for corruption, she was pressured by the agent to bring me to a meeting with her and the agent to discuss the progress of finding the desired site. In other words, she was being pressured to produce me at a meeting to discuss the project and undoubtedly to implicate me in the bribery scheme. That pressure forced Pat to reveal that she had not been bribing me, as she had led the agent to believe. This is how I learned of the showdown between Pat and her undercover FBI agent.

Jewel Thomas, the mayor of the neighboring city of Brighton, told me how she ended up testifying before a federal grand jury in Pat's case. Pat had made a late-evening emergency call to Jewel, asking her if Pat could come and pick her up to go to a very important meeting with her at a motel in Homewood. She needed Jewel's cooperation, she said. Once in Pat's car with her and her black male driver (Pat did not drive), Pat explained the deal to her. Pat said she was working with a businessman to find a site for a garbage disposal project in Birmingham. She told Jewel that she was unable to come up with a Birmingham site and she wanted to tell the businessman that she had turned to Jewel to find a site in the city of Brighton. Pat promised Jewel six hundred jobs for her city from the project and other benefits if she would go along with the plan. Unbeknownst to Pat and Jewel, Pat's black driver that evening (who had driven her back and forth between Birmingham and Montgomery and to attend to her other legislative business for years) was wired by the FBI. Her trusted driver was an FBI informant.

Pat had fully briefed Jewel by the time they arrived at the motel. The only one not prepared was Pat's business partner, the undercover FBI agent, whom I assumed I'd met at the fund-raiser. Pat and Jewel walked into the motel room where the agent and several other persons, no doubt FBI agents, were waiting. "Where is Mayor Arrington?" the agent impatiently asked. According to Jewel the room was equipped with cameras. I believe they had planned a big "welcoming party" for me. Pat responded to the inquiry about my whereabouts by saying, "Oh, Birmingham didn't have any suitable sites for the project so I'm getting a site in Brighton." The long-running entrapment had been sprung but there was no Arrington, the major target. It was now clear to Pat as well as Jewel that the operation had been an FBI sting operation. As they left the motel and the angry agents, Jewel noticed that the car in which they had ridden to the motel had been under helicopter surveillance during the entire trip. Weeks later, in the grand jury room, Jewel was confronted with the tape of the conversation that took place in the car on that evening. That and the other events that transpired made her realize what she had almost been caught up in. The U.S. attorney asked Jewel if she had agreed to help Pat for bribe money. She denied that she had done so. This grand jury would lead to Pat's indictment on corruption and her eventual imprisonment.[8]

There remains, however, a mysterious development during the grand jury hearing that I still don't understand. It involved yet another accusation by Pat Davis. At one point during the hearing, Pat and a close female friend of hers, whom I knew well, were asked about the whereabouts of some bribe money paid to Pat. They alleged that the money was at the friend's home. The prosecutor very cleverly asked the judge to recess the trial for a while to permit the women to retrieve the money and bring it into the court. Of course Pat was lying about the money and during the recess rode directly to my home instead. I was not home but she told my wife Rachel she needed to borrow several thousand dollars from me for an emergency. Rachel went to a back room of the house and called me on my mobile phone just as I was driving up to the back of my house. She told me the story and said, "Don't come in while she's here. She's clearly in trouble." After about thirty minutes Pat left and Rachel called me to come in. I would learn later that when Pat left my home she went to the home of State Representative John Rogers and attempted to borrow the money from him. Why would Pat, who had lied about my involvement in the bribery all along, now run to my home to borrow money? Didn't she know that she was either tailed or brought to my house by a federal operative? Was it another last-ditch effort by the feds to lure me in the trap? Was Pat led to believe that she could still get a break if she delivered me? I don't know the answer, and I don't like what I think the answer is. Pat was convicted on December 20, 1989, for extortion and sentenced to six and one-half years imprisonment on February 1, 1990.[9]

THE FEDS SPREAD THEIR ENTRAPMENT NET

With the tragedy of Robert Mousallem and the fiasco of Pat Davis, one might think the FBI might cease their efforts to entrap me. Quite the contrary: they were gearing up for an all-out effort to succeed.

In late 1989 a local businessman named Henry Johnson (who was also a close friend of Willie Davis, a former administrative aide on my staff), the person the FBI had mentioned at the Montgomery meeting of Alabama black elected officials at the Dexter Avenue Baptist Church of Montgomery in the summer of 1989 (see chapter 7), had been indicted and convicted by the feds in what they said was a scheme to milk the Birmingham Transit Authority of funds. As Johnson's trial proceedings show, he had entered into a contract to service some new city buses acquired by the Transit Authority. The services were never provided and Johnson was accused of being in cahoots with the transit's manager, Al Richards, and other unnamed persons to fraudulently collect $50,000 to $70,000 from the arrangement. (Richards would later be indicted but his indictment was thrown out because of fraudulent FBI evidence used to indict him.)

I knew nothing about the transit scheme until Henry Johnson approached me to say that FBI agents questioning him about the deal repeatedly tried to get him to admit that I had received some of the funds from the deal. It was at this point that I first learned of the deal. After his conviction Johnson told me that Bill Barnett approached him on several occasions, telling him that he was facing a two-year prison term that Barnett could make go away if Johnson provided him with incriminating evidence on me. Johnson had no such evidence and did not attempt to create any. Before Johnson was sentenced, on a busy interstate highway a block from city hall, Johnson's van was struck by another vehicle and forced across several lanes. As Johnson emerged from his vehicle to examine the damage he was struck by a vehicle driven by a local sheriff's deputy and instantly killed.

Bill Barnett then turned his efforts to entrap me toward a local white businessman who operated a large business in Alabama and possibly had IRS problems. I'm not sure why he was chosen; I barely knew him. The man was approached by FBI field agent Whitaker and several other agents and asked to become part of a scheme to offer me a bribe in exchange for some city business. They had two meetings with him at Lloyd's Restaurant on Highway 280 to lay out their plan and told him that a well-known black businessman friend of mine would bring him to my office. Troubled by the offer and the pressure for an answer, he revealed the offer to his attorney, whose office was in an adjacent city. With his OK, his attorney called my attorney, Donald Watkins, and told him of the FBI trap. On that very evening my attorney drove to the other attorney's office and obtained a sworn affidavit from the businessman detailing the FBI's efforts.

Barnett next turned to a man named Jay Kelly, who had been working as an FBI operative, to help the FBI successfully carry out sting operations on a tax evader. In exchange for his role as an FBI stooge, his own punishment for his tax violations would be reduced to a recommendation of probation. This was the same Kelly who had attended my first Mousallem meeting with a small group of white men at Denny's restaurant in Roebuck. At the time Barnett approached Kelly about me, Kelly was awaiting a decision from Barnett and other federal agents on the outcome of his pending bribery charge. We immediately made this information regarding FBI entrapment efforts on me available to the media. But anyone following these developments and who had any knowledge of federal investigations had to see that the U.S. attorney's investigation was reaching a phase where I would become the target of the investigation.

9

FEDS DESIGNATE ME AS A TARGET
OF GRAND JURY INVESTIGATION

With harsh accusations being hurled in the media by my attorney and the U.S. attorney's office, the spotlight stayed on these developments. Each complaint we filed against the U.S. attorney was made public. Eventually, at our request, the U.S. Office of Professional Responsibility (OPR) headed by David P. Bobzien began an active probe into Frank Donaldson's investigation of me. Bobzien's office was charged with investigating complaints against the U.S. attorney and its FBI agents. But his small staff consisted of only three attorneys to look into complaints across the entire country. Their active investigations irritated Donaldson's office, especially when they found the U.S. attorney's staff had violated some professional standards. Shortly after the OPR's report was made public, Donaldson set about to get higher-ups in the Justice Department to overrule the OPR's finding, but clearly the pressure was on.

With the local publicity on the federal investigation of me, community and business leaders began calling on the U.S. attorney to complete the investigation, which was a source of negative publicity for the city. Donaldson and Whitaker made public statements that the investigation was not aimed at me but at excessive complaints about city hall corruption. This was, of course, a lie. I had always been the target of the FBI-U.S. attorney entrapment schemes. We knew well that at a time of their choosing they would step forth and announce that the investigation was targeting me—using their well-known, shopworn statement of "we just went where evidence led us."

With the 1991 mayoral election approaching, Donaldson and Barnett began to make their major moves to bring me down. By the fall of 1990, the federal investigation of Marjorie Peters and the new Birmingham Civil Rights Institute (BCRI) was moving toward a conclusion (see chapter 7).

Frank Donaldson now informed local media that his office was beginning an investigation of the City of Birmingham's Minority Participation Program. Led by Bill Barnett, the FBI, and the IRS, the investigation was swiftly launched with a subpoena to the city for a complete listing of all vendors that had held contracts with the city over the previous five years. The feds were limited by federal law to going no further back than five years. In response to that subpoena, the city generated a list of over 25,000 names. From among the list the feds chose all of the minority vendors and subpoenaed the city's file on each. The tension between the U.S. attorney's office and the city was stretched to the breaking point, with each publicly charging the other with misconduct.

By August 1991 the federal grand jury indictment of Peters was in and her trial set for September, two weeks before the Birmingham mayoral election. She would be, as discussed earlier, tried in October, would be found guilty, and would appeal her conviction to a higher court, which ordered that she be granted a new trial. When the new trial began in January 1992, Peters, apparently financially and emotionally exhausted from the long ordeal, entered a plea bargain with the U.S. attorney's office in exchange for a lesser sentence and began serving her time.

On October 8, 1991, I was reelected mayor for a fourth term with 63 percent of the vote after repeatedly stating publicly that Donaldson and Barnett were trying to sabotage my reelection. Black voters, many apparently resentful of the feds' constant harassment of me, voted for me in large numbers. White voters, who had never given me more than 10 to 12 percent of their vote, reduced their support for me by half, to around 5 percent; the old racial cleavages of Birmingham were alive and well. In our ongoing struggle with Barnett he used the tactic of reissuing subpoenas to the city for its files, claiming that the city had not complied with his earlier subpoenas. We had responded to every subpoena and saw Barnett's action as one more example of harassment. In a hastily called meeting with my defense attorneys it was decided that we would again deliver several boxes of city files that were subpoenaed to the federal grand jury room by two of our defense attorneys, Kenneth Thomas and Henry Gillis. This time we decided that the files would not be given to Barnett, who was conducting the investigation before his grand jury. Instead our attorneys would place the boxes in the possession of the foreman of the grand jury, a white man from Parrish named James Byrd. After all, we decided, it was, by law, the foreman of the jury who was supposedly in control and not Barnett. Under no circumstances, we decided, were Thomas and Gillis to give the files to

Barnett. Instead, they were to read a statement to the grand jury pointing out that we had fully complied earlier with all grand jury subpoenas and viewed the reissuing of subpoenas for duplicate material a form of harassment.

When Thomas and Gillis reached the grand jury room at the appointed time with the boxes, Thomas read the statement and proceeded to walk over to hand the boxes to the foreman of the jury. An angry Barnett rushed up to Thomas and attempted to wrest control of some of the boxes from him. Thomas refused to let go of the boxes and a wrestling match over the boxes ensued between our two defense attorneys and Barnett before the grand jury. Unable to take the boxes from our attorneys, Barnett rushed from the room and returned with two U.S. marshals, ordering them to seize the boxes and place Thomas and Gillis in detention. For several hours the marshals held them in a locked room of the federal courthouse before finally releasing them. Nothing else came of that incident but Barnett never again lost any of our subpoenaed documents. I immediately sought a meeting with Donaldson, who had assured me that he would always be accessible to me. I called his office but he was in New Orleans. His secretary said she would reach Donaldson in New Orleans and have him call me. In about thirty minutes he was on the phone with me from New Orleans. I explained to him what had occurred before the grand jury between Barnett and my defense attorneys over the city files. He said he would be back in Birmingham the next morning and he and I would meet to discuss the incident. When I called his office the following morning he refused to speak with me. In fact, Donaldson and I never spoke to each other again. I did send him a letter on January 11, 1992, expressing my disappointment with his failure to meet with me as he had promised.[1]

Meanwhile the hostility between the two sides continued. In Birmingham, the police captain summoned a City Council staff person named Paul Gentle to an investigative meeting at the federal courthouse where he was questioned about any knowledge he had of questionable activities by me at city hall. That Sunday evening, Gentle, accompanied by his young Indian girlfriend, came to my home to tell me about his experience. He drew a sketch of the room he was taken to and wrote down the names of everyone in the room and where they sat and stood while questioning him. We immediately turned that information over to OPR investigators and the media. One of the U.S. attorneys participating in that inquiry was Leon Frank "Bud" Kelly, a first assistant to Donaldson. A month later after the news media reported on the questioning of

Paul Gentle, Kelly filed a defamation suit against me in state court in Shelby County, claiming he had not participated in the meeting.[2] I was sure that Kelly would not take such drastic action without Donaldson's approval. Kelly went outside Jefferson County, where Birmingham is located, to the nearly all-white Shelby County, where I had absolutely no support. The presiding judge of Shelby County Court, whom I believed Kelly "shopped" for, would immediately find that I had defamed Frank Kelly. My attorneys quickly took the decision to an appeals court that reversed the decision in our favor.

Tarlee Brown Implicates Mayor

On September 6, 1991, Barnett played his "ace card." On that morning I was hosting the mayors of Alabama's six largest cities at the downtown Harbert Center. The meeting was one of a series of meetings in which we went to each member's city to discuss strategies for increasing our cities' influence in state affairs, especially in gaining a fair share of state appropriations. The session ended with a noon luncheon. As I was being driven by one of my security officers back to city hall, about six blocks away, we quickly noted that Joe Cole, a paralegal on Donald Watkins' staff, was driving erratically in our direction, darting across the median stripe dividing the street. We pulled over and Cole stopped his car and ran over to my car. He gave me the bad news. Tarlee Brown had just been marched before federal judge James Hancock with my nemesis, Bill Barnett. Barnett read from a statement prepared by him and signed by Brown, stating that on certain dates he had come to my office at the request of Marjorie Peters and paid me a bribe of $5,000 for one of the city contracts I had given him. The appearance of Brown had been carefully orchestrated for maximum media exposure.[3] In fact, Cole had learned of Brown's pending appearance earlier that morning from a friendly reporter at the *Birmingham News*. He called to tell Cole that he, the reporter, had received an anonymous phone call telling him to be in Judge Hancock's courtroom at 11:00 that morning. The reporter quickly realized that this was a move by Barnett and probably involved the investigation of me. Were we aware of the 11:00 drama, the reporter asked? We were not, but Cole decided he would be in Hancock's courtroom at 11:00, where Brown testified before the judge about his alleged payoffs to me. I was rocked by the action and angry. I gathered with my attorneys at city hall to decide our next move. Soon we got a copy of Brown's written statement before the judge. Barnett and Brown had made the fatal mistake in manufacturing their lie of naming in the proceedings the dates that Brown had allegedly paid me off at city hall.

Where was I at that time and date, my attorneys wanted to know. It occurred to me that my executive secretary, Caroline Knowles, maintained a written record of every person who visited my office plus a record of all my activities, including travel, for every day of the week. If someone not on the appointment schedule showed up and met with me, Caroline simply wrote in the name and time. She kept each daily log in a file by month and year for the office archives. An examination of my appointment book for the date of the alleged payoffs showed that I had been out of the country for two weeks, leading a citizens' delegation in Israel. How could I be in two places at once? There was no question I was in Israel. Our delegation had been accompanied by local Birmingham reporters.

Watkins seized on the lie to call an early-morning news conference to brand the U.S. attorneys a liar and produce the indisputable information about my whereabouts on the alleged city hall payoff day.[4] Barnett was stung! Soon reporters rushed to us claiming that Barnett and Brown had claimed Brown gave me a second bribe in city hall again naming the date. Wrong again! Another lie, we shouted. My schedule logs and pictures on the front page of the *Birmingham News* showed me at the Democratic National Headquarters building in Washington, D.C., surrounded by foreign ambassadors from several countries, attending a luncheon fund-raiser for my upcoming October 8 reelection campaign.

In a few days Barnett issued a subpoena for the last five years of my appointment logs, which he had not known existed until we used them to reveal his lies. I announced that I would not turn my logs over to Barnett and permit him to use them to construct yet another lie to entrap me. I would, I announced, turn my records over to the U.S. attorney general in Washington, D.C., for examination and prove my daily whereabouts for the five years in question. My attorney quickly wrote a letter to U.S. Attorney William Barr, offering up my records. He refused them, stating that we should deal with the local U.S. attorney, Frank Donaldson. I decided I'd go to prison before I turned them over to Donaldson. That's exactly what Donaldson had in mind for me. I would eventually go to federal prison for contempt of a court order to hand over my appointment logs.[5]

Exactly who was Tarlee Brown, the FBI informer Bill Barnett was using to try to get me indicted for corruption under the federal racketeering statute (RICO)? He had become a major player in the federal drama. As a business partner and close friend of Marjorie Peters, he had turned over evidence that helped send Peters to prison in the probe of their role in the development of the Birmingham Civil Rights Institute. Now he had become the only person among many who had been approached by the FBI to level a charge of corruption against me.

Brown was a member of the architectural firm of Milkey and Brown Associates of Atlanta. His partner, Milkey, whom I would meet later in the firm's Atlanta office, was a white man who, like Brown, had respected architectural credentials in Atlanta. I found Brown quiet, easy to talk to, and likable. When I learned he was an Alabama native from the Demopolis area we connected. (Livingston, where I was born, is also in western Alabama.) We both appeared to take some pride in our similar rural Alabama roots.

In August 1984 I appointed Brown to do an architectural feasibility study of the renovation of Boutwell Auditorium. The feasibility fee was $25,000, which Brown agreed to rebate to the city if his firm was selected as the architect for the renovation based on the study. His firm was selected for the job and given a nine-month contract of $240,000 for the project.[6]

Until Tarlee Brown showed up in the federal court of Judge Joe Hancock on September 6, 1991, with Barnett to testify that he bribed me, our relationship, while not close, was, I thought, solid. There had been only one discordant incident between Brown and me. It occurred in 1990 when Cecil Jones of Jones Engineering was given the bid to design the city's new road to the new race track being constructed in the eastern area of the city. Jones hired Brown as one of his subcontractors for the job and also because Brown was a minority. One day Jones came to my office to tell me that Brown had overcharged his firm $200,000 for time Brown had worked on a project. What advice did I have for him on this matter, Jones wanted to know. Brown was under contract to Jones, not the City of Birmingham, but I recommended that Jones immediately recoup the $200,000 from Brown, which he did. Brown later spoke with me about his disagreement with Jones but decided he would not pursue the matter any further.[7] Of course when Brown leveled his bribery charge against me I immediately ordered the city finance director to stop honoring any invoice from Brown on any city project. It turned out that there was an outstanding invoice from Brown in the amount of $86,625 for design work on a Birmingham Board of Education school project.

The city also notified the Alabama Board of Architects about Brown's "confessed crime" of bribery. The board set a hearing to revoke his Alabama license. On the day of the hearing in Montgomery on license revocation, a member of the board called my chief of staff, informing her that the board had just received a request for an attorney to appear at that afternoon hearing as a character witness for Brown. His name, the board member said, was Bill Barnett. Barnett was attempting to protect Brown. On hearing that, one of my attorneys called a reporter at Birmingham's Channel 6 and said he might want to be at the board's meeting that afternoon. Of course, Barnett did not know that we or the media knew of his planned appearance on behalf of Brown. Barnett was embarrassed to learn that the media from Birmingham were present when he arrived at the meeting, where his name had been entered on the agenda to represent Brown. Upon seeing the media Barnett withdrew his request to appear and left. The reporter then rushed back to Birmingham to Donaldson's office and asked him, on camera, why his office was appearing on Brown's behalf. Donaldson just sat before the camera with an angry glare, refusing to utter a word.

We alerted the media to every move the feds made and each time embarrassed them. Soon Donaldson would file a motion with the court for a gag order against my attorneys. The order was denied.

To this very day I have not spoken with Brown since he leveled his accusations against me. After the investigation was over and Judge Hancock, the prosecutor's favorite judge, had given Brown a slap on the wrist—probation for his admitted felonies of bribery and tax evasion while using the Brown sentences to level a thinly veiled attack against me—Brown approached Watkins several months later asking if I would see him and accept an apology from him.[8] I said, "No thanks."

I believe that the "real deal" with Brown and Barnett can be found in the files of the October 29, 1987, indictment of Brown's daughter Audra Lambert and her husband, Vincent Lambert. Brown's allegations to Barnett led my attorneys to conduct a full background check on Brown. The following are some pertinent points that investigation turned up.[9]

1. On October 29, 1987, Brown's daughter Audra Brown Lambert and her husband, Vincent Lambert, were indicted in federal court in Atlanta for conspiracy and possession with the intent to distribute several kilos of cocaine that they had flown from Miami to Atlanta with co-conspirators. They were arrested on returning to Atlanta and going to the bus station to obtain the cocaine from the co-conspirators, who had accompanied them to Miami. Vincent Lambert was also charged with firearm violation for weapons found at their residence (drugs were also found).

2. When arrested, Vincent Lambert told agents that he and Tarlee Brown were co-owners of a used-car business from which drugs were sold.

3. Vincent and Audra Lambert were convicted by a jury on all counts. Audra was sentenced to seven years' imprisonment (Lexington) and Vincent to fifteen years in Atlanta, beginning September 1988.

4. Investigators took a statement from a prison mate of Vincent Lambert's, Reginald Grandison, saying that at the time (August 1991) Brown was bargaining a plea with Barnett to implicate Arrington. He was also trying to bargain with Barnett for the early release of Audra from prison. Grandison claimed to have worked the drug trade with Vincent and stated that he thought Tarlee Brown financed his son-in-law's entry into drug peddling.

Whatever the truth, Brown appeared to have a good motive to bargain a plea with Barnett. If Brown's allegations of bribery of the mayor on one or two occasions that he and Barnett presented to Hancock were factual, how does one account for the dates they alleged the bribes occurred at city hall when I was undeniably out of the city?

GRAND JURY SUBPOENA

In December 1991, Bill Barnett had the federal grand jury issue a subpoena naming me as the "target of the investigation," a fact that Donaldson and Barnett had vehemently denied they planned up until this time. According to the subpoena, I was being investigated for potential violations of the Hobbs Act, wire and mail fraud, racketeering, political corruption, and tax evasion. Such charges, if sustainable, would mean possibly a lifetime of imprisonment and federal confiscation of every item of value belonging to me.

Later that month, after kidney stone surgery, I appeared before the grand jury and Barnett and denied the charges. But after Barnett warned me that my statements could be used as self-incrimination, I pled the Fifth Amendment and refused to produce my personal daily schedule and diaries for 1985–91.[10] Barnett and Donaldson filed a motion with the federal court to force me to produce my schedules and diaries. On Friday, January 17, 1992, Judge Edwin Nelson ordered me to produce my schedules and diaries for the grand jury. I would have seven days to produce the documents for the jury. Each day of delay would result in a $1,000 fine. As mayor, the judge ordered, I would also spend four days—Sundays through Thursdays—imprisoned, being allowed each week to return to my office for city business on Friday and then back to prison until I complied with the court order. My attorney appealed Nelson's ruling to the federal appeals court and lost. My offer to turn the documents over to the Justice Department in Washington was refused by the attorney general.

On Friday, January 24, 1992, after a rally led by black ministers at the historic 16th Street Baptist Church, hundreds of demonstrators, mostly black, marched me, handcuffed and chained, three blocks from the church to the federal courthouse and surrendered me to federal marshals to be taken to Maxwell Federal Prison in Montgomery.[11] I had originally been scheduled to be imprisoned at Talladega (Alabama) Federal Penitentiary but Senator Howell Heflin intervened with the Bureau of Prisons and got the approval for me to go to Maxwell—a less harsh institution.

The federal marshals whisked me to the holding area of the third floor of the courthouse and placed me in belly chains and handcuffs for my trip to Maxwell. I had just a few items to take with me in my attaché case, including my medications. I had earlier asked my attorneys if I needed to take pajamas and they thought that was a joke. I was for real.

Justice Department Intervention

On Friday morning at about 9:30, one of my defense attorneys, Joe Whatley, arrived at the mayor's office. He had just received a call from Frank Donaldson. According to Donaldson, Washington had instructed him to offer me a compromise deal to avoid my going to prison. The Justice Department would now accept my earlier offer to U.S. Attorney William Barr; the only condition was that the documents would be turned over to a U.S. attorney from the Washington office and Donaldson, jointly. I had earlier offered to turn the subpoena documents over to Washington, saying I didn't trust Donaldson and Barnett. Would I accept the compromise, Donaldson asked Whatley. Whatley asked for an hour to confer with me and to get back to Donaldson.

In my office my attorneys and I agreed to accept the deal. Then we made the mistake that played into the hands of Donaldson, who opposed Washington's instructions. "Is there any other condition we want to ask for?" asked one of the attorneys. Then someone, maybe I, said, "Let's tell them we accept it providing Bill Barnett is removed from the investigation." Whatley reached Donaldson with our response. Removing Barnett was taken by Donaldson as my rejecting the offer from Washington. But as far as I know Donaldson never mentioned the Barnett request and may have never gotten back to Washington. Instead, according to his office, he left for a speech at Samford University (Birmingham), giving instructions to his staff to leave the office early—at noon, to avoid the anticipated demonstrations by my supporters. Later, my attorneys, waiting for a reply from Donaldson on my proposal, could not locate him. His office was closed and his staff gone. There was no way to reach him. So the rally at 16th Street Baptist Church and my surrender to the marshals proceeded that afternoon.

As I waited in the federal holding pen for transportation to prison by the U.S. marshals, Donald Watkins walked in. "I've just received a call from the Justice Department. They wanted to know what had gone wrong with the deal that was offered," he told me. Apparently Donaldson had told Washington nothing and they had been unable to reach him that afternoon. "The deal is still on," Watkins said. "If we accept it, we'll work out the details tomorrow and you don't have to go to prison."

I thought to myself, there is no way I can walk out of here now without going to prison. Some key supporters had just dispersed from around the courthouse. What will they think when they turn on the ten o'clock news tonight and learn that I never went to prison? I looked at Watkins and said to tell them we'll work it out at the prison tomorrow. Watkins smiled approvingly. In a matter of minutes I was placed in a prison van with dark-tinted windows and whisked out the federal courthouse yard while a couple of decoy vans went out a different gate to distract the crowd still standing outside the building. Five blocks west on 4th Avenue North, the van exited to Interstate 65 heading to Montgomery. Worn and weary from the two-week ordeal, I fell fast asleep and did not wake up until the van was entering the gate to Maxwell prison, about ninety miles and an hour and a half later.

MAXWELL FEDERAL PRISON

The staff at Maxwell was mostly black and each person I had contact with showed great respect and sympathy toward me. I wondered if they were just concerned or embarrassed that the first black mayor of Alabama's largest city was in prison.

Inside the first building, I was asked to turn in all my belongings and I was taken into a small closet where my civilian clothes were exchanged for prison garb. I was then given a medical check. The processing officer explained to me that I could choose between being separated from the prison population or being placed in an isolated holding area. He said, however, that he thought it would be better for me to be intermingled with the prison population than to be isolated and totally alone. I agreed. After processing, I was walked over to the prison dormitory to which I was assigned. En route to the dorm, the security guard cautioned me to watch what I said. He warned me that many inmates were "snitches" and would seek any information from me that they could, hoping they could use it to bargain with federal officials for a less harsh sentence.

The regular prison workday had just ended and most inmates were in their assigned dorms or participating in some extracurricular activities as inmates are permitted to do between dinner and the 8:00 bedtime. One could go fishing on the banks of the river, where the prison was located, play tennis or some other sport, do arts and crafts, or, if you had prior approval, board the prison bus to go to classes at the nearby community college.

As I entered the dorm, many inmates rushed to greet me. They had been following my case on television and knew I was en route there. Some offered me chips and soft drinks from a small refrigerator in the sleeping area. I was assigned to the top bunk of a two-bed bunk. The only question I asked of them was if we would be permitted to watch the upcoming Super Bowl game on Sunday. They assured me that we would.

The security officer showed me to the laundry room, where I was to find linens and towels and uniforms on a certain day. One inmate escorted me to the cafeteria, noting that it was near closing time for dinner. Back out on the ground I noticed several long lines of inmates waiting to use one of the monitored pay phones. I joined one line and slowly worked my way to the phone and called home and spoke with my wife and daughter.

At about 8:00 all lights were out and everyone was due in bed. I fell asleep only to be harshly awakened at about 11:00 by lights coming on and whistles being blown. The officers yelled out, "Bed check! Everybody up and by your bed!" When the inmate count was complete, we were ordered back into our beds and the lights turned out. The bed check and count were repeated around 3:00 A.M.

The next morning, after shaving, dressing, and eating breakfast, we left for our work assignments. Those like me who were without a work assignment were told to meet in the gym. There were quite a few of us at the gym because there were not enough tasks for all the inmates. Finally an officer told us to pick up a shovel and broom and go to the yard. I was assigned to the "cigarette butt" detail—walking around, looking for cigarette butts to be placed in the garbage receptacles.

Two of my attorneys, Demetrius Newton and David Johnson, arrived at the prison and met with me to discuss the process of turning over the subpoenaed documents to the Justice Department. The federal attorneys, after receiving my documents, were to have Judge Nelson authorize my release to my attorneys. I waited all day, working in the yard and waiting for my attorneys to come for me. At one point, security had an inmate who was serving time as a member of the Colombia drug cartel take me back to my dorm to show me how my bed was to be made each day.

By about 5:00 P.M. I had heard nothing from my attorneys and I was preparing for another night at Maxwell. Then security summoned me to the phones. Joe Cole was calling to tell me Judge Nelson had signed my prison release. Did I want Cole to come for me now or wait until tomorrow? "No," I said, "come get me now."

On Saturday, January 25, 1992, the *Birmingham News* reported that Donaldson said he had repeatedly talked with my attorneys on Thursday, trying to reach a deal that would keep me out of prison. But he said my attorneys had blown the deal and tried to revive it on Friday but he had refused. Of course Donaldson had done no such thing. The details of the compromise worked out with the Justice Department were not widely reported. The most misleading representation in the media was that of Michael Riley, a reporter whose February 5, 1992, *Time* magazine story suggested that I had "caved in" to get out of prison and it all may have been just a media ploy.

While a small group of the city's corporate community, led by Dr. Neal Berte of Birmingham-Southern College and James Lee Jr. of Pepsi Cola Buffalo Rock, worked tirelessly to head off the growing dispute with the feds, quite a few were miffed at me for refusing to honor the federal subpoena and said so publicly.

Barnett's Many Subpoenas

Bill Barnett stepped up his investigation of me after I was released from prison. He inundated Alabama with subpoenas for my records. Any institution that had any financial dealings, charitable or otherwise, with me became the target of subpoenas. My mother (who was over eighty years old), my maid, and my children were served with subpoenas to appear before IRS agents with records. U.S. attorneys tried unsuccessfully to get them to appear without an attorney. FBI agents masquerading as service men for the local utility companies came to my home allegedly to check malfunctioning gas lines but really to survey my yard with metal detectors.

Grand Jury Investigation Ends

The investigation of me by the U.S. attorney's office is fully documented by the FBI files, which are now part of the Arrington Administration Archives and available at the Birmingham Public Library Archives. Altogether the investigation spanned two decades, and by its own files and admissions, the U.S. attorney found no criminal violations by me. Within a short time span, however, a grand jury investigation of me was launched.[12] The groundwork for this new investigation had been carefully laid over several years by Donaldson and Barnett. At their disposal during all of these investigations were the full resources of the FBI, the IRS, and several other government agencies. The investigation lasted two years. The maximum time for a grand jury to sit is two years. Had the investigation continued, it would have required the convening of a new grand jury.[13]

Elsewhere in this memoir I give a brief history of the Jefferson County Citizens Coalition (JCCC), a grassroots political organization I founded in 1975 with some other black elected officials (see chapter 12). For nearly twenty years it was undoubtedly one of the most powerful black political groups in Jefferson County. But it, too, drew the ire of the FBI. The FBI repeatedly infiltrated our monthly meetings with their spies, some of whom I knew and who admitted that they were FBI operatives. Their tasks were to report on all of our activities, political and social, and on who was dating whom among the members. Why the government spends millions of tax dollars on such muckraking confounds me. But it continues in many, many places in our democracy—the kinds of things we are taught are done only in communist countries or under dictators.

I distinctly recall the case of a young man I shall simply refer to here by the first letter of his name—"T." T. was widely known in Birmingham's black community for his paraprofessional health screening programs. He was active enough at his work to secure a small federal grant to support his activities. At some point he wrote a small check to himself on his grant account and was caught. To avoid prosecution he was immediately put to work by the local FBI to spy on me and the JCCC. He was so bothered by this that he took the risk of traveling sixty miles to another county to speak with an attorney friend of mine and asked him to alert me to what he was being forced to do. I would later have several secret conversations with T. about what the FBI was asking him to do. He was given an FBI agent and the presiding Circuit Court judge, Joe Jasper, as his "handlers." He had to report to them on a regular basis and was often hooked up to a lie detector, supposedly to see if he was telling the truth about us. One day he reached a friend of mine in great desperation and at great risk of revealing his contact with me to his handlers. Frustrated at finding no law violations by me and probably little other dirt, the judge ordered T. to determine the precise route I took home most days from city hall and whether I drove there alone. He did and reported back to them. Then the judge divulged his plan to have a sixteen-year-old troubled white girl hail me down under the pretense she was having auto trouble. She was to ask me for a ride to a nearby service station and once there to claim I had tried to molest her. T. rushed to find me to divulge the scheme and to make sure I didn't stop anytime to assist a young white girl. I assumed he thought that an altruistic fellow like me might easily be ensnared by such a trap.

When a business partner of mine who owned a funeral home ended up buying an old office building—the Ramsey-McCormick Building—from the city and the sale was approved at a City Council meeting, the local HUD manager, Richard Compton, filed a complaint with HUD's inspector-general for investigation, noting that the city had once used some of its HUD funds to help acquire the building. The inspector-general reported the case to the FBI, which investigated the matter and finally concluded I was not guilty of violating any federal statute. The truth was that I did not know my partner had purchased the building until it was before the council for approval. The building, which was in terrible disrepair, had been given to the city some years earlier under an agreement in which the city would assume the remaining short-term mortgage of about $400 per month. This monthly rate was paid by the city's Community Development Department with HUD funds. Months earlier, with a single tenant in the building, my partner learned that the city owned the building, a fact that the city director of community development had forgotten until my partner went to his office to inquire about purchasing the building. The department head, Bob Land, later told me that the FBI came to see him about the role I had played in the sale. His department had lost track of the city's ownership of the building. It was but one more example of how the government bureaucracy let matters fall through the cracks—maybe a big one this time. But I was not surprised. I had learned during my first year as mayor that the city did not have records of all properties it owned. A later audit, ordered by me, showed that the city owned more than 1,200 pieces of real estate.

I always suspected the HUD manager who did his job so well was motivated by his dislike of my public criticism of President Reagan for killing a number of HUD housing assistance programs. While I was always sure that Reagan didn't give a spit about my criticism of him, the local Republicans at the HUD office were furious—so much so that they sent their favorite black Republican, Joe Dickson, a high school classmate of mine, to warn me that I should cease my negative comments about the president. Dickson was serious when he came to see me but I could not help but laugh in his face.

Richard Scrushy, then CEO of the largest chain of rehabilitation hospitals in the United States, Canada, and Britain and a strong supporter of the city and its local charities, built his international headquarters (10,000 employees) in Birmingham. I could always count on Scrushy to support a worthy cause. In September 1991 he sponsored a $100 per plate fund-raiser luncheon for me at the Birmingham-Jefferson Convention Center. According to the *Birmingham News*, 1,600 people attended.[14] The evening before the luncheon, Barnett publicly named me as an unindicted co-conspirator in the Marjorie Peters fraud case. I was embarrassed, not only for myself but for Richard Scrushy. Richard got up at that luncheon and told the audience that the U.S. attorney's office had lied in naming me as an unindicted co-conspirator.[15] I thought that took courage. But within the next week or so the FBI agents were at his headquarters questioning some of his physicians and other employees about his company's compliance with federal regulations. This was nothing more than an attempt by the FBI to intimidate him for what he had said at the luncheon.

The Public Corruption Unit of the Justice Department had told Donaldson several months prior to this that he did not have the evidence to proceed with an investigation of public corruption against me. So he, Barnett, and the IRS managers had been busy trying to build a tax evasion case against me. When it came time to produce a case or find another "pot," the IRS told my attorney that I had avoided reporting a portion of my income over the previous five years. According to the IRS, I had underreported my income by about $20,000 in each of three years and about $80,000 in two years. The IRS had arrived at the numbers based on the growth of my "net worth." The amazing thing to me was that in computing my annual income from all sources the IRS had arrived at the almost identical numbers each year that my CPA firm had calculated. The difference was that my CPA was arguing that I overpaid my taxes and the IRS was arguing that I had underpaid my taxes. Off both sides went to the Washington office of IRS for a review. IRS officials thought the numbers were questionable but not conclusive enough to prosecute. But the call on an indictment was left to Donaldson's successor, Jack Selden.[16] Thank goodness Donaldson had been forced into retirement. I don't know if what I'm about to say is factual but one of our sources on the U.S. attorney's staff told us that at a meeting to review the evidence for or against an indictment, Selden found the evidence lacking. Barnett did not give up, however, according to this source; he copped a plea with Selden: "Well, just let me send it to a jury and let them decide." Fortunately for me, Selden said no. Barnett, who had the grand jury waiting in their last day of session, would not go to the grand jury room but sent one of his assistants to dismiss the jury.

On November 12, 1992, Selden wrote my attorney saying that the grand jury investigation had ended with no indictment.[17]

On November 15, 1992, we had the dedication for the new Civil Rights Institute.

On July 29, 1993, the federal court granted my attorney's motion to strike my name from the records as an unindicted co-conspirator in the Marjorie Peters Civil Rights Institute fraud case.[18]

10

THE BIRMINGHAM CIVIL RIGHTS INSTITUTE (BCRI)

The comments here about the birth of the Birmingham Civil Rights Institute (BCRI) from an idea conceived by one of Birmingham's mayors and nursed into reality by the successor of that mayor and a small group of dedicated, Birmingham-loving citizens, through struggle and pain, are not intended to be a complete history of the development of this magnificent idea and institution.[1] I will leave the recording of the full story of the development of the BCRI to two individuals who are the true heroine and the true hero in bringing the BCRI to life. One or both will no doubt, despite their demanding schedules and responsibilities, write the BCRI's full history. Either will do it with the characteristic articulate style and intellectually analytical capacity for which each is well-known. Their ability to do this far exceeds my ability to do so. Indeed, they are the ones who directed the development of the BCRI and know the story better than anyone else—including me, though a lot of my blood, sweat, and tears went into developing the BCRI. During my sometimes long twenty years as mayor of Birmingham, I was most fortunate to have some very bright, well-educated, hardworking young professionals to help and guide me in nearly all of my work as mayor—people like Odessa Woolfolk, a Birmingham native and graduate of Talladega College, who was never a paid member of my staff but always worked as if she were. It is her love of Birmingham that drives her. Then there is Edward Lamonte, a graduate of both Harvard University and the University of Chicago and Distinguished Howell Heflin Professor at Birmingham-Southern College, who served on my mayoral staff for many years, nearly half of them as chief of staff—the person who really runs the day-to-day operations of the City of Birmingham. There are others who helped build the BCRI who should be mentioned, including Virginia Williams, a Mississippi native, former beauty queen, and my chief of staff after Edward Lamonte who was blessed with great administrative talents; Mike Dobbins, a bright and gifted city planner who eventually left my staff to accept a professorship at the University of California at Berkeley; Bill Gilchrist, an Atlanta native and MIT graduate who worked on the project and now leads the city's Department of Planning and Engineering; and Harvard graduate Art Clements, who worked for the Atlanta-based Russell Company as the project manager for the BCRI project. Together these young professionals, each many years my junior, represent one of the greatest talent pools that any city has ever assembled.

Odessa directed the development of the BCRI and its adjacent park, which features the "Freedom Walk" and statues that tell the story of the important Birmingham civil rights movement. Edward Lamonte was given the responsibility of the city's chief liaison for the BCRI project. He and Odessa had been peers on the faculty of the University of Alabama at Birmingham in the urban studies department. These two young scholars are my nominees for writing the history of the BCRI.

I will tell the story of the BCRI from my own memories and using the public relations accounts released for the institute's dedication. I will also include excerpts from the City of Birmingham's own investigation into the local U.S. attorney's allegations of fraud in connection with the design and construction of the BCRI. The latter represents the painful part of this story—a story that I believe to this day was political, fraudulent, calculated, and a great injustice to our city. But through that storm the sun still brightly shone as the BCRI became a reality.[2]

The Dedication

On November 15, 1992, right on the heels of the three most turbulent years of my twenty-year tenure as mayor (much of it having to do with the BCRI), the Birmingham Civil Rights Institute held its opening. A huge crowd had gathered and included dignitaries of modern America's most important human rights movement. As I stood among the special gathering, my lingering anxiety subsided and the anger I had nursed for months seemed to vanish. I thought, "This day is worth all we've gone through." This magnificent end justified the turbulent and sometimes bitter journey to this day. I hoped the martyrs of the civil rights movement and its many unsung heroes and heroines were satisfied.

AN IDEA BORN

If the idea of a BCRI belongs to anyone, it belongs to David Vann. In the mid-1970s during his time as mayor, Vann began to share with the City Council his idea that Birmingham should have a civil rights institute to tell the story of Birmingham's perseverance and triumph over racial bigotry, and to try to explain to the world that constant struggles against such bigotry and hate are what shaped and finally saved Birmingham. The institute would be one of the symbols of the true conversion of a once frightened, violent, and race-driven city into a more tolerant and peaceful one. Vann went as far as setting down in writing his proposal for a program and organization for the institute, which the BCRI Study Committee would use in the beginning of its work.

For those who knew Vann, his idea, though radical for Birmingham even in the early 1990s, was no surprise. Vann had always been radical by Birmingham's standards in his search for racial accommodations in a city where race and hatred sat on the throne. He was so out of step with the thinking of Birmingham's white majority that some openly said that he was a communist.

When no one else would fill the void of mediator between blacks and whites when King, Shuttlesworth, and Gardner led the assault on Birmingham's policies of racial apartheid, Vann stepped in to do so. When some of Birmingham's young white professionals decided that the only way to set Birmingham on a different and peaceful course was to rid it of Eugene "Bull" Connor and the city commission and replace it with a more representative mayor-council form of government, Vann was key among the efforts of the Young Men's Business Club to organize the referendum for changing the form of government. He became the main strategist for collecting and certifying voter petitions calling for a referendum. Without David Vann's leadership, I believe the referendum effort would have failed. It was not only hard work that confronted those working for the needed petitions but there was always the shadow of Klan-led bombings and beatings for those who dared to oppose the status quo.

It was commonly said of Vann that "he couldn't be elected dogcatcher in Birmingham." Vann persevered, however, and was eventually elected to the highest office in the City of Birmingham. I'm not suggesting that getting there was easy for Vann. In 1964, he ran for Congress and tried to take a more conservative stand, calling for a bipartisan letter-writing campaign to help defeat the civil rights bill that he referred to as "a fraud."[3] But white voters just shook their heads—Vann couldn't be elected dogcatcher.

I had heard and read about Vann, but I had not met him until I ran for City Council in 1971. Vann and I were elected to the City Council that year, marking a radical shift in the voting power in Birmingham. Though his peers did not choose him as council president, he still became its most influential member, serving as Finance Committee chair. It was his sheer brilliance about municipal government that catapulted him into a leadership role in the council. As a brilliant and clever tactician, he operated almost as the de facto mayor.

I was deeply impressed by Vann and his obvious intelligence. He spent little time in his law practice but hours and hours at city hall in his part-time elected position. He loved what he was doing and he loved Birmingham. As political allies, he and I spent many hours together. No one knew more about Alabama's municipal annexation laws than Vann or how best to find their loopholes. Even after I succeeded him as mayor, he stayed on as one of the city attorneys to serve as my architect for some bitter but successful annexation battles that doubled the size of Birmingham and saved its municipal tax base.

As a mayor, he was not a good administrator; he did not delegate responsibilities and was too "hands on." He plotted one successful political battle after another and raked in millions of dollars in federal grants for city projects. But he got around to implementing few because he was so busy planning how to get the next federal grant.

But Vann would stay in city hall long enough to see his dream of the Civil Rights Institute become a reality. On June 20, 1986, Odessa Woolfolk held the first meeting of the Civil Rights Museum Task Force at the downtown Redmont Hotel. On August 20, 1986, the task force finished the BCRI Mission Statement. Despite setbacks, this task force never halted its work, carefully planning step by step as if success were assured.

FINDING A BCRI SITE

With the help of Vann and my staff, I chose the site on the corner of Sixth Avenue and 16th Street North as the future home of the BCRI. It was the ideal site, directly across the street from the 16th Street Baptist Church where racist bombers killed four young girls in a Sunday school class on September 15, 1963. Across the street to the east was Kelly Ingram Park, the site at which Bull Connor, his police, firemen, and police dogs halted every civil rights march headed out of 16th Street Baptist Church intending to march three or four blocks to city hall. Connor never permitted civil rights protestors to reach city hall.

The block of land on the corner of 16th Street and Sixth Avenue North was purchased for the BCRI in 1990. The city paid the property owner $720,500 for the land, which the *Birmingham News* reported on April 19, 1990, was appraised by the Jefferson County Board of Equalization for $369,900.[4] I was not bothered by the purchase price because the board always assigned a lower market value to property than it actually brought on the market. Alabama law assesses property by classes, supposedly related to use. Its classification system is a direct product of the power of large corporate landholders to lobby the state legislature for low property taxes. Taxes on real estate in Alabama rank among the lowest, if not the lowest, in our nation. Hardly a soul sells his property for the market value assigned by the board.

The groundbreaking for the BCRI was set for June 1990.

Funding the BCRI Project: Bond Issue Fails

In 1986 I asked the City Council to approve a resolution permitting the city to borrow funds for certain public improvements, including the planned BCRI, by issuing city bonds authorized by voter referendum. The council called the bond referendum for July 8, 1986. The referendum also required voter approval of a tax increase of about $10 a year per home to repay the total debt.

I was optimistic that voters, especially black voters, would favor the referendum. The BCRI, though opposed by most white voters, would gain favor with black voters, I reasoned. I had also carefully studied the voting results of every successful bond referendum passed in Birmingham dating back to the late 1960s. As many as five or six bond elections had been called and passed. But as the record will clearly show, every bond election that passed in Birmingham during that time was passed on the strength of black voter support. Not a single bond issue during this period had passed in a predominantly white voting box in Birmingham. Each bond referendum consisted of "propositions" for each project to be financed with the bond money. Not a single "proposition" of a bond referendum, except for the one to build a new city jail, had ever passed in a predominantly white Birmingham voting box. On the contrary, no bond issue of this period had ever failed in a single predominantly black voting box. Since the city had a special fund (called a "sinking fund") generated from annual property taxes that could be used only to pay off bond debt, there was seldom a need to ask voters to increase their taxes to permit the city to issue bonds. However, the July 1986 bond vote that included the BCRI among the several propositions such as street and sewer improvements required a tax increase. The bond issue was soundly defeated in white and black boxes alike. I was crushed! My disappointment, which I wore on my sleeve, was the subject of many local media stories for the next couple of weeks. There was no $10–$13 million to develop the BCRI.

Apparently feeling sorry for their first black mayor and his "crying the blues" about the failure of the bond vote for the BCRI, a group of black neighborhood leaders came to city hall to lift my spirits. I had not done a good enough job, they said, of explaining the importance of the vote to black voters. I should try another such referendum and they would get out the black votes needed to pass it, they said. After much behind-the-scenes lobbying by the council, I succeeded in getting the council to call another bond election of $110 million that included money for the BCRI. It would also require a modest tax increase. The council set the bond referendum for May 10, 1988. I planned carefully and worked hard—mainly in the city's black neighborhoods—to rally support for the 1988 bond referendum. Polls had clearly shown that there was less than miniscule voter support for the bond issue among the city's white voters.

From the outset of the first serious discussions about building the BCRI, the corporate community had told me that it was a bad idea. Henry Goodrich, the CEO of the SONAT Corporation in Birmingham, had come to my office to tell me that the corporate community did not support the idea of the institute. They believed, he said, that it would only serve as a reminder of an old, violent, racially bigoted Birmingham of the past—a Birmingham we should all want people to forget. "If you do this," he said, "it will only open old sores." He also brought with him and left with me a clipping from the *Memphis Commercial Appeal* announcing that the city of Memphis planned to convert the old Lorraine Hotel in Memphis, the assassination site of Dr. Martin Luther King Jr., into a civil rights museum. "We don't need two such institutes here in the South," he said, trying to convince me to drop the idea. I had considerable respect for Goodrich. He was, after all, quite active in supporting worthy city events, such as the Birmingham Museum of Art and our symphony. He could also be counted on to give a sympathetic ear to any idea I had that I convinced him had merit. On top of that, he was generally recognized as the "bell cow" of Birmingham's corporate community. I told Goodrich that I would not abandon the institute idea. I redoubled my efforts to rally black voter support for the institute, while saying as little to white voters as I could about it. I was already sure whites would vote against it. The less I reminded them of the upcoming bond referendum, the better, I thought. My actions did not go unnoticed in the white media, however. Leaders of white neighborhoods were redoubling their efforts to defeat the referendum. An anti-tax and anti-Arrington administration group calling itself the Tax Busters, led by Joseph Boohaker and former Birmingham mayor George Seibels, mounted a vigorous campaign against the upcoming referendum in both white and black neighborhoods.

Seibels in particular led a "disinformation campaign" among the public housing residents against the referendum; my strategy had called for working for a large turnout among public housing residents, explaining to them that they were not affected by an increase in the tax of homeowners. But as I stomped door to door in public housing asking for support, I often encountered Seibels, who was going door to door telling the residents that their rent would increase if the tax referendum passed. This of course was not true. He handed out yellow Tax Busters leaflets warning them of the rent increase. Seibels was against the tax increase and, I presume, the BCRI. He had a strong dislike for me and had publicly blamed me for his defeat for his third term as mayor of Birmingham in 1975 (see chapter 3).

On May 10, 1988, referendum day, I was out early encouraging public housing residents to vote. Their response to me was noticeably one of annoyance. Some residents who were seated on their porches would get up and go inside when they saw me approaching. When the polls closed, the referendum had been soundly defeated a second time. This time it passed in the predominantly black boxes, but the overall black voter turnout was dismally low. On June 7, 1988, Odessa wrote me to say that the institute task force thought that we should proceed with other fund-raising activities.

Licking my wounds, most of which had not healed from the defeat of the first referendum, I began to search for other ways to fund the BCRI. I asked City Attorney James Baker to check with the city's bond counselor to see if there was any city financing authority or legislation to create one that could fund the BCRI. On May 21, 1990, he suggested that the City Council create a Commercial Development Authority under the state constitution, section 11-54-170, which lists "museum" construction as one of its permissible projects. If we were to choose this route, we would have to amend the BCRI charter approved earlier to use the term "Museum" instead of "Institute" in its name. We had selected the term "Institute" after much debate because we envisioned the BCRI as sponsoring numerous seminars and similar activities usually not associated with "museum."

Finally, the staff came up with the suggestion that the city sell a building owned by the city's Building Authority and that currently housed the Southeastern Regional Social Security Office. The sale of that facility for $7.2 million in revenue bonds from the Historical Preservation Authority, and $2 million in city warrants, generated $9.2 million that would eventually be used toward the $12 million BCRI cost. Work on the BCRI accelerated.[5]

THE BCRI TASK FORCE

As noted, the BCRI Task Force under the guidance of Odessa Woolfolk guided the step-by-step process of developing the BCRI. In the face of repeated disappointments, questions about sources of funding, and alleged improprieties by a firm that served as a consultant for the BCRI project, the task force never wavered. Instead, it meticulously laid out the plans, the mission, and the charter of the future BCRI. Never once did the task force say, "Wait, let's see what happens next," or "Is the BCRI really going to become a reality?" As the work of the task force and the board continued, the scope of the project expanded to include a civil rights "Sculpture Garden" and Freedom Walk in Kelly Ingram Park. The park was completely renovated and several nationally known artists were commissioned to provide sculptures that would depict the story of the highlights of Birmingham's civil rights movement. Odessa and I traveled to the studios of the various artists to monitor their work and to give the city's approval to the work.

I first reviewed each piece of sculpture selected for the park, and the task force and the artists were commissioned to proceed. Along the way one snag developed—not with the task force or the artists but with some of the civil rights "foot soldiers." The dispute began when I selected a photograph of three ministers kneeling to pray by Kelly Ingram Park after Bull Connor halted a

Current and former Birmingham mayors at a 1985 gathering; from left, Richard Arrington Jr. (1979–99), David J. Vann (1975–79), George G. Seibels Jr. (1967–75), and Art Hanes (1961–63). Courtesy of the City of Birmingham Public Information Office.

Mayor Arrington with attorney Donald Watkins, 1988. Courtesy of the City of Birmingham Public Information Office.

Mayor Arrington presents the key to the City of Birmingham to civil rights pioneer Rosa Parks. Courtesy of the City of Birmingham Public Information Office.

Near the end of construction on the Birmingham Civil Rights Institute in 1992. In the foreground is the 16th Street Baptist Church, site of the infamous bombing that killed four schoolgirls on September 15, 1963. Photo by Bill Ricker.

Solidarity march from the 16th Street Baptist Church to the Birmingham Federal Courthouse, where Mayor Arrington would surrender for incarceration on contempt charges. Courtesy of the City of Birmingham Public Information Office.

David Vann at groundbreaking ceremony for the Civil Rights Institute, 1991.
Photo by Bill Ricker.

protest march that they were leading. The ministers in the photos were the Reverend A. D. King (the brother of Dr. Martin Luther King), the Reverend John Porter, pastor of the Sixth Avenue Baptist Church (Birmingham), and the Reverend Nelson Smith, pastor of New Pilgrim Baptist Church (Birmingham). The city, with Odessa's leadership, would later arrange for John Porter and Nelson Smith to travel to Washington, D.C., to serve as models for James Kaskey, who sculpted *The Kneeling Ministers,* which is now at the southeast entrance to Kelly Ingram Park. Several concrete boulders, four of which are sheared off at the top, representing the four young girls slain in the 16th Street Baptist Church bombing, flank the sculpture. It rests on a diagonal line that runs from the sculpture across the park to the front entrance to 16th Street Baptist Church.

Just after Odessa and I gave final approval to the wax or clay model of the statue that was to be cast in limestone (which is abundant in Alabama), Odessa learned from the Reverend Fred Shuttlesworth and the Reverend Abraham Woods Jr., two prominent leaders of the civil rights movement in Birmingham, that they and some of the other active participants in the movement objected to including the faces of two of the ministers who were the models for the statue. If those faces were not removed from the statue, they said, they would lead daily protest marches to the park, the site of the statue, until it was removed. They questioned whether two of the men depicted had been prominent enough in the civil rights movement to deserve to be memorialized by the statue. After enduring the hostility of much of the white community over the project, I was now faced with threats of protests over the statue from civil rights leaders. I finally relented and had the artist remove the faces of all three of the ministers and replace them with anonymous models we hired from the Washington, D.C., area. The unpleasant and embarrassing task of informing each minister that his likeness was being replaced and the reason why fell to Odessa. This action upset the congregations of Sixth Avenue Baptist and New Pilgrim. But their pastors asked them to remain quiet and support the project. Out of respect to their pastor and their city, they contained their seething anger.

The renovated park was given a new theme, "A Place of Revolution and Reconciliation," which was intended to convey the confrontation between the demonstrators and city officials and the eventual nonviolent resolution of the conflict. I personally chose that theme one evening during a conversation with

Mike Dobbins on a return flight to Birmingham from New Orleans. Mike had invited me to speak to some distinguished city planners and architects who were attending the Urban Land Institute Conference in New Orleans. Some of them noted Birmingham's increased use of environmental landscaping, art, and districts such as our Civil Rights District to enhance the visual and artistic quality of our downtown area. Mike, who had contributed most to that impetus, kindly gave me credit for being behind that effort. As a result, the group invited me to do a slide-lecture presentation on the recent changes in downtown Birmingham. Heading home on the flight, we discussed the ongoing work in Kelly Ingram Park. Somewhere in our conversation I blurted out to Mike that the Civil Rights District, in my mind, was a symbol of both the revolution and the reconciliation of the civil rights movement in Birmingham. Mike apparently liked what I had said. He shared my comment with Odessa, who shared it with her task force, who thought it was a fitting theme. Thus, this was my major contribution to our Civil Rights District.

Strong, dedicated men and women who love the City of Birmingham would not let the dream of the BCRI be shattered. Indeed, they knew in their hearts that a beautiful dream fulfilled is the redemption of a potential of a people—a potential too long delayed in my city.

11

Keeping the City Viable
Annexations and Economic Development

The flight of the suburban middle class from the City of Birmingham, followed by a significant number of jobs, had a great destabilizing impact on the city. In addition to slowly sucking the economic lifeblood from Birmingham, suburban communities continued to leave the heavy burden of financing most of the social amenities that contribute to a good quality of life for the entire metro area on the City of Birmingham. Their failure to contribute to the cost of the symphony, the museums, the zoo, the botanical gardens, and similar amenities created a situation in which Birmingham, with its lower per capita income, was paying for suburbanites' benefits. Birmingham continues to carry the major burden of economic development of the metro area. Approximately 60 percent of jobs in the metro area are located inside the corporate limits of Birmingham. The major costs for economic development efforts in metro Birmingham are borne by the City of Birmingham.

I knew that Birmingham would remain viable only if it broke out of the ring of suburban cities surrounding it and developed economic initiatives that created the new jobs the city needed to create a strong tax base. I thought that the way to ensure the city's long-term economic viability was to use the dual-track strategy of downtown renewal and aggressive annexation of potential commercial areas.

The municipal tax structure in Alabama is built around commercial development or businesses. Without adequate business development, the city's tax base dries up, followed by a decline in basic city services, such as police, fire, and sanitation services. Government workers and city equipment cost considerable amounts of money. The only source of revenue for cities is *taxes*. More than 75 percent of Birmingham's annual revenue comes from the following sources: sales taxes, occupational job taxes, and business license taxes. If there are no businesses, there are no jobs, no business license taxes, no sales on which to collect taxes, and so forth. That, one would think, is easy for elected officials to understand. However, according to Birmingham City Council candidates in 1985, one of my greatest political sins was expanding Birmingham into suburban areas and creating jobs as a base for city revenue. Many of those candidates ran also wanting to know why I did not put that economic development money and efforts in the older, deteriorating inner-city areas. Of course, I would have loved to do that if I could have found businesses that were willing to invest in the inner-city areas, but they were few and far between. It was very clear that taxes for services for inner-city Birmingham were flowing largely from the newly annexed commercial areas of Birmingham. Please remember that property taxes in Alabama are among the lowest of the nation! Only about 8 percent of a city's budget comes from property taxes.

ANNEXATIONS

Alabama has archaic annexation laws, a very real concern for a central city like Birmingham, which is surrounded by thirty or more small suburban municipalities. There are three ways that Alabama municipalities may annex properties or expand their corporate limits.

1. Citizens may petition for annexation of property that is adjacent to or contiguous to the city's corporate boundary. This process can work well for an individual property owner or a small number of unincorporated properties adjacent to the corporate boundary of the annexing city. It also works quite well for a larger unincorporated community, where the overwhelming majority of property owners of the community are desirous of annexing, usually to obtain some municipal benefit like fire protection or garbage collection. Petitions from an overwhelming majority make it easy to obtain the number of petition signatures of property owners to meet this annexation statute. However, this method does require a high percentage of property owners residing in each quarter/quarter section of an area to sign the annexation petition. Hence, if there is opposition, the annexation effort can be easily defeated.

2. The state legislature can annex or de-annex property by majority vote of both houses, whether such properties are contiguous to a city's boundary or not.

3. A 1908 constitutional act permits a municipality to annex property on its own initiative if a majority of people living on the property (may or may not be the property owner) vote for annexation. This type of annexation is initiated by a resolution of the City Council, giving a precise legal description of the area to be annexed. The resolution is then sent to the probate judge of the county in which the property is located, who sets the date for the annexation vote. This is usually referred to as the "tax exempt" annexation method because the annexed area is exempt from municipal taxation for ten to fifteen years. The area may waive its tax exemption by majority petition and get full city services. If the annexed area remains tax exempt, the annexing city is obligated to give the area only police and fire protection.

In 1981, the Alabama Supreme Court ruled that an interstate highway or state highway could be used in an annexation call for the purpose of making separate pieces of properties contiguous, setting off a flurry of what came to be called "long lasso" annexations.[1] The city of Tuskegee and a property owner used Interstate 85 to make a race track that was fifteen miles northwest of the city, contiguous to Tuskegee, and thus annexable. A year later, the City of Birmingham launched several similar annexations. This time, the state Supreme Court ruled such annexations as unconstitutional, putting an end to a long list of planned "long lasso" annexations.

In June 1975, under the administration of David Vann, Birmingham annexed (tax exempt) a community known as Garden Highlands and 4,000 acres of adjoining property owned by U.S. Steel. Jefferson County commissioner Tom Gloor vigorously and unsuccessfully protested the annexation.

In May 1975, Birmingham called for a tax-exempt annexation vote in an area of Jefferson County called Birminghamport, which is located on the Warrior River. This was an effort to extend Birmingham's corporate limits to the port area so that Birmingham could implement an economic development program for a major port facility in Birmingham. I worked closely with Vann in that annexation effort. The plan called for a small black community called Booker Heights to vote its area plus contiguous port property into the city of Birmingham. Vann and I worked closely with S. C. Perryman, who pastored in Booker Heights, to gain the support of the 50–60 voters in the area. Perryman was our leader in pushing for this important annexation, but one week before the election we learned that Perryman had switched sides and was quietly opposing the annexation. He joined ranks with Gloor, who was fighting the annexation. On referendum day, May 25, the annexation failed because of a tie vote. After the failure of the annexation, Gloor worked with the nearby city of Maytown to annex enough property to block any Birmingham access to the port area.

In December 1976, Birmingham annexed the eastern communities of Briarmont, Airport Hills, and Pine Knoll Vista. These, like Garden Highlands and Booker Heights, were all-black communities that wished to receive city services. Mason City, an all-black area in southwest Birmingham, was also annexed. In addition, voters in the struggling black cities of Brownsville and Roosevelt City opted to unincorporate and vote themselves into Birmingham in order to receive city services and to avoid bankruptcy.

Dolomite, a small black community that had no fire or garbage services, was also part of the annexation plans. Its two adjacent, predominantly white cities of Pleasant Grove and Hueytown rejected Dolomite's request for annexation. The community had lost several homes to fire because it had no fire protection. When Dolomite approached the City of Birmingham, asking to be annexed, Birmingham was willing to do so. There was one problem: Birmingham and Dolomite were not contiguous at any point and U.S. Steel owned the only possible land corridor that could make the property contiguous. Local U.S. Steel officials strongly fought Birmingham's efforts to annex a narrow corridor of U.S. Steel property. Even a corridor an inch wide would make Dolomite and Birmingham contiguous at some point and would thus allow the annexation. I finally took the fight to annex the corridor to a U.S. Steel executive at its national headquarters in Pittsburgh. We were finally permitted to annex a twelve-inch corridor of U.S. Steel property to link us with Dolomite. The executive who gave the green light requested one commitment from me—that we would not use the corridor to also annex the huge U.S. Steel plants in the area. Annexing those plants would have brought millions of tax dollars into the city's coffers, but I gave my word and we were committed to it. We finally annexed Dolomite. While we did not bother the U.S. Steel plants, we used the Dolomite annexation to also annex a corridor that takes the Birmingham corporate limits within feet of Birminghamport.

In 1984–85, I began a major annexation push by Birmingham, which brought a loud protest from the suburbs and their state legislators.[2] We were moving eastward, annexing 4,900 acres of undeveloped U.S. Pipe property and then turning south, racing through a twenty-five-foot-wide corridor between the cities of Irondale and Leeds, on into Shelby County, toward Lake Purdy, which was the city's river water supply. The hue and cry got louder. We finally got through that twenty-five-foot corridor, beating Leeds and Trussville, who were trying as fast as the law permitted to annex properties that would make their boundaries contiguous and block Birmingham from gaining access to the properties leading south into Shelby County. We beat them by holding special council meetings on a Saturday and a Sunday to annex through the unincorporated gap of property between those two cities.[3] They thought that they had us stopped, and they would have in another week. However, David Vann came up with the Saturday-Sunday strategy and to this day, I am not sure that they know what hit them. The city of Hoover and its state legislators tried to undo our annexations in the legislature and then before the Alabama Supreme Court. They lost at each turn. All of a sudden, they acted as though we were taking property within their cities. Several years later they were carrying out similar annexations for their cities.

Then we began an annexation program targeting the fast-growing Highway 280 corridor. Our first successful annexation there was the annexation of the site that became the Colonnade Office Complex and Retail Center. On that one, I had to fight David Vann, who was attorney for the Atlanta (Carter) Development Firm that owned the property. On all the others, Vann was leading the way as the city's strategist and annexation attorney. The 280 program brought in Perimeter Square, Grandview I and II, and the Summit Shopping and Residential Project. In the latter, we were aided by the Overton Community, a black area that needed city services but had been turned down by the city of Irondale when it requested annexation. Our 280 program took us south on 280, past Inverness, down to the Brook Highland Shopping Center, and on to Lloyd's Restaurant.

Not every annexation plan was a success, though Birmingham did double in size during my administration.[4] Two critical misjudgments, one by Vann and one by me, greatly hurt our efforts, as did an outright betrayal by one corporation.

The first was the 1985 Vann miscalculation. We had an ambitious plan to go eastward along I-59, annexing thousands of acres of U.S. Steel and Tutwiler property. The nearest city to the property was Irondale. Our plan was to use the votes of a small, unincorporated black community, adjacent to Irondale, which Irondale refused to annex. We were assured of winning the annexation election because the voters wanted to be a part of Birmingham. A few weeks before the scheduled election, Vann and our community development director, Bob Land, decided to drive throughout the targeted area. Much to their surprise, they found out that part of the area contained dozens of apartments, all occupied by white residents. Vann had been relying on an old set of outdated maps to draw the proposed annexation area. The old maps did not show new residential developments. We knew at that moment, with all of the controversy surrounding the upcoming annexation vote, we had lost.

I made two bad mistakes that good politicians never make. First, I took the word of officials from three development firms. They said that they would willingly annex their properties to Birmingham if we first permitted them to complete portions of their planned office commercial developments in areas that we had included in the annexation referendum. The first involved the area now known as Liberty Park and Old Overton. Those properties were included in our Overton annexation referendum, which would later be successful. But a few weeks before the scheduled annexation election, officials of Drummond and Torchmark, the developers, lobbied me to remove their property from the annexation call. It was less costly, they said, to develop their property outside of the city with its stricter building codes and then annex the property after the buildings were constructed. To show their good faith, they would willingly annex two pieces of developed property in the area. I was too stupid to ask for a legally binding, written agreement. I took them at their word and removed their property from the annexation call. When the property was developed, I approached them about annexing their property, as promised. Instead, they tried to annex it to the city of Mountain Brook first. After that failed, they succeeded in getting the property annexed to the city of Vestavia via legislative act.

The second mistake was taking the word of Daniels Realty, a developer, regarding the Rust Engineering site on Highway 280. The city had a long-standing agreement with the parent company of Rust, then in Houston, Texas, to keep Rust within the corporate limits of Birmingham. Under that agreement, the city underwrote the expenses for the search for and evaluation of a new Rust site. Local Rust officials made several attempts to get its corporate headquarters' approval to locate on sites outside the city and got a "No." Finally, David Rosendale, of the Birmingham Rust office, working with Bill

Richardson of Daniels Realty, approached me about supporting a plan for Rust to relocate just outside the city limits on property under development by Daniels. The Daniels property was already under development and Daniels wanted to complete it before annexing it to the City of Birmingham. If I would write the Rust corporate headquarters, stating that I was agreeable to the Rust-Daniels plan, Rust would move to the Daniels site and upon completion of the Rust campus Daniels would annex the property to the city. I agreed. When the project was completed, they reneged on their promises.

We did succeed in January 1985 to get the legislature to de-annex 4,000 acres of property from the city of Fultondale and annex it to Birmingham for development of a planned theme park.[5] The request was made by the property owner. Several years later, when the theme park project did not materialize, Birmingham supported legislation to de-annex the property from Birmingham and annex it again to Fultondale, as it had been agreed at the outset.

One of the city's most successful annexations was the annexation of the Oxmoor Valley Industrial and Research Park site of nearly 5,000 acres.[6] The city purchased the first 3,000 acres (4.7 square miles), financed portions of the infrastructure, and got two corporate firms to join in the purchase of the remainder of the site, held by U.S. Steel. Today, Oxmoor Valley remains a major generator of key commercial projects and new jobs for Birmingham.

I have spoken here mainly to how our annexation program undergirded our economic development, with a focus mainly on commercial properties. However, most commercial annexations were possible only because they were contiguous to residential properties whose residents favored annexation. Several other economic development initiatives were also undertaken during my tenure.

THE GREEKS AND BLOCK 60

Block 60 is the name and number on the downtown real estate map for the block bound by 4th and 5th avenues and 19th and 20th streets north. It could be called the heart or center of northern downtown or the city center—a prime piece of real estate. Block 60 would also become the name for one of my administration's early downtown economic development projects.

In March 1979, the City Council approved a contract for the preparation of a downtown master plan. On May 5, 1981, the City Council approved the preliminary plan, laying out the long-range plans for downtown redevelopment. As the plan was being refined, the city adopted what it called an "Early Action Program" of the plan. This included the first redevelopment program of the new master plan. We wanted to immediately implement the Early Action Program to bring credibility to the entire long-range plan. The first step was to redevelop Block 60 by constructing a new $125 million hotel plus mixed residential and retail facilities on the block. In July 1980, the city asked interested developers to submit their proposal for redeveloping Block 60. More than a dozen developers submitted proposals. In August 1980, Metropolitan Properties was selected by the city as developer for Block 60 and their plan was approved in September 1981.[7]

The first step now was to have the developers purchase Block 60 from its several owners. The developers, with the city's assistance, set about to acquire options to purchase the property by December 31, 1982.

The most contentious negotiations over the purchase of Block 60 occurred between the developer and Cameron Grammas, a Greek American who owned a significant part of the block. An option to purchase his property was finally negotiated. As the deadline approached for exercising the purchase options, Metropolitan Properties was still unable to secure the financing required, forcing the city to step in at the last minute to arrange the financing.[8] On December 31, 1982, Grammas's attorney, Gusty Yearout, another Greek American who was supposed to handle the closing for Grammas, was reportedly in California and would not return to Birmingham for several days. When he did return, he said that his client did not wish to sell because the deadline of December 31 had passed. In essence, the much anticipated and closely watched sale of Block 60 did not go through. A third Greek American, John Katopodis,[9] was a member of the City Council and the greatest "in-house" detractor for the project. He constantly expressed skepticism publicly about the administration's ability to pull the project off. Some people speculated that Katopodis wanted to see the project fail because he planned to oppose me in the upcoming mayoral election, which he did. The failure of the Block 60 project was a great blow to my administration and to the revitalization of downtown Birmingham.[10]

The Financial Center

One of my administration's first successful downtown projects was the development of an office building called the Financial Center. It is located on half of the block diagonally northeast of Block 60, the former site of an old Birmingham hotel.[11] When the hotel was demolished because of its poor condition, it left half of the block in the very heart of downtown vacant—a further indication of a dying downtown. I got the owner's permission to lease the property to the city for a minimal fee to enable us to make it a green space until such time that I could develop a suitable project to put on the property. Again, Katopodis, his eye on the upcoming mayoral election, was very critical of the proposed green space, which turned out quite well. He also spoke of it as one more example of my administration's inability to provide the leadership needed for the economic welfare of downtown.

At about this time, a large suburban development known as Riverchase was under way and was certain to suck jobs out of downtown. I observed that one of the key investors in the project was Equitable Life Assurance Company. Its CEO was Coy Ekuland, a name familiar to me because he was an active supporter of the National Urban League. With the help of James White III, a local investment banker and financial advisor to the city, I got an opportunity to meet with Ekuland in his New York office. At that meeting with him and White, I told Ekuland of my concern about the plight of downtown Birmingham while also noting that his firm was investing in Birmingham suburbs. I asked if it were possible that his firm might invest in a major downtown Birmingham project. He promised to look into it. In about a week he called me to ask if Equitable's investment in what is now the Financial Center would help our downtown. I said, "Indeed, it would." He proceeded to put the financing for the project in place.

Industrial Parks

Earlier, I mentioned the Oxmoor Valley Industrial Park development. It was one of a dozen such parks that my administration developed. Oxmoor, of course, is by far the largest one. However, the others also have had significant impact on the creation of jobs for Birmingham. Our Airport Industrial Park filled as fast as we could develop it. Other parks were not very long in reaching their capacity, too. When I flew to Michigan with the head of our Metropolitan Development Board and enticed the Olgihara brothers of Japan to select Birmingham over other southeastern sites for their new southern plant, we had an industrial park site ready for them—a key to their site decision, I believe. Birmingham was Olgihara's second U.S. plant site. It has undergone one significant expansion since locating in Birmingham and I anticipate a third expansion soon. From its Birmingham plant, it produces all major exterior parts for the Mercedes Auto Plant in Tuscaloosa, about forty miles down the interstate. Olgihara also produces exterior body parts for auto plants for General Motors in Michigan, Nissan in Tennessee, and Ford in Georgia. I anticipate that one day, after Olgihara is able to meet the growing demands of Mercedes-Tuscaloosa, it will begin supplying its contracts in Tennessee and Georgia from Birmingham rather than from its Olgihara plant in Michigan.

Birmingham's industrial park program has been a major job creator for our city. I just wonder what we could have been if Vann's attempt to annex the Birminghamport property in 1975 had succeeded. Can you imagine a major industrial park sitting right on the Warrior River in Birmingham? Well, maybe not. Imagination has sometimes been a scarce commodity in metro Birmingham.

Controversy over Land Purchases

This seems like a good place to mention one of the controversies that I became involved in as I pursued the city's economic development program. This is not a particularly big one, but it serves as a good example of what I often encountered. The plan was to quietly purchase properties along the Eighth Avenue corridor and solicit proposals for redevelopment of the corridor. By owning the properties, the city could control what type of development went there and offer certain tax incentives to developers. When the city purchased a 5,000-square-foot lot from black state senator Earl Hilliard for $165,000, the media had a field day, yelling, "Foul, corruption!" I had purchased property of a close political ally and paid $165,000 for it, when the tax assessor said its market value was only $34,950! An appraiser had set its value at $165,000. The controversy continued for a couple of weeks, leading the State Ethics Commission to investigate the transaction. In the middle of the controversy, I attended my monthly breakfast with the Birmingham corporate leaders. As soon as we turned our attention to the agenda for the morning, Richard Pizitz, one of the corporate officials who was present, stood and assailed me for the property deal I made with Hilliard. From the looks on the faces of the group, most believed that I committed a corrupt act. I tried to remind them of something that I believed they all knew—that market values assigned to properties by the tax assessor are always two to three times less than the property brings on the market. I said to them, "Nobody in here would sell his property for what the tax assessor of the county says its market value is." I noted, for example, that a state-owned property in the same Eighth Avenue corridor, in the adjacent block, was appraised by the tax assessor to have a market value of $566,000 and we paid the State of Alabama $1.2 million. This was at the same time that we purchased Hilliard's property. The Elks property in the same area, according to tax assessor records, was worth $423,000. We paid $1.06 million for it, and so on. Neither they nor the media seemed to have any problem with our paying three to four times the tax assessor's value for other properties of comparable location to the Hilliard property. I left the meeting that morning feeling that I had not convinced a single person that the Hilliard property sale was "legit." It was not until I was hauled before the State Ethics Commission and was able to show conclusively that the purchase was not different from dozens of other commercial property purchases made by the city or from hundreds of other pieces of commercial properties sold throughout the city by others in the past year that the fuss subsided. The latter was easily shown by looking at the real estate publication listing all property sales in the city. It showed that every piece of commercial property sold during that year brought at least three times more than the tax assessor's records said its value was. Not a single commercial property, of the hundreds of property listed, sold anywhere close to what the tax assessor said its value was. The Ethics Commission was satisfied, though I'm not sure about my corporate friends.

MINORITY BUSINESS ENTERPRISES PARTICIPATION

"There is no doubt that Birmingham and other cities in the South have had a sorry history of both private and public discrimination. Happily, this era is long past. It is impossible to locate and compensate the victims of such past discrimination, and the fact that there was past discrimination cannot justify reverse discrimination of other minorities *unrelated* [emphasis mine] to the past acts." This ruling from Jefferson County Circuit Judge Marvin Cherner on March 31, 1989, cut me deep. At first I felt pain and anger cascade through every fiber of my being as I read his words. Then, in a few minutes, I felt just numb. City attorney Donald Watkins brought me a copy of the order. In a matter of minutes, I was at my desk, writing my own news release in which I tried to express my anger at Cherner's ruling.

What was it about Cherner's ruling that evoked such emotions on my part?

It could not have been just the fact that the ruling declared the city's Minority Participation Program unconstitutional. The city had been in and out of court since 1973, fighting to defend its minority participation programs and eventually losing each fight. Maybe it was just that I expected something different from Cherner. I did not expect a decision in the city's favor but perhaps I was just hoping it might happen. The order was the culmination of a long and sometimes bitter fight with the Associated General Contractors Association that cost the city in excess of $2 million in legal fees. I was prepared to accept defeat, but not a "stinging defeat." Cherner's order added insult to injury and rubbed salt in the wounds with three short sentences that were included in his twenty-seven-page order and a one-page quote from a speech by then Assistant U.S. Attorney William Bradford Reynolds in a speech on October 5, 1983, to the University of Virginia School of Law that Cherner "provided an eloquent statement of reasons why any affirmative action program undermines the fundamental principles embodied in the 14th Amendment to the U.S. Constitution."

Before the Associated General Contractor's case asking the court to declare Birmingham's Minority Participation Program unconstitutional went before Judge Cherner, I knew Cherner only by his reputation among some local attorneys, including several black attorneys who argued cases in his court. Their perception of him was that of a judge who was bright, perhaps the brightest in his circuit, and fair. Not that they ever thought him radical or liberal, just smart and fair. One day, during a short recess in the long-running arguments before Judge Cherner, he did not leave the bench while the hearing was recessed. Instead, he sat there, looked out at me seated at the defendant's table and asked me to come to the bench. Looking me in the eye, he hunched over slightly in his chair and said, "Mayor, I just don't understand what you and your people are thinking. What do you expect? Nobody is just going to give you a handout. You just have to work hard and earn what you get. My father came to this country, a Russian Jew and worked in the mines to get ahead. It seems to me you people don't want to get out and work hard."

"Judge, we have worked hard in this country, too. We just want a fair shake like others get." This was a part of what I said to him during the five- to ten-minute recess. I think I knew that Cherner could not see the issue as we saw it.

But months later on March 31, 1989, I was standing by my desk in the mayor's office, reading his order in our case. He acknowledged without a doubt "that Birmingham and other cities in the South have had a sorry history of both private and public discrimination." "Happily," he wrote, "that era is long-passed." "Long-passed?" I thought to myself. Where in the hell has this man been living? For the past ten years we had been embroiled in bitter legal wrangling over exclusion of blacks from business contracts in the public and private sectors of Birmingham. The City of Birmingham, but not the county's other thirty or more municipalities, was in the early stages of a federally drafted consent decree to open up fair hiring practices for blacks. The other municipalities were on the sidelines, watching us fight the battle but doing nothing about their own sordid record of racial discrimination in hiring. How could that era be "long-passed"? Then came Cherner's coup de grâce in his order. "It is *impossible* [emphasis mine] to locate and compensate the victims of such discrimination." Impossible to find the victims? This is Birmingham! This is 1989! Civil rights demonstrations had taken place in Birmingham just two generations ago. "How can you not find the victims when you walk past them every day?" I tried to say in my news release on the order.

I did not know at the time that Cherner considered me a "racist." He would tell a friend of mine that about a year or so later. My friend had just narrowly lost the race to retain her seat as a Jefferson County Circuit Court judge. She lost because her opposition portrayed her, to the white voters, as an ally of that police-hating, race-baiting Arrington. When she told a reporter that she thought her "race" had been a factor in the defeat, Cherner reportedly called her to his office and admonished her never to say that again. "You lost because you're allied with Arrington. That man is a racist," she said that he told her.

FIGHTING FOR MINORITY PARTICIPATION

The entire history of blacks in Birmingham has been one of a struggle for justice, for being seen and treated as human beings. Thank God I can say, at this time, that my city, Birmingham, has made dramatic and incredible strides over the last two decades to expand constitutionally guaranteed rights to its black citizens. It's the thing I'm most proud of about my city. I rank Birmingham's racial progress right up there with the abandonment of apartheid in South Africa. I never thought I would live long enough to see either.

The fight for minority participation was not limited just to getting city and private business contracts for minority enterprises. The fight was on a much wider front—voting, employment discrimination, judicial discrimination, law enforcement discrimination, public accommodations discrimination, and, in general, just about everything involved in daily life.

The fight for Minority Business Enterprise (MBE) participation in city contracts was launched in 1974 when the Birmingham City Council adopted Ordinance 74-2 requiring assurances of nondiscriminatory employment practices. This is the ordinance Mayor George Seibels vetoed. It was passed over his veto, which cost him his reelection. In May 1977 Ordinance 77-81 required that within thirty days of an award of a city contract, the contracting party must provide the city with an analysis of its workforce by race, sex, and national origin. In October 1977, Mayor David Vann acted under Ordinance 77-81 and, following the federal requirement of the Public Works Employment Act (PWEA), required that minority firms be assured of at least 10 percent of the contract amount. Cities using PWEA funds were required, by federal regulation, to assure the minimum 10 percent minority participation.

Associated General Contractors (AGC) Attack

On November 30, 1977, AGC sued in Circuit Court, seeking to have the city MBE Ordinance invalidated. They sought an immediate preliminary injunction against the city. In January 1981, Circuit Judge William Thompson declared the city's 10 percent MBE ordinance invalid.

Nine days later, the city adopted Ordinance 77-257 and later adopted 79-140 (August 1979), declaring its findings of historical patterns and practices of racial discrimination and denial of city business to minorities. A goal of 15 percent MBE participation was established for contracts of $20,000 or more. Bidders were required to make and document good faith efforts to meet the goal.

AGC again asked the court to invalidate the city's new MBE ordinance. This was the case that was heard in the court of Judge Marvin Cherner. Cherner's March 31, 1989, ruling invalidated the city MBE ordinance.

On April 1, 1989, I issued an executive order, putting a moratorium on all city contracts until I found a way to promote MBE participation. On April 3, 1989, the city successfully appealed to the Alabama Supreme Court for a temporary stay of Cherner's order. This request had come shortly after the U.S. Supreme Court ruled in the Virginia Croson case, establishing some MBE participation guidelines. The city asked the court to grant it time to change its MBE program and bring it in line with the new Croson ruling.

AGC and City Search for Solutions

During the Supreme Court–"granted" appeal and the time for a hearing on the case by the court, AGC and the city began serious discussions to resolve the issue of how to promote fair MBE participation in city and private construction contracts. The cost of the litigation to the city at this time was about $2 million.

With the appeal granted, I removed the moratorium on city contracts while asking the city's corporate community to join the city and AGC in a dialogue to help find a solution that included voluntary minority participation, bonding, financing, and management training for MBEs.

The city's corporate community responded immediately by providing important human, financial, and professional resources. The effort quickly brought together more than 100 business and community leaders. On April 21, 1989, these leaders joined me at a working breakfast at Birmingham-Southern College. The host for the meeting was Dr. Neal Berte, president of the college. He was also an active participant in resolving many of the urgent community issues that were confronting Birmingham. From this meeting and numerous follow-up work sessions, the Birmingham Plan emerged. The Birmingham Plan is a series of voluntary programs designed to overcome historical economic inequities and promote greater economic inclusion of minorities and disadvantaged persons in the Birmingham economy. The Birmingham Plan is one of the most significant achievements of the Birmingham community. It stands as a symbol of what a united community can achieve. The legal fight over Birmingham's MBE participation ordinance had taken thirteen years, millions of dollars, and endless efforts. The Birmingham Plan would be fashioned into a consent decree through city ordinances, cooperation, and compromise among AGC, the city, and the corporate and civic communities.

On January 17, 1990, Judge Marvin Cherner approved and entered a consent decree in the case of *AGC vs. The City of Birmingham.* There are many other important developments that contributed to Birmingham's success in fashioning its MBE participation programs. Although not all of them can be mentioned here, I should note that prior to the Birmingham Plan, when the

University of Alabama at Birmingham's Health Foundation was preparing to construct its outstanding Kirklin Medical Clinic designed by nationally known architect I. M. Pei, the controversy of MBE participation was an issue. The foundation's president and internationally respected heart surgeon, Dr. Kirklin, took note of the issue and its impact on the city. He asked me to have lunch with him in his office. He began by telling me that he was concerned about having fair minority participation in the clinic project and in the city in general. He said to me, "I have not had a lot of experience in resolving these kinds of racial issues. I grew up in Minnesota where race was not a controversial issue. We want to do what is right. My project manager tells me that there is not enough MBE construction capability in Birmingham for us to get more than two or three percent MBE participation in the clinic project. I would like for you to tell me how much MBE participation we can achieve." I told him that with a concerted effort, we should certainly get 10 percent MBE participation, maybe more. From that meeting with Dr. Kirklin and subsequently with my chief of staff, Dr. Edward Lamonte, the Kirklin Clinic project became a pilot program for MBE participation. Three minority firms, representing about 20 percent of the contracts, would be selected to participate. Lamonte would be the project monitor, carefully evaluating the performance of the MBE participants. That way, according to Kirklin, the community might come up with the right blueprint for promoting successful MBE involvement.

I want to close this discussion with some brief comments about the efforts of minority contractors to make the city MBE program work well. My overall evaluation on this point is mixed. From the very outset, back in 1975, there were black, so-called contractors who were willing to serve as "minority fronts" for a few white firms in exchange for compensation. They fronted as construction material suppliers or construction participants when, in fact, they were neither. Their behavior and sellouts made our efforts much harder. A few were "whiners," always complaining about not being included and just hoping for some "handout." Many wanted and tried to participate but lacked the business background to meet requirements for maintaining business records. One may be an outstanding brick mason but care little for the paperwork that is required of the contract or even for proper payroll records. They were deficient in management skills and only a minority of them took advantage of the city's MBE programs, taking special training courses or seminars to develop their management skills. Frankly, some of them had subsisted as small operators in their vocations and could not afford the time for seminars. Still, there were some notable successes.

One day, five young black construction contractors came to my office. They wanted to tell me how much they had been helped by taking the classes in the construction science areas that were offered by Auburn University through our MBE program. Not only did they tell me in some detail about how the training positioned them to bid successfully for work that they would have otherwise not gotten, but they requested that the city have Auburn University provide several other specific courses they needed. That made my day! We undergirded our MBE in every conceivable way. We organized the Minority Business Contractors Association, provided the funds for staff and legal services, and tried, unsuccessfully, to get the association to organize a lobbying capability in the Alabama legislature. Satisfactory MBE participation in private and public construction contracts still has a long way to go to achieve satisfactory results in metro Birmingham. In 2007, Birmingham's city government still confronts the issue, but I remain confident that the goal can be achieved. I think that two ingredients are essential. First, the City of Birmingham's black-dominated government must obtain a considerably larger number of major public construction projects. Unlike the city of Atlanta, which has successfully completed major construction projects like its regional international airport, the Georgia Dome, a regional public transit authority, and similar projects, heavily subsidized by federal grants, the City of Birmingham has had no comparable success. Its efforts at a regional transit system have failed repeatedly, and its MAPS program, including a dome facility, failed. Consequently, the "pie" has been smaller and the minority slice in Birmingham remains relatively small. Second, the rapidly expanding suburban area of Birmingham, which has small minority political influence and places little to no priority on encouraging MBE participation, must push for programs of MBE participation. Until the current Jefferson County Commission took office in 2002, the county did little about MBE participation. That is now changing for the better with the new commission. Concern and commitment about MBE participation by Jefferson and Shelby counties and growing suburban areas, like Hoover, are needed for the MBE participation programs of metro Birmingham to achieve a fair result.

12

The Jefferson County Citizens Coalition (JCCC)

The Birth of New Politics

During my first four-year term on the Birmingham City Council (about 1973), the City of Birmingham proposed a General Obligation Bond Referendum.[1] That referendum, which had to be authorized by a majority of city voters, would provide funds for a number of city public improvement projects. I researched the results of past successful city bonds referendums and was fully aware that the city's growing number of black voters determined the fate of the city's most recent successful bond referendums. Previous referenda had passed, by sizable majority, in predominantly black voting boxes while failing in predominantly white boxes. This was a voting pattern that clearly continued through 1999. During this period, only one proposition in a bond referendum would receive a majority in a predominantly white box. That proposition was for the construction of a new city jail.

As the 1973 bond referendum approached, I thought a good political strategy for the city's black community was to tie our support for the upcoming bond issue to a guarantee by the city that minority or black businesses would receive city contracts for work financed by the bond proceeds. At that time, no bona-fide black businesses had received city contracts. To adopt and implement this strategy, I sent invitations to the city's numerous black civic leagues, inviting them to attend a strategy meeting on the upcoming bond issues at the 16th Street Baptist Church. At the time, the city had not developed its Neighborhood Association Program, which later created more than ninety neighborhood associations. The city's black neighborhoods had long ago organized civic leagues, largely for the purpose of fighting for and increasing black voter registration and neighborhood improvement.

When I arrived at the church for the 7:00 P.M. meeting, the church was packed. The turnout far exceeded my expectations. I explained my proposed strategy to the group which included organizing what I called "an umbrella group" to which all existing black civic leagues and political organizations would belong. It would allow the black community to speak with a single voice on issues such as supporting the bond issue in exchange for guarantees of black participation in the city public improvement projects. On March 22, 1973, the idea was unanimously approved and a small committee that included attorney Oscar Adams, Walter Jackson, Lee Loder, and several others was appointed to approach the city and county governments about our proposal. Our new umbrella group called itself the Citizens Coalition. The committee appeared before the Birmingham City Council and the Jefferson County Commission, explaining what assurances we sought in exchange for support of the bond referendum. The county government had no pending bond referendum and took no action after listening to our concerns.

The Birmingham City Council reacted immediately. It appointed a council committee of three—Russell Yarbrough, David Vann, and me—to meet with representatives of the new coalition to explore ways to implement minority participation in city projects. Mayor George Seibels gave the idea lukewarm support. Several meetings were held between the committees of the council and the coalition. Good faith efforts were promised to include black contractors in future city work but the actual results, following the passage of the bond issue in question, were not productive. It would take several years before the city began to adopt minority participation programs. However, what was more important was that Birmingham's black community was beginning to flex its "political muscles" at a time when the number of blacks on the voter rolls was increasing and they were speaking with a single political voice. Collectively, we called ourselves the Jefferson County Citizens Coalition.

Undermining Black Political Solidarity

Before the existence of the coalition, the city's fathers never had to deal with the demands of a united black political entity. A decade or so earlier, the city had to learn to deal with the solidarity of the civil rights movement in Birmingham that was led by Reverend Fred Shuttlesworth, Reverend Edward

Gardner, and Dr. Martin Luther King Jr. Now it was faced with the birth of black political solidarity.

It was my belief at the time that the individual organization that stood to gain the most from the coalition was the city's only black political organization, the Jefferson County Progressive Democratic Council (PDC), headed by attorneys Arthur Shores and David Hood. The council was the black arm of the Alabama Democratic Party and rallied black voters' support through its sample ballots that were distributed at black churches before each election. Despite the suspicion of many blacks that the Progressive Council was directed to endorse candidates by Bob Vance, chairman of the Alabama Democratic Party, it was still a strong force as the only black political organization in the county. I was a member of the PDC and I knew that on issues of major import, the council followed Vance's recommendations in endorsements. I had personally witnessed Vance change endorsements made by the council's membership to those he preferred. As one of the two black City Council members on the PDC, I had enough privilege to know some of its "inside workings." Black voter support of the PDC was never near total or solid. There were always dissident voices accusing the council of being a "puppet" for white Democrats. I believed the formation of the coalition would significantly broaden the base of support for the PDC. The agreement reached in the formation of the coalition was that the council would be our "political arm" and the coalition would not make political endorsements, especially of candidates for office. I knew at the outset that David Hood, president of the council, would never support any organization that threatened its political influence. The coalition needed a respected political organization to give clout to getting elected officials to respect its concerns.

Of course the city's white power structure sensed the danger of a united black political voice and no doubt feared it. They were accustomed to dealing with and manipulating the PDC or the Alabama Christian Movement for Human Rights (ACMHR), led by Reverend Edward Gardner. Gardner had staged a long-running series of protest rallies against racial injustice in Birmingham and he was respected in the black community. There was never any question that he more than paid his civic dues—and long before King came on the scene to lead the Birmingham civil rights movement. Yet, Gardner was a known factor to the white power structure and they believed they knew how to deal with him. Anyway, they preferred "a devil" that they knew. They would not sit still and watch the coalition become a force.

This fact became evident when I received a phone call several weeks after the coalition was organized from Reverend Gardner, who stood strongly with the coalition. He told me he was withdrawing the ACMHR from the coalition. I asked him why. He said that he had received a call from Vincent Townsend of the *Birmingham News*. Townsend, he said, wanted to know whether he, Gardner, was still the black leader or was he giving that mantle to me. Nothing I said to Gardner could change his mind. The first break in our solidarity had occurred. It was regrettable, but nothing close to fatal. Gardner's organization was a "direct action" group that stirred the pot with street demonstrations. We could succeed without ACMHR being "inside the tent." They could go on with their protests and we would still benefit from them. It was the next break from the coalition ranks that hurt and led us to reassess our strategy.

I got a call from Bernice Johnson, president of the Black Democratic Women's Club, a member of the PDC, and an unwavering political supporter of mine. No other black woman in Birmingham wielded the influence of Bernice Johnson. She invited me to meet with her and David Hood that afternoon at the downtown Holiday Inn-Civic Center.

At that meeting, Johnson and Hood told me that the PDC was a part of the Alabama Democratic Party. They were "uncomfortable" with attorney Oscar Adams, one of the few black Birmingham Republicans, speaking for their organization under the umbrella of the coalition. (Adams would later become the first black on the Alabama Supreme Court.) "A Republican could not speak for Democrats," they said. This was a reference to the fact that Adams was chairing the coalition's Negotiating Committee, which had also appeared before the City Council to set forth our demands for black participation in future city contracts. My contention that what we were fighting for went beyond political party lines did not faze them. They were withdrawing from the coalition. Left with what we considered "no political arm," we soon decided that the coalition would make its own endorsements and distribute its own sample ballots. Our political influence would come through the officers of our civic leagues who were members of the coalition. Since these individuals were already well known in their communities and respected by their neighbors, our influence in those communities was instantaneous.

Within a year, 80 percent of voters in predominantly black boxes were voting for candidates and issues recommended by the Jefferson County Citizens Coalition. Soon, no black in Birmingham could gain elected office without coalition support. It had become, according to the *Birmingham News,* a "powerful political machine."[2] Although the coalition did not formally incorporate until September 1983, it was the dominant force to deal with in Birmingham politics for the next two decades.

Many coalition members reveled in the fact that the local media often referred to the coalition as a machine, despite my warnings that this was only their way of telling their readers that we were a "dangerous group worth close watching." It was their way of setting us up for "assassination," I warned. But a truly strong black political group with considerable power in the black community of Jefferson County was heady stuff and we loved to stop and "smell the roses."[3]

In the 1981 City Council election, the coalition experienced its first strong attack from the local media. At that time, all council members were elected at large and six of the nine members were white. After considerable debate over what strategy was required to elect a majority of blacks to the council, the coalition adopted the unwise strategy of endorsing an all-black slate.[4] The basic rationale was to deny votes to strong white incumbents thereby enhancing the chances of winning for three of the strongest black candidates. Since I was mayor and the coalition founder, it gave my detractors an opportunity to portray me, the mayor, as the racist many whites believed I was. Also, the white media used the all-black slate to fire up and turn out a large white vote. One of the white candidates thoroughly infiltrated our strategy sessions using, as her informer, the black assistant superintendent of Birmingham Public Schools. He suddenly became an active volunteer on our strategy committee, recorded our plans, and took them to the white candidate he supported. And of course, worst of all, all black candidates but one lost. Black voters who had endured years of racial injustices under lily-white governments resented the idea of a black mayor now playing the race card.

As the coalition grew I was careful as its first president to avoid what I saw as some of the major mistakes of the once-powerful PDC. I had the good fortune of becoming an "insider" in the council because I was the city's second black elected official. The PDC was glad to have me as a member of its inner circle where few members caucused with David Hood prior to meetings of the general body and decided on strategies to use to get the body to adopt the program we had already decided on. This method of operation kept the power of the PDC in the hands of small, select groups that in reality decided on who could and could not join the organization and which candidates the organization would support for political office. The general membership was kept in the position of being our "rubber stamp." The way the PDC operated made it the focus of constant criticism from outside observers, new applicants for membership in the PDC, and some of the loyal PDC members. Our president was considered "dictatorial" and our organization operated as a "closed" organization.

I nearly broke ranks with the PDC before the birth of the coalition over its refusal to accept young blacks seeking political office into its membership, thereby limiting their chance of getting elected. An endorsement from the PDC was essential to winning Jefferson County's black vote. I had barely won that endorsement when I first won a City Council seat in 1971. Inside the organization I was constantly rebuffed by our president as I tried to get new young blacks admitted to membership.

The PDC was also criticized because it was legitimately the "black arm" of the Alabama Democratic Party and therefore supported Democratic Party candidates only. The organization also received its major financial backing from the Alabama Democratic Party.

Now as coalition president I was careful to get our membership to open the organization to any and all comers—those who meant us well and those who did not. I indoctrinated the membership with the idea that if a core of our membership remained united we could permit dissent and still maintain majority rule. Founding members of the coalition became "blood brothers," steering the organization. Every issue could be debated and every member could debate, but a final decision would be determined by the body. Our monthly meetings had a regular attendance of 100 or so persons. Around election time the attendance usually doubled. Oftentimes new members joined just before an election, often as part of a ploy to support a particular candidate for endorsement in an upcoming election. These repeated efforts by candidates failed as our "conservative core" membership always carried the majority vote.

Membership dues in the coalition were kept at five dollars for years and then eventually went to ten dollars per year. But it was the written policy of the body that no person would be denied full membership because of inability or failure to pay annual dues.

The main strategy of the coalition was to be an "open organization" that welcomed new members, especially aspiring young political candidates. No one could ever accuse us of barring anyone or ignoring younger and often more dissident members. Our policy was to seek out young people with leadership potential and bring them into the fold. That policy worked fairly well, but not perfectly. Indeed, we successfully supported some young candidates for city boards, City Council, and the state legislature. In fact no black candidate from Jefferson County won without our endorsement. But there was always competition from the older coalition members who were the core of the coalition's strength. These were the "carryovers" from the old days of the civic leagues. They were older, often with less formal education than the younger members, but they maintained, rightly, that "they had paid their dues" and were entitled to some of the harvest—of being the first of their race to hold these important offices. Though a member seeking to fill a vacancy on an important board, such as the Housing Authority, could not fully understand all of the bureaucratic policies and sometimes arcane policies of that body to the extent that his competition for the position may be a young bright attorney, they believed they outranked the young person on "dues."

The coalition also was a nonpartisan organization, even though 95 percent of its endorsees for political office were Democrats. This simply reflected two things: 1) the black community's pro-Democratic allegiance and 2) the opposition to the nearly all-white Alabama Republican Party made up largely of former "Conservative Democrats." "Conservative" in Alabama political jargon always connotes something about "race." In fact, Alabama would not have any politics if there were not some racial underpinning. Of course it's not nearly as bad as it used to be. We're halfway home on racial tolerance but still have a long way to go. And it's a situation where the pot can't call the kettle black.

Unity of the coalition membership was also undergirded by the desire to support me as "their council member" and later as the first black mayor. This was especially true of the older members. When I was elected mayor I resigned as president of the coalition and was succeeded by Simmie Lavender, Ben Greene, and Lewis Spratt, all "old-timers" from the civic league days. Spratt would eventually get elected to the state legislature on the strength of his coalition ties. Lavender won a constable seat and Greene was my right-hand man when I was mayor.

As is true with most institutions in the black community, the coalition could not have succeeded without the strong women of the organization. They carry more than half the load for the group. Yet in the coalition, even with its "openness" policy, women could not get elected president. Most of the old-timers loved women but didn't think they should be president. That was a man's job. A few of our hardworking women left the organization when a strong woman candidate for president was defeated. Of course, there were also a few women who didn't revel in the idea of a sister being president.

In addition to the strength the coalition derived from having the old civic league, new leaders in the forefront of the organization solidified the organization's political status by forming a strong alliance with the county's black ministerial alliances. After all, the black church is the center of the black community's religious, political, and civic leadership. Visible black ministerial support was like a "laying on of hands"—a blessing in our black community. Hardly any black ministers attended a coalition meeting but nearly all were kept abreast of all we did and asked for the coalition's support. Most adopted me as the "political leader," asked me to attend their business meetings, and pushed our political agenda with their members.

After nearly two and a half decades as one of Alabama's strongest political forces, the organization began to lose its strength. Weakness came from within first. For years our members labored in numerous political campaigns for candidates we supported strictly as unpaid volunteers. Our candidates made contributions to the organization to help cover expenses of ballot printing, getting out the vote, and so forth, but no money was given to individuals working in the campaigns unless they had signed on to work as staff for a given candidate. In the latter case, the coalition's policy required that that member make known his position and limit himself in debate and voting on matters directly related to the candidate he worked for. This policy worked quite well for us. As the years wore on we made the mistake of letting volunteers get paid to work political races as coalition members. This led to an influx of individuals who had never been volunteers but joined the volunteer ranks for the money. Soon some of them became sellouts, switching their allegiance and that of the organization to the highest bidder. It eroded the group's reputation as an ethical political group as well as our unity—which had been the strength we were built on. We were further weakened by abandoning another policy we had adopted at the outset. One of the strengths of our organization was having "block captains" in every black neighborhood. Block captains took on the responsibility of organizing voter turnout in their neighborhoods. Each captain was assigned certain polling boxes and given a minimum percentage turnout for a box. Block captains gladly competed against one another for the highest percentage of voter turnout and took great pride in that fact. Our policy was that no elected official could head up the block captain program of the area he served. It was reasoned that making an elected official head of a block captain program gave him a decided advantage over any competitor he might have. Equally important was the fact that as long as an elected official had to rely on the organization for support, his loyalty to the organization remained strong. We had made good examples of what happened to those who betrayed us by defeating three young state legislators. Others got the message. It was quite frankly a "fear factor" that politicians respect. If they fear that they will be defeated because the members believed they were not effective or loyal, they adhered to the group's position. When we decided that the organization would permit elected officials to become the head of block captain programs for their districts, it was a big mistake. Most worked to shift block captain loyalty to them rather than the organization, which slowly wore away the bonds of unity.

When I left the mayor's office in July 1999 and took a low-key posture within the organization, there was great division over who should lead the coalition. I worked to get a young businessman named Dale Bloomer, who had been a loyal, but not activist, member, to seek the presidency. He was a successful small businessman with good organizational skills. He was elected president and led the organization with efficiency and vision, slowly gaining the support of the doubters in the group. He also fit the description of "new," "young," and "educated" leadership. We were, at last, moving away from the old practice of the black community leaders "taking leadership to the grave" with them. We were reaching out, embracing young blacks with leadership potential, bringing them into the inner circle, and ensuring future generations of good leaders. It was truly tragic and unfortunate when Bloomer passed suddenly one morning from a massive heart attack. The doors were thrown wide open for a fight over the leadership of the coalition. The jockeying for position was incessant and divisive. The result was a fragmented and weak organization that members drifted away from. Today the struggle to rebuild a defunct and once-powerful political group continues. The leadership for that task has not been found. There are other political organizations in our black community but none truly strong and none that can demand the attention of the city leaders and politicians. The fragmentation of Birmingham's and Jefferson County's black political officeholders is a tragedy. Each black elected official is an "island," none appearing to understand that each one is stronger if they work as a unit.

A New Citizens' Voice: The Citizens Participation Program

Federal revenue sharing with local governments was adopted by Congress in 1972. In addition to providing local governments with some of the tax dollars collected by the federal government, the program required local governments to establish a Citizens Participation Program (CPP) to provide greater citizen input into the expenditure of the funds. This new revenue sharing program led the City of Birmingham to create a Community Development Department in July 1972 and a CPP as mandated by the federal Department of Housing and Urban Development. Mayor George Seibels proposed a CPP which, in the opinion of several council members, provided for very limited citizen input. His proposal was debated by the council for several months and never adopted. At the February 5, 1974, council meeting, Councilman David Vann introduced an ordinance to create an elected CPP board or Citizen Advisory Board (CAB) based on a division of the city into twelve CPP communities. Under the Vann proposal the elected CAB would organize a number of citizen committees to provide input to the CAB. The Vann proposal was viewed by a majority of the City Council and Mayor Seibels as providing unprecedented power to citizen committees. The Vann proposal was defeated by a vote of 5–3; Angi Proctor and I supported the Vann proposal. The defeat of Vann's proposed ordinance was a victory for Seibels, who had lobbied the council to get the proposal rejected. Nina Miglionico, who was also a supporter of Vann's proposal, was absent from the February 5 meeting.

Following that meeting Vann suggested to me that we seek greater citizen input into the organization of the CPP. I immediately began to contact black neighborhood leaders to explain how Vann's proposal would empower citizens, giving neighborhoods a powerful voice in determining priorities for the city's federal revenue dollars. After contacting several neighborhood civic league presidents and getting their support for Vann's proposed CPP, I asked Ruby Williams to appear at the March 12, 1974, City Council meeting to speak on behalf of the Vann proposal. Ruby, who stood about 5'2″ and was of medium build, was the vocal and feisty president of the Public Housing Tenants Council and the Welfare Rights Organization. She was a combat veteran in local politics, having been the spokesperson for public housing residents and welfare recipients. She had waged numerous public verbal battles with politicians on behalf of her organizations. With her no-nonsense voice and keen mind, coupled with her strong commitment to the members of her organization, she seemed always ready to take on the next issue-dodging politician. She was certainly fired up on March 12 and she let the council have it for opposing citizen input into city government. Her supporters packed the council chambers that day and egged her on with amens and applause. When she had finished, the council agreed to set a special public hearing to get greater citizen input on how the CPP of the City of Birmingham should be structured. A formal vote of the council on that hearing was taken on April 7 and October 8 was chosen as the date of the hearing, to be held at Boutwell Auditorium. More than 500 citizens showed up for the hearing and called for the council to adopt the Vann proposal it had earlier rejected. After that hearing the council unanimously adopted the Vann proposal and set November 19 as the date of the first CPP election. The Birmingham CPP immediately gained nationwide recognition and maintains it today as a model for citizen input into local governance.

The civic league presidents and other participants in civic leagues who had labored for years to give Birmingham's black citizens a voice in government were immediately chosen by the city's neighborhoods to lead their CPP. Initially there were 80 neighborhoods grouped into 12 communities, based solely on the geographical boundaries the neighborhoods had traditionally recognized. The new CPP with its first CAB holding its first meeting on February 22, 1975, represented a new and powerful voice for all of Birmingham's neighborhoods. The number of neighborhood associations grew to 99 and the CABs expanded to 23. The CABs had direct input from their neighborhoods on the development of the city's public policy, including appointments to city boards, and, most important, the shaping of the budget priorities of the city—not just the city's federal revenue sharing budgets but the total city budget. The elected officials of the city, the mayor and council members, were keenly aware of the political influence of the CPP and gave careful consideration to its recommendations. This is what Vann had envisioned in February 1974 when he launched his effort to structure a CPP in which citizens' voices would be heard. The influence of the CPP was also what some of those who initially opposed

Vann's concept of the CPP feared. The CPP would become a strong watchdog over the city's elected government. Then there was another fear that many CPP participants would use the program to launch their own political careers. That, too, became a reality as many CPP officers sought and won races for City Council and positions on many of the city's strong public policy-making boards. In other words the CPP became a fertile training ground for those wishing to enter city politics. It was effective because the CPP was a testing ground of one's ability to lead and maneuver through the politics, bureaucracy, and red tape so common to government. If one could prove his/her mettle by delivering for his/her neighborhood, it was believed he or she could do the same at a higher elected office.

The CPP was a great catalyst for the growth of the Jefferson County Citizens Coalition since most of the black civic league leaders had joined the coalition and given it instant credibility. Now these leaders had moved to a higher plane—the CPP—and they were lifting the coalition up with them.

THE BIRTH OF THE ALABAMA NEW SOUTH COALITION (ANSC)

The JCCC restricted most of its political efforts to Jefferson County, but it played a key role in forming a statewide, predominantly black political organization called the Alabama New South Coalition (ANSC). Since Jefferson County was the site of the largest bloc of black voters in Alabama, the coalition was recognized statewide.

In early 1985 I was approached by attorney Michael Figures (state senator from Mobile), attorney Hank Sanders (state senator from Greene County), and attorney Earl Hilliard (state senator from Birmingham) about leading an effort to organize a new statewide political organization. The only black statewide political organization in existence at the time was the Alabama Democratic Conference (ADC), the "black arm" of the Alabama Democratic Party. Its longtime leader was Joe Reed of Montgomery. Everyone who would eventually play a role in the founding of the ANSC was a member of the ADC. Many of them had been disenchanted for years with Reed's dictatorial leadership style.

My participation in organizing the ANSC was considered pivotal since I was the mayor of Alabama's largest city and had statewide name recognition only slightly second to that of Governor George Wallace, according to state polls. I rebuffed the first efforts to lead in organizing the ANSC, telling the senators that I thought such an organization would often divide and fragment the political influence of Alabama's black voters. "We should form a new organization only if it can do a better job than the ADC," I told them.

At a follow-up meeting several months later, held in the mayor's office in Birmingham on a Saturday morning, the senators and several other prominent black political and civic figures argued their case for the new statewide black political organization emphasizing the fact that the organization would address issues of black economic improvement, youth development, and a number of other very relevant issues for Alabama's black community. They also correctly noted that the ADC was committed to the Democratic Party, largely funded by the party, and worked to endorse Democratic candidates only. It had no agenda to address the multifaceted problems of Alabama's black community and no capacity or desire to influence candidates other than those of the Democratic Party. They said that the black community of Alabama needed and deserved much more. At that meeting we decided to organize a new organization. At my insistence, we decided that we would invite Joe Reed and other ADC officers to participate in the organizing meeting that was set for December 14, 1985, in Selma. A list of invitees was compiled and invitations were mailed to them. I personally mailed an invitation to Reed, but he did not attend the Selma meeting, although he was seen in Selma that day.

Nearly one hundred black political business and civic leaders and about two dozen white political and civic leaders met in Selma on December 14, 1985, to discuss the proposal for an organization. Among those present at the Selma meeting and leading the organizational efforts were attorney J. L. Chestnut, Michael Figures, Earl Hilliard, Hank and Rose Sanders, John and Carol Zippert, Fred Horn (state senator, Birmingham), Dr. George Grayson (state representative, Huntsville), Lewis Spratt (state representative, Birmingham), Lucious Black (representative, Sumter County), James Thomas (representative, Lowndes County), Jenkins Bryant (representative, Perry County), James Buskey (representative, Mobile County), City Council members John England (Tuscaloosa), Jeff Germany, Eddie Blankenship, and Linda Coleman, all from Birmingham, and Simmie Lavender, president of the JCCC. The group meeting unanimously issued a call for a statewide political convention in Birmingham on January 24–25, 1986.

From the beginning, ANSC grew into the dominant black statewide political organization, a status it still enjoys today.[5] Its community development agenda is still by far the most inclusive of any black Alabama organization.

Significant efforts were made in 1987–88 to merge the ANSC and ADC. As president of the ANSC, I was chosen to represent the ANSC in the discussion with Joe Reed. He and I eventually agreed to a merger, which included a plan to alternate the presidency for the first four years between a former ADC member and an ANSC founder/member. The ANSC Executive Committee rejected the merger when Reed refused to agree that he would exempt himself from service as president in the soon-to-be-merged organization.

13

POLITICS AND FOOTBALL
The University of Alabama, Auburn, UAB, and the Magic City Classic

LEGION FIELD

On August 30, 2004, the mayor of the City of Birmingham announced that the University of Alabama Crimson Tide would cease playing football at historic Legion Field. The announcement was the culmination of many years of political maneuverings and the steady decline of the over 80,000-seat field.[1] Time and wear have taken their toll on the "Grey Lady" named in honor of our war dead. After the Mercedes automobile symbol was placed atop the large Legion Field scoreboard to commemorate Alabama's major success in attracting a Mercedes plant to the state—the first "foreign" plant Mercedes built outside of Europe—we were all happy that Alabama had outbid its fellow states and we wanted a way to celebrate that victory. But we were soon to hear from some chapters of the American Legion who thought that it was inappropriate, to put it mildly, to place a Mercedes symbol on a site honoring American war dead. They said that much of the Nazi war machine had been built by Mercedes and was directly responsible for the deaths of some of those the field honored. This never became a big public issue for obvious reasons. But at our first opportunity, the upgrading of our scoreboard, we quietly removed the Mercedes sign, promising to find another "appropriate site" for it. We have not yet found a place for it.

Legion Field and Alabama Crimson Tide football had a tremendous economic and civic impact on Birmingham. So with the declining fortunes of Legion Field came some negative impact on Birmingham's economy and civic pride. Birmingham was proud to have Legion Field designated by the University of Alabama and the NCAA as a "second home stadium" for the Tide. One man who looms large in Alabama's football history is responsible for the designation of Legion Field as an Alabama/Tide field. He is Paul "Bear" Bryant.

The Bear and Legion Field

If you are a football fan who lives in Alabama, no matter your team allegiance, you know football is next to God in Alabama and God and Bear Bryant are held in nearly equal esteem, especially by Tide fans.

Bear loved playing at Legion Field. That alone accounts for Legion Field's status during Bryant's tenure as head coach of the University of Alabama football team (1958–82). If Bryant said that Alabama plays at Legion Field, Alabama plays at Legion Field. If he says that Legion Field is a fine facility, Legion Field is a fine facility. There was no questioning the man's wisdom about anything connected with Alabama football. But as I will further note below, the death of the legend Paul "Bear" Bryant cast the future of Alabama Tide football at Legion Field in question. That fate was in place long before the upper deck of Legion Field was found to be too much of a safety risk to continue using and would have to be scrapped. The upper deck was constructed at Bryant's insistence that more seats were needed. More revenue thus came in for Tide games. It is also interesting to note that the upper deck, shiny and new for the first Tide game, was declared unsound by engineers a week or so before it was to open. Bryant requested—and, I am sure, received from Birmingham—special compensation for the lost revenue from those unused seats. But it was only Bryant who could have quieted a revolt from thousands of fans with tickets for seats in the deck to watch the Tide play. His unwavering demeanor about Legion Field saved the city from an exit of Alabama football from the stadium. But isn't it strange that Tide football at Legion Field ends with a story about the declining upper deck. But we all should have seen it coming. While other major southeastern cities built new stadia and domes and southeastern colleges renovated and enlarged their stadia, dear old Birmingham was stuck with its usual status quo—making some improvements but refusing to build a new stadium. Even when there was a plan proposed during my administration to upgrade Legion Field and to add a new baseball facility for the Birmingham Barons baseball team, rather than playing at Rickwood Field, the idea was rejected. With the same lack of a sense of community that characterizes metro Birmingham today, a new Baron Stadium was built in the suburb of Hoover. What a nice little minor league stadium! But other southeastern metros were coming together and building new major sports facilities at the time. Birmingham and its suburbs are still fighting their "civil war." The suburbs want nothing to do with Birmingham if they can help it—except the jobs that the city works to develop and upon which much of their livelihood depends— five days per week, 8:00 A.M.–5:00 P.M., and zip! Nearly every thriving sub- urban area even has its own "civic center." Together they could have built a new major civic or convention center that would have enabled the metro area to compete for the huge dollars of big conventions. But they said no to that also— especially in the suburbs, killing programs like MAPS. Who wants to help Bir- mingham?

The anti-Birmingham attitude of the suburbs is really not a new phe- nomenon. It has been a part of the behavior of much of the metro area for about five or six decades. Fight Birmingham! In the state legislature and any- where else it dares to raise its ugly head! Even the "one man, one vote" decision of the Supreme Court of this land could not affect that behavior—any more than *Brown v. Board of Education* could rid the area of "separate but equal" school facilities. I think the real problem here is that our system never taught us the true meaning of that word "equal."

I should not fail to mention the role of racial bias in the decline of Legion Field. After all, "the black Bull Connor," as some called me, should not fail to blame race for all that goes wrong. Legion Field has always been located in a so-called inner-city environment. Just across the street from the stadium to the southwest is a large public housing project that in the days of "separate but equal" had all-white residents. Since the mid-1950s the project residents have been overwhelmingly black. In fact, black residents surround Legion Field. So how does racial bias fit into the decline of the facility? Some university officials were concerned about crime in the area. That fear escalated after a white citizen leaving a night game of the Birmingham Stallions—one of sev- eral of Birmingham's professional football teams—was stabbed by a black man within a block of the stadium and right in the midst of hundreds of other fans walking to their parked vehicles. I was told in no uncertain terms at my next monthly breakfast meeting with city corporate leaders about how unsafe Le- gion Field was. Several made it clear that they never let their wives or daugh- ters attend any event at Legion Field because it is located in an unsafe commu- nity. To my knowledge the incident following the Stallions game was the most violent occurrence connected to an event at Legion Field. Several years later,

I received an irate letter and call from Cecil "Hootie" Ingram telling me that the son of one of his staff had been attacked in a nearby phone booth by some criminal element and had sustained serious facial lacerations. This occurred at an afternoon Alabama game at Legion Field. Both incidents were turned over to police officials for investigation. At every Alabama game played at Legion Field, our police department placed an extraordinarily high number of officers throughout the Legion Field community in an effort to provide security for everyone in the area. Physical assaults on fans in the areas during Alabama games were practically nonexistent over the decades, except for the two incidents mentioned above. Our police department had created what they called a complete safety belt around Legion Field for any major event occurring there. The plan used officers in uniform, in plainclothes, in police and civilian vehicles, and our entire mounted police force. The crimes that occurred in the area at these events were mainly breaking and entering of vehicles where personal items were stolen. A police report after each major event showed that only a few incidents of that kind occurred—usually in vehicles in some very remote area. But even so, I was fully aware of the city's need to make the Legion Field area perhaps the safest area in our city during a major event.

I had the occasion to speak with Coach Bryant a few days after an Alabama game at Legion Field when five or six cars were reported to me by police as having been vandalized. I called him to express my concern about the vandalism and to assure him that we were redoubling our security efforts in the area. He thanked me for calling and said, "Let's make it as safe as we can." Then he added, "Mayor, don't get too upset about those incidents. We have quite a few more cars vandalized when we play games here on campus than we do when we play there." It did not appear to me that Coach Bryant viewed Legion Field as a dangerous place for Alabama to play its games. However, following his death in 1982, the perception among a couple of top Alabama executives that Legion Field was an unsafe site would increase.

The Parking Problem

Legion Field was a 1920s facility and never had adequate parking for major events like big college games. Fans were urged to ride special city buses between their hotels and Legion Field in order to eliminate much of the traffic congestion before and after games. The vast majority of those living at hotels did ride the buses, but hundreds of others inched their vehicles along in heavy traffic lines to find a place to park by the stadium. About half of those drivers parked in the yards of homes near the stadium or at other private lots as the parking on the stadium lots quickly filled up. As far back as I can remember, parking on privately owned property was the practice at Legion Field's major events. Residents in the area seemed to welcome the opportunity to make a few extra dollars by permitting fans to park on their property, including in their yards. Hours before a game, people in the surrounding neighborhoods stood on the streets waving flags at drivers and trying to herd them into their parking spaces. This system worked well for years and city officials were usually pleased that residents rarely complained about the intrusion into their residential areas. After every major game, the streets of the neighborhoods would be littered with beer cans, whiskey bottles, and other trash. The city street and sanitation crew was on standby following every game to immediately clean the streets left littered by happy fans. The standing rule was that all streets around the stadium had to be clean before noon on the day after the game. So our crew began cleaning the streets just as fans drove away from the stadium. We also issued decals to residents in the area for their vehicles. The vehicles with decals were permitted to enter and exit their neighborhoods during the games. During my second year in the mayor's office I had the staff of our Park and Recreation Department, under which Legion Field is administered, to survey every stadium in the Southeastern Conference (SEC) to determine the number of parking spaces available to vehicles on game day. Only the University of Tennessee's stadium in Knoxville provided more stadium-area parking than Legion Field. The City Council then authorized the purchase of as much property as available around Legion Field and its conversion into parking lots and neighborhood parks or recreation sites. Our goal, which we achieved, was to have as much parking at Legion Field as any SEC stadium. Of course it was not enough to accommodate the Legion Field crowds, but at least we were no worse off than other SEC stadia.

So the congested parking situations worked itself out quite well for decades. The exception was during my second year as mayor. During that time, I was embroiled in a public verbal battle with the Birmingham FOP over the issue of "police brutality" toward citizens, as discussed earlier. As I noted, the practice at Legion Field for decades was for residents to park vehicles on their properties for a fee. The city never considered this a commercial activity under its code and never required those residents to purchase a parking or business lot permit.

On a Saturday when an Alabama game was being played at Legion Field,

Birmingham police swept through the community arresting residents who were parking vehicles on their property and taking them to the city jail. The charge was operating a business without a license. The officers told those arrested that they were acting under order from the mayor's office. This, of course, was a lie and aimed at embarrassing me. It infuriated the community. The following Monday, I met with the residents at the Smithfield Housing Community Center. They were livid with me; but it slowly began to dawn on them that this act was a trick of the police to set them against me. They quieted down and together we vowed that such an incident would never occur again. We established a neighborhood community to coordinate parking plans with a member of the mayor's staff.

AUBURN AND LEGION FIELD

For many years, the Auburn Tigers played three of its home games at Legion Field including their games against Alabama when Auburn was designated the home team. But by the late 1970s, Auburn had stopped playing games at Legion Field, except for the Alabama game. I made several unsuccessful efforts to get Auburn to bring some of its games back to Legion Field. I visited the campus as part of a continuing dialogue with Auburn's business and athletic department executives about coming back to Legion Field. We received the gate and concession receipts for Auburn games and I offered to have the city contract with the university guarantee that playing at Legion Field would benefit Auburn economically more than playing on the Auburn campus. For a while it appeared that we might succeed in getting Auburn back at Legion Field for several of its home games. Then, without explanation, the effort died. I made one last-ditch effort to get Auburn back to Legion Field. I asked Gusty Yearout, Pat Sullivan, and two other well-known distinguished alumni, all four former football greats at Auburn, to meet with me. In our meeting, I expressed my deep interest in having some Auburn games at Legion Field. All four said that they too would like to see Auburn return some of its games to Legion Field. They generously agreed to form a committee and visit Auburn officials to try to get an agreement from the university to play some games at Legion Field. They briefed me on their first meeting and planned a follow-up visit. But it never happened, or if it did, I never heard about it.

Shortly after Pat Dye was appointed football coach at Auburn and before he coached his first game there, I had the privilege of meeting him at Legion Field. We were attending a Carver High School—Birmingham football game. Coach Dye came up to me and introduced himself. He immediately began talking about his plans for Auburn football recruiting, including his plans to recruit competitively in the Birmingham area. For this reason he said that he also planned to play some games at Legion Field. I was quite pleased to meet Coach Dye and to know that he wanted to play in Birmingham. This never happened; instead, after Auburn enlarged its campus stadium, Dye moved the Auburn game with Alabama to Auburn when Auburn was the home team. The first development that probably changed Dye's mind about playing in Birmingham occurred about a week after our meeting at Legion Field. The *Birmingham News* reported on a talk he gave before the Montgomery chapter of Auburn alumni. When he mentioned his intention to play more games in Birmingham, the audience booed him, according to the report. I suspect that was the beginning of the end for Auburn and Legion Field under Dye.

It was Auburn's interim president, Dr. Wilford S. Bailey, who eventually made it clear to me why Auburn was not interested in playing at Legion Field. Our conversation took place at Legion Field during an Alabama-Auburn game and just minutes after an embarrassing display by a Birmingham police officer working at the stadium. The president of the university attempted to enter the stadium to go to the president's box. The officer stopped him from entering the gate. After the president identified himself, the officer still would not let him enter until the officer's supervisor got to the scene and authorized his entry. This rightly angered Dr. Bailey. He said to me, "This would never happen to the president of Auburn at Auburn." He was right. Then he went on to tell me that Birmingham is an "Alabama town," not an "Auburn town" or a "neutral site." He noted that city employees working the stadium gates at Auburn games played there usually wore University of Alabama caps. "This is an insult to our university," he said. Now I understood why Auburn did not want to play in Birmingham.

Ray Perkins

Coach Bryant retired and handpicked Ray Perkins to succeed him as head football coach at Alabama. My first meeting with Coach Perkins was on the afternoon of July 23, 1985, at Legion Field. He was there to inspect the stadium and to discuss extending Alabama's contract to play at Legion Field for another ten years. In that meeting, he informed me that Auburn was planning to move its game with Alabama at Legion Field to Auburn. It was the first time I had heard about the plan. He was not interested in Alabama playing at Auburn and thought that he could halt the Auburn plan if the city would amend its contract with Alabama to make it a rent-free game. I agreed to that request. But in about a year, Perkins had left Alabama, and Auburn, with its newly enlarged stadium, was preparing to leave Birmingham.

Steve Sloan

By now Steve Sloan, a former Alabama quarterback, was the athletic director at Alabama. I visited him in his office at Alabama—a courtesy visit I had told his secretary when I requested the meeting. But I also had uppermost in my mind getting Sloan aboard the movement to stop Auburn from moving their Alabama game to Auburn. But as soon as I mentioned the game and asked for Sloan's support of the "stop Auburn" move, he minced no words in telling me that he thought that Auburn had a right to choose where it played its home games, including the Alabama game. I was mildly surprised. An Alabama athletic director not opposed to playing at Auburn! Sloan told me that Alabama would continue to play at Legion Field but would not try to dictate to Auburn. Our meeting ended much sooner than I had anticipated.

Auburn Departs

I was out of options for keeping Auburn in Birmingham and left with going to court to try to enforce the contract Auburn and Alabama had to continue to play each other in Birmingham. Jim Baker, our city attorney, reviewed the contract. A copy was on file at the Legion Field office. He and several outside attorneys he consulted were initially of the strong opinion that Auburn was obligated to play Alabama at Legion Field through 1991 unless both universities agreed to a change of site. They based their opinion on the SEC contract signed by Paul Bryant for Alabama and Athletic Director Jeff Beard for Auburn in 1972 and amended by letter in January 1980.

In 1972, Alabama and Auburn contracted to play each other at Legion Field through 1987. In January 1980, Lee Haley, Auburn's athletic director, wrote Bryant requesting his approval for the Alabama-Auburn game from 1988 through 1991. In February 1980 Bryant responded by writing "approved" on Haley's letter and returning it to Haley enclosing a letter outlining the contract extension.

I conferred with Alabama officials to make sure they had no opposition to the city filing a suit against Auburn's effort to move the site of the game, since we would also have to make Alabama a defendant in the suit along with Auburn.

On January 8, 1988, I filed suit in Jefferson County Circuit Court against Auburn and Alabama to enforce our interpretation of the contract. The case never went to trial. City attorneys recommended to me that we accept Auburn's proposed settlement. Auburn would agree to play its home game against Alabama at Legion Field up to 1997 but not thereafter. Auburn played at Legion Field for one more year—1998. Alabama was the home team.

Cecil "Hootie" Ingram

In September 1989, Cecil "Hootie" Ingram became Alabama's athletic director, succeeding Sloan. Within a month, the local media of Birmingham and Tuscaloosa were reporting that unnamed University of Alabama officials were very critical of the deteriorating condition of Legion Field. I interpreted these reports as a preface to Alabama's attempt to get out of its contract to play at Legion Field. Six years remained on the contract and Alabama had made significant renovations to its stadium in Tuscaloosa. On November 8, 1989, I met with Ingram in his office and presented several alternative plans for making improvements at Legion Field, consistent with Alabama's wishes. The plans we presented were based on earlier discussions with Steve Sloan, who had requested that Birmingham provide a skybox-type facility at Legion Field that was comparable to those recently constructed at Alabama's Bryant-Denny Stadium. The plans also included enlarging team dressing rooms to accommodate eighty players, upgrading restrooms, adding 5,000 premium seats, and enlarging the press box. In exchange for the improvements the University of Alabama would extend its current contract to play at Legion Field for an additional nine years, giving us a new fifteen-year agreement under which Alabama would play at least three games each year at Legion Field and a possible fourth game if the schedule permitted.

I eventually negotiated an agreement with Ingram for the extended contract, giving a twelve-year commitment to playing at Legion Field through July 2002 and stadium improvements costing the city $12 million. The university was permitted to choose and manage the architect for the Legion Field upgrade. The renovated Legion Field would "footprint" some aspects of Alabama's stadium. The city would end up making approximately $16 million of improvements at Legion Field. Alabama committed to play at least three games per year at Legion Field through July 2002. The city and the university jointly released a public statement on April 21, 1990, confirming our new agreement. The Legion Field improvements were to be completed by August 15, 1991.

Chinks in the Armor

At the end of the 1990 Alabama-Auburn game at Legion Field, a number of fans climbed the fence around the playing field, avoided a cordon of officers, and ran onto the playing surface. Many of them were taken into custody by police and placed under arrest. Other fans rained empty liquor bottles down on the field in protest. In the end, those who were arrested, all university students, were released an hour later with no charges.

Apparently the university received a number of complaints about the detention of the students by Birmingham police. I wrote a letter to the university's newspaper, *Crimson-White,* apologizing for the incident even though the students had been unruly. George Arnold, editor of *Crimson-White,* had promised me via phone that my letter would be printed by *Crimson-White.* It never was.

Dr. Roger Sayers, president of the University of Alabama, protested strongly to me about the incident. He insisted that Birmingham officers assigned to work Legion Field at the Alabama games get special training by the head of the university police department. He visited the city to confirm that the city fulfilled the special training commitment and presented the university with a written security plan for Alabama games at Legion Field. We complied with all of his requests, but the relationship between the city and the university was deteriorating.

The City Commits the Stadium to UAB

The contract between the University of Alabama and the city stated that any other college games played at Legion Field during the period of the contract required the university's prior approval. This had been a clause of the contract dating back to Paul Bryant's days. I assumed Bryant had the clause put in the contract in anticipation of the day that the University of Alabama at Birmingham, once a branch campus, would want to field a football program in the same NCAA class with Alabama. That day came in early 1994. The University of Alabama at Birmingham (UAB) announced that it would begin to play 1A football. It requested the city to permit it to play its home games at Legion Field.

I believed that the University of Alabama's main campus in Tuscaloosa (UA) would not look with favor upon UAB's decision. But based on rumors and difficulties with UA, I believed it was wise for Birmingham to begin nurturing its own 1A program because UA was less than happy playing at Legion Field. I also believed that UA would not want the negative publicity of publicly opposing its sister school by opposing UAB's use of Legion Field. On August 2, 1994, accompanied by Larry Striplin, a local Birmingham businessman and member of the city's Park Board that administers Legion Field, I went to visit Ingram to discuss UAB's use of Legion Field. Ingram told us that UA had no objection to UAB's using the field as long as UA retained its priority on game dates there. Ingram had also told me in an earlier meeting that he had no objection to Alabama's two historically black universities—Alabama State and Alabama A&M, playing their annual Magic City Classic game at Legion Field on the last Saturday in October. Based on the letter, I encouraged the black colleges to enter into a ten-year contract to play the classic at Legion Field. It was already the longest-running continuous football classic played at Legion Field, but there had never been a multiyear contract between the city and those two schools to make Legion Field available for the classic. The arrangements were made on a year-to-year basis, with alumni associations of the schools alternating yearly as host for the game. I also encouraged presidents of the two schools to contract with a local promoter to market the game and to guarantee the schools a larger gate. With their permission, I got the firm responsible for marketing the Tide games to make a proposal to the schools for the Alabama State-Alabama A&M games. Several proposals were made but never accepted during my mayoral tenure. At that time, Ingram agreed that UA would not schedule any of its Legion Field games on the last Saturday in October to avoid any conflict with the Magic City Classic. He put strong emphasis on his respect and support of Alabama State and Alabama A&M and said that the Tide would never want to be in conflict with them about the classic date.

A Visit with Dr. Sayers

By the end of the 1994 football season, rumors and news reports said that UA planned to discontinue playing games at Legion Field. There were then seven years left on the city's contract with UA for playing at least three games a year at Legion Field. We had made $16 million of improvements at Legion Field to keep Alabama. But our relationship was becoming more difficult. There was increasing pressure on UA from the corporate community of Tuscaloosa to play all of its home games in Tuscaloosa, which essentially meant leaving Legion Field. The Tuscaloosa media were strongly behind the proposed move and at times, I thought, so were the Birmingham media.

Soon, contrary to an earlier promise, UA scheduled a Legion Field game on the last Saturday in October, which conflicted with the Magic City Classic. Ingram said the only solution to that conflict was to move one of the UA games that year from Legion Field to Tuscaloosa. I saw it as an appeasement move toward the Tuscaloosa corporate community and a violation of Ingram's earlier commitment to avoid a date conflict with the classic. But the game was moved to Tuscaloosa. Again in September 1995 UA proposed to schedule its 1997 and 1999 Legion Field games against Tennessee on the last Saturday in October, saying it was due to restructuring in the SEC schedule. I interpreted it as an effort to get the Tennessee game moved to Tuscaloosa. The university's contract to play at Legion Field required that the Tennessee game be played at Legion Field. I immediately asked SEC commissioner Roy Kramer if the SEC schedule could be adjusted to avoid the Alabama-Tennessee game being played on the last Saturday in October. The commissioner adjusted the schedule to avoid the date conflict.

I took that as an ominous move about the Tide's intentions. I quietly appealed to a couple of Birmingham representatives serving on UA's Board of Trustees to get UA to honor its contract with the city that ran through July 2002, but I got little encouragement and no help. I would soon learn why. A UA board member tipped me off to the fact that UA was quietly completing architectural plans for expansion of its campus stadium. The expansion was being underwritten partially by $4 million from Tuscaloosa's corporate community. Dr. Sayers had revealed the architectural plans to the board after one of its meetings and after the *News* reporters had left. With nowhere else to turn, I visited the chancellor of the university system and explained my concerns about UA's not honoring its contract with the city. For the first time, I was given some comfort. He told me in no uncertain terms that UA would honor any contract it had with the city.

On January 19, 1995, I had an appointment with Dr. Sayers at his office to reiterate Birmingham's commitment to its contracts with UA and our expectation that UA would do likewise. Complaints from Ingram about Legion Field were continuing to come in. We thought some of the complaints were unfounded and could possibly be used as a condition for UA to withdraw from its contract with the city. So, in a rather bold move, I decided to go over Hootie Ingram's head to Dr. Sayers. I asked Larry Striplin to accompany me to the meeting with Dr. Sayers. When we arrived at Sayers' office, he was there with Ingram, who appeared very unhappy that I'd gone to Sayers. The discussion in Sayers' office was uncomfortable for me. I was left with the understanding that Sayers and Ingram were definitely on the same page. Ingram reminded me how Alabama's football had helped build Legion Field. Sayers wanted me to clearly understand that the university would hold the city to every letter of our contract. Soon Ingram had his staff visiting Legion Field to inspect it. In one lengthy letter he wrote, he listed fifteen items from "no clean towels in the dressing room for the team at half-time of a recent game to possible structural problems at Legion Field." I called Legion Field to inquire about the towels in the dressing room: "Totally untrue!" the staff said. "There is still a laundry basket full of clean towels in the dressing room."

Bob Bockrath

When Hootie Ingram left the athletic director's office at UA he was succeeded by Robert Bockrath. Dr. Andrew Sorenson was now the president of UA. Bockrath, unlike his predecessors at UA, was an "outsider" (not from the University of Alabama family). That was an oddity and a bad omen. When it comes to football, the university has never been fond of outsiders. In fact, Coach Bill Curry had been treated with open hostility by Alabama football fans. He was not an Alabama Bear Bryant boy and he dared let his team lose two games in a season! I knew Bockrath had a tough row to hoe.

On March 30, 1998, the city had a professional structural engineering firm conduct the annual safety inspection of Legion Field. The firm reported that certain structural improvements were needed in order to ensure the safety of those using the stadium. The cost for the improvements was estimated at $2.1 million. The city's first concern was whether the improvements could be completed by August 1, several weeks before any game was scheduled at Legion Field for that year. The city was given that assurance by the firm chosen to make the structural improvements. The expenditure of $2.1 million was not already in the city's current budget so I had to go to the City Council for a budget amendment for the work. Some of the local media immediately began to speculate that the only reason I'd gone public with the announcement about the needed work was in order to push for a favorable referendum vote in August on a proposed new dome stadium.

Bockrath did not read it that way. In response to my letter to him informing him of the improvements and assuring him that the work would be completed by August 1, he questioned whether the city would have the work completed by then. He further suggested that we should agree that Alabama's three 1998 Legion Field games would be moved to Tuscaloosa. Bockrath was making another attempt to get Alabama games out of Legion Field. The Legion Field improvements were finished by mid-July. In some of our earlier negotiations, he had informed me that after the current contract between UA and the city expired in July 2002, the university would move all of its games to Tuscaloosa. In a series of quiet meetings, Bockrath had told me that prior to his becoming athletic director, the university had executed a contract "between it and the cities of Tuscaloosa and Northport" that required the university to play specific games in Tuscaloosa and to move the Tennessee and Auburn games to Tuscaloosa no later than 2002. At one point in April 1998, I had agreed to amend the contract to permit the Tennessee and Auburn games to be played in Tuscaloosa in exchange for the university switching two of its games scheduled for Tuscaloosa to Birmingham. Tennessee had won the national championship and Bockrath wanted the upcoming game on the campus. Since Alabama also had to play Auburn at Auburn every other year, he wanted the Auburn game to be played on campus. He made a very convincing argument for his case and I agreed. But when he told me that the Alabama-Tuscaloosa-Northport agreement, in which those cities contributed funds toward stadium improvements at Bryant-Denny, precluded any game swaps, the deal fell through.

Our negotiation continued into 1999 with Bockrath proposing to pay the city $350,000 compensation per game if we agreed that the university could move its games from Legion Field to Tuscaloosa. As a part of the proposed deal, he would extend Alabama's contract to play at least one game at Legion Field for several years. He and I reached two agreements that permitted the Tennessee and Auburn games to move to Tuscaloosa for compensation. In exchange, Alabama would play several non-conference games at Legion Field for another five years. He would later tell me each time that the Tuscaloosa-

Northport Committee rejected the deal. It appeared to me that Dr. Sayers and Hootie Ingram had given control of the sites for Alabama games to the cities of Tuscaloosa and Northport.

I sensed that Bockrath was under increasing pressure in Tuscaloosa to get Alabama out of Legion Field. In February 1999, he wrote offering another deal. In that letter, he also wrote, "This proposal *adds* two years to our presence in Birmingham (through 2003 instead of 2001) plus increases the compensation for moved games to $350,000 each. From our standpoint it meets the condition of the Tuscaloosa agreement, adds 6 games to the Bryant-Denny inventory and gets Tennessee and Auburn in our stadium. The last point could be critical in our drive for the championship in each of the next three years." I countered Bockrath's proposal with the proposal titled the "Second Amendment to Agreement Dated September 30, 1985, Between the Board of Trustees of the University of Alabama and the Birmingham Park and Recreation Board," which was accepted. My negotiations with UA had finally ended. I knew at the time that I accepted the amendment that I would soon announce my plan to resign from the mayor's position in July 1999.

The Southeastern Conference Championship Games

In 1991, the twelve colleges of the Southeastern Football Conference established a season-ending championship game between its east and west division champions to begin in the 1992 football season. Several cities were invited to submit competitive proposals to host the championship game. The City of Birmingham, the Birmingham Football Foundation (newly formed by the corporate sector), and the Birmingham Chamber of Commerce made a joint proposal to host the game. Our proposal guaranteed $120,000 for the scholarship fund of the SEC and projected revenue of $6.7 million per game. The proposal was for five years, 1992–96. The SEC was guaranteed minimum revenue of $4.5 million a year after the first year. Should the revenue be less than $4.5 million, the city was obligated to make up the shortfall and both parties were to determine if new terms were to be negotiated. Birmingham's official negotiations were assigned to the Birmingham Football Foundation (BFF). The Birmingham team put considerable effort into lobbying to be the host city for the SEC championship. Our proposal was deemed to be the best, and Birmingham was selected to host the game for five years. If the city met all terms of its agreement with the SEC, it had an option to extend the contract for another seven years through 2003, providing it expanded the number of skyboxes available at Legion Field.

Revenue from the game for the second year failed to reach the $4.5 million minimum guarantee by approximately $300,000, triggering the thirty-day cure and renegotiation clause of the contract. The BFF began the negotiation with SEC commissioner Roy Kramer. The BFF informed me that the renegotiations were proceeding well and that curing the $300,000 shortfall would probably not be required.

The SEC championship was the brainchild of Kramer, who had left his position at Vanderbilt University to become SEC Commissioner. I had been told by some members of the corporate community that Kramer had assumed that the SEC office located in metro Birmingham would be relocated to Atlanta. It was reported that in anticipation of his Atlanta office, he had his personal belongings shipped there. In anticipation of the Atlanta move, the City of Birmingham submitted a proposal to the SEC to construct a new $2 million downtown SEC headquarters and lease it long term to the SEC for a dollar a year. We believed that the SEC would not turn down a new rent-free facility and that Atlanta would not attempt to top our offer. In fact, the SEC was seeking Atlanta not the reverse. The SEC accepted the Birmingham offer and moved from its suburban location in metro Birmingham into the new downtown facility. We calculated the offer to be economically good for the city. With the SEC headquarters in Birmingham, we reasoned that the SEC would influence a number of athletic events to be played in Birmingham. The assumption was wrong. Not only would Birmingham soon lose the new SEC championship game, but it would fail to successfully compete for NCAA basketball tournament regionals because our coliseum had only 17,000 seats, short of the minimum number of seats the NCAA would eventually require for a regional tournament site.

The negotiations on resolving the SEC football championship problem were going well, I had been told. Less than a week later, a short article in the *Nashville Tennessean* reported that the SEC athletic directors had voted to move the championship game from Birmingham's Legion Field to Atlanta's Georgia Dome for the upcoming year. I didn't believe it. No one—the BFF, the chamber, or the commissioner—had told the city about its decision. I attempted to reach Commissioner Kramer in his office, but he was abroad attending the Winter

Olympics. The BFF officials professed to be surprised when I contacted them. To this date, I am not sure that they were. In desperation, I called the president of the SEC, who was also the president of the University of Tennessee. He confirmed that the decision to go to Atlanta had been made more than a week previously at a meeting of the presidents and athletic directors. I asked him if he did not think the City of Birmingham was at the very least due the courtesy of being told that the negotiations were being terminated and the game moved. He thought I had been told of the decision. He apologized and said he thought nothing could be done to change the decision. About an hour later, Roy Kramer called me from the Olympic game site in Europe and tersely told me of their decision.

Apparently while Kramer was negotiating with BFF officials, he was also concluding negotiations to move the game to the Georgia Dome in Atlanta once the thirty-day contractual "cure period" had passed.

14

STEPPING-STONES
Transition and Reconciliation

In the first chapter of this memoir I quoted the 1971 statement from Birmingham's Centennial Committee that noted that although the city had faced some struggles and disappointments in its first one hundred years, we should know that these are only stepping-stones to greater things for the city.

Nearly three decades later I was ending my fifth and final term as the city's mayor. Surely there had been some progress during that twenty-year period and there had been some sorrows that we could use as stepping-stones to higher achievements. I'd like to take a quick look back and reflect on the transitions of that period. Much of it I call progress; some was disappointment. But even the disappointments are, I hope, only stepping-stones to a brighter future and to bringing back the "magic" to our once Magic City.

> We are losing a very good general.
> —*Birmingham News* editorial, July 10, 1999

> For 20 years Mayor Arrington fought his way through the arena, moving this city forward against an often hostile environment.... He lived life in a fish bowl filled with contention. For that effort, for his dedication to the city, and his many, many successes, a loud, sustained standing ovation is in order as he leaves city hall.
> —*Birmingham News* editorial, July 18, 1999

These two excerpts represent the finest tributes paid to me by the media. No politician can afford to ignore what the media tell the public about his service. It was quite satisfying to me to end my political career with a fine tribute from Alabama's major newspaper.

It has been difficult to choose what I believe are the most appropriate topics for this memoir. I remain haunted by the many topics I have not discussed here or those that I wanted to explore more, such as the city's very fine and nationally recognized citizens' participation program, or the long struggle to make regional cooperation between the thirty-plus governments of Jefferson County a reality. The latter certainly ranks as one of our disappointments or sorrows, something which we failed and still seek to achieve.

I also served in city government during a period of significant transition for metro Birmingham, a transition fueled by economic growth and diversity, social and political change marked by increased tolerance among the metro-area citizenry, and political change that opened the doors of political participation, including political offices, to all of Birmingham's citizens. That transition occurred in such a relatively short time that I consider it nothing short of dramatic. Surely for me, the dramatic transition that took place in metro Birmingham on the heels and shoulders of the Birmingham civil rights movement and during my succeeding twenty-eight-year tenure in city government was unimaginable during my childhood and early adult years. Even in hindsight I see it as nearly incredible. How could a metro area leap from the darkest depths of division and bigotry to the increasingly enlightened metro area that Birmingham had become, starting in the 1980s? Nearly everyone familiar with this story finds it compelling and promising. I devote portions of this chapter to a discussion of these important transitions.

It is probably human nature to look back over a task completed twenty years or so earlier and try to assess how well or how poorly it was done. Such reflection inevitably leads me to think, "If I had only known going into the job a fraction of what I knew as I left, how much better a job I would have done!" Such hindsight is probably every mortal's regret.

Beginning a Period of Transition

Transition, of course, is change and is by its very nature ongoing. But I speak of transition here in the context of progressive change. A decade and a half before I took the first oath of office as Birmingham's mayor, the city had gone through a period of perhaps its most significant transition. It was the 1960s period of the Birmingham civil rights movement briefly mentioned several times in this memoir but fully documented in the pages of history. While that movement had been borne out of years of sorrowful racial strife, it became the stepping-stone to a better day for our city. It also was the stone upon which the progress of my time in office would be built. With the process of reconciliation of blacks and whites in Birmingham set in motion, we were able to push ahead to make city government include all citizens.

When I placed my right hand on the Bible, held by Alabama chief justice Janie Shores, to take my sworn oath of office as mayor of Birmingham on November 13, 1979, its once-booming steel economy upon which the city's economy was built was stagnant and dying. By 1981, the nation was in the grips of a recession with the highest unemployment rate in the United States in forty-one years. By 1981, unemployment in Birmingham was about 24 percent and the city was being buffeted by suburban flight—the loss of jobs and the middle class to the surrounding thirty-plus suburban communities. The most urgent tasks facing the city were rebuilding its nearly bankrupt economy. The beginning was tough. Just a few weeks into my first year as mayor, a rumor surfaced that the U.S. Steel (USS) plant, which employed about 3,000 workers (its labor force had been nearly 30,000 during good economic times), was about to close its operation. I nearly panicked when I first heard the rumor. I called the local headquarters of the company and asked to meet with its top local executives. My request was quickly granted. In my meeting with the executives, I inquired about the company's plan for its Birmingham-area plants and spoke specifically about the rumor I had heard about the plants' shutdown. The USS officials quickly assured me that the rumor was totally unfounded and that the company had no plans to cut back its operation. I left the meeting relieved that there was not more bad economic news to deal with. So I was somewhat shocked and angry when within the next three weeks or so, the company's public relations office announced that USS operations in the Birmingham area would cease within the next thirty days. I can now only speculate that the company did not want to make an earlier announcement about its plans to close. Even if the officials had been honest with me about the company's plans, there was nothing I could have done about it. But by denying the truth, it avoided pressure from the city about losing 3,000 jobs. Still, I thought that the company, once the city's leading corporate citizen, owed the city the courtesy of informing city government about its plans earlier than it did. But several case studies that I would later review on USS's poor corporate leadership style in its Birmingham-area operations showed that the company's handling of its plant closing was consistent with the manner in which it dealt with its responsibilities as a major corporate citizen of Birmingham. The Harvard University Business School had cited USS management style in the Birmingham area in several of its case studies on corporate management styles. They took note of the failure of USS to provide any leadership in the City of Birmingham's brewing racial crisis during the 1950s and 1960s. Its "hands-off" style was cited as an example of poor corporate-community relations and leadership.

Now the city was faced with an additional labor crisis. Steelworkers at USS, with the aid of a strong union, who enjoyed high hourly wages and fringe benefits were not only out of work but faced the prospect of seeking training for jobs that paid only about a third of the hourly wages most had at USS. In summary, the impact of the USS shutdown was devastating for an already debilitated Birmingham-area economy. The challenge of rebuilding our economy would claim much of the city's resources and energies for the next decade. But the challenge was even bigger than just rebuilding a weak economy. There was rebuilding to be done in other areas that were important to the city's welfare.

Juggling Major Transition

From this bleak day onward, we began a major journey back toward viability. By late 1980, the City of Birmingham was "juggling" transitions in three major areas at the same time. Any one by itself was enough to challenge the will of our city. Birmingham was simultaneously facing economic transition, political transition, and racial reconciliation (or social change). There was not time for the city to deal with only a single one of these transitions while deferring the others to the future. The city's economy was in a ditch. Something had to be done quickly. Political transition, borne of the civil rights movement of the 1960s, especially the 1965 Voting Rights Act, combined with suburban flight, had ushered in a period of growing black political strength in Birmingham. The number of black participants in the city's overall governmental structure was rapidly growing in a community where blacks had been barred for years from service on city boards and elected offices. Now the city had its first African American mayor—a development that probably came ten years earlier than the city fathers and most citizens had anticipated. Now the city got busy implementing new programs aimed at racial reconciliation and increased biracial communication. Between 1975 and 1980 the Birmingham community had created more programs aimed at biracial communication and cooperation than perhaps any other city in America. After all, it had waited a couple of decades later than other southern cities to work earnestly on the problem. It was only after the 1960s civil rights movement that the tough work of enhancing racial tolerance began in earnest. There was a lot of healing to do.

ECONOMIC TRANSITION

When I was elected mayor, my staff immediately set to work to develop and implement strategies that could bring the city economic relief. Realizing that the municipal tax structure in Alabama is heavily weighted toward commercial development, we began urgent dialogue with our corporate community and played heavily on the theme of public-private partnerships. The response from the corporate community was positive. I later noted at a 1993 Economic Development Conference that the Alabama Development Office Report listed 210 new or expanding manufacturing companies in Birmingham, representing $117 million in new investments. Only a fraction of these companies received financial assistance from the city. Nevertheless, we believed that city incentives would be a major catalyst for new business investments.

We quickly took stock of municipal resources the city had available to serve as a catalyst for economic progress. As noted earlier, my predecessor in the mayor's office, David Vann, had accumulated a significant number of federal grants for the city but had implemented few of the programs the grants supported. There was also a good amount of federal community development funds. Within months, we were using every federal grant to create incentives in the private sector for economic development.

Our Economic Development and Community Development Departments, working with Operation New Birmingham, a public-private partnership focusing on redevelopment of our City Center, began a campaign of "job retention," conducting citywide surveys of our business community to assess their perception of the city's most urgent needs and how the city was responding to their needs. We ascertained which businesses were pleased or unhappy with city services and got suggestions on how they thought the city could improve the business environment. We learned how many had plans for expansion and job creation and which businesses were thinking of leaving the city. From this information we initiated a successful "job retention" program and a "rebate program" for every city business that made improvements to its physical plant. By 1982 we had provided incentives for 137 firms, which we calculated as 6,337 jobs retained at a cost of $200 million to the city. The tax return on the city's $200 million investment would more than quadruple the city's investment in the first couple of years.

The blighted City Center was also a major target from the beginning of my administration and for the succeeding nineteen years. The rapidly expanding University of Alabama at Birmingham (UAB) buoyed the Southside of the City Center with its nationally recognized medical center. New facilities and new jobs were brought on line by UAB. Construction, professional, and service sector jobs expanded on the UAB campus at a pace that soon made it the city's number one employer. Its tremendous growth continued throughout my administration's twenty-year tenure. More than any other single entity it became our city's saving grace. It was also a strong partner with city government, and much of the city's economic recovery was a result of the strong leadership of the presidents of UAB from 1950 to 1999. Aside from the positive tax impact UAB had on the city, it contributed much to the city's social and civic structure, bringing highly trained professionals into the civic fabric of the city's communities.

But aside from the economic growth spawned by UAB, other City Center projects were under way. In the first three years of my first tenure as mayor, $650 million was invested in new and renovated office buildings in the City Center, much of it tied to city incentives of building new parking decks and doing extensive streetscaping. During the same tenure period, the city used its financial resources to provide new infrastructure for three new industrial parks that created 2,200 new jobs. The city's economic transition from an industrial economy to a service, biomedical, engineering, and banking economy was clearly picking up steam.

By the end of my second term, 1987, the city had invested $200 million into revitalization of residential neighborhoods, new streets, street lighting, and parks. An additional $13 million underwrote the public-private redevelopment of the Five Points South commercial area.

In succeeding years, the city's economic redevelopment continued to thrive. Sixty-five square miles of commercial properties were annexed to the city and developed, eventually becoming the major cornerstone of the city's tax base.

By the end of 1998, I was able to give Birmingham citizens a highly favorable report on the city's economic rebirth in my January 1999 State of the City Address. What follows are some excerpts from the address.

The City of Birmingham has a significantly stronger and more diversified local economy than it did twenty years ago. To some extent we are sharing in the overall strength of the national economy, but I regard the real improvements in our local economy during the past twenty years as one of the major success stories of my administration. . . .

The measures we have taken to strengthen the city, and thereby the entire metropolitan area, include our downtown and neighborhood commercial revitalization programs, industrial park development program, aggressive housing assistance program, and a variety of financial incentives to encourage business development within the city. The following statistics compare the city in 1977 with the present (all dollar amounts have been adjusted for inflation): Unemployment has dropped 33 percent, and the city is now on track to record the lowest annual unemployment rate in the 1990s, posting a 4.5 percent unemployment figure in the third quarter of 1998. The General Fund balance has increased 80 percent to a figure of more than $40 million. The Sinking Fund, established by constitutional amendment in 1920, receives ad valorem tax proceeds that can be used only for payment of bonds issued for general municipal or school purposes. The Sinking Fund has increased 32 percent during the past twenty years, now standing at $71.3 million. The number of housing units in the city has increased 12 percent to more than 117,000, and the number of square feet of rentable office space in the city has more than doubled and presently stands at more than 6.5 million square feet.

Two particular strategies have contributed to Birmingham's economic strength: annexation and downtown revitalization. Since 1980, the City of Birmingham has annexed 62.72 square miles, bringing into the city primarily vacant land with high development potential for office and retail activities, which strengthen the tax base of the city. The City of Birmingham has the financial capacity to provide necessary infrastructure for commercial development in this recently annexed territory and, indeed, has played a major role in most of the commercial development, which has occurred in the 62.72 square miles of annexed properties. These annexations have resulted in a 63 percent increase in

Birmingham's area since 1980. The economic development that has taken place in the annexed area has contributed significantly to our strong present-day tax base.

My administration has also maintained an aggressive commitment to the strengthening, revitalization, and redefinition of downtown Birmingham. . . .

Indicators of strength are unmistakable: the City Center is the second largest banking center in the Southeast after downtown Charlotte. More than 80,000 people are working in the City Center, which is more than ever before in the history of Birmingham. The number of vacant buildings has declined by nearly 40 percent in the last three years.

The city made a major commitment to assuring its continued economic strength by establishing the Birmingham Fund in 1994. This endowment fund was created when the city realized $87 million in cash after the Industrial Water Board property was conveyed to the city at no cost in late 1993: the Birmingham Fund now stands at nearly $100 million and has generated approximately $5.6 million per year, with one half of this amount added to the principal and one half appropriated to the General Fund.

The city has extremely favorable bond ratings in recognition of its economic strength; indeed, few cities have stronger ratings. Standard and Poor's December 1998 AA rating noted the city's large and diverse economic base anchored by a strong service sector; described Birmingham as the business center of Alabama; commented on the city's sound financial performance with large reserves and operating surpluses over the past four years; and commended the city's sound financial management practices. In short, the state of the city's economy is sound and is recognized as such throughout the nation.

In the period of nearly two decades, Birmingham had completely transformed its economy into one of the strongest and most diversified municipal economies in the Southeast. To be sure, there had been some notable failures such as the 1980s Block 60 program and the 1999 billion-dollar MAPS program. But sandwiched in between those failed programs were many successful programs, and surely the fact that the overall crime rate in Birmingham by 1999 was at the lowest in twenty years contributed to economic rebirth.

With a healthy economy, an inclusive political structure, and growing biracial tolerance and cooperation, a city that as recently as the 1960s was referred to in the national media as the Johannesburg of the South could proudly claim that it was a "city born again." The credit belongs to its people, who managed major transitions of political, social, and economic change in an amazingly short period of time.

I see all of the above-mentioned transitions as of major importance to Birmingham during my tenure as mayor. I should not leave the impression that other developments mentioned in this work did not represent, in the final analysis, important contributions to the city's progress, even those that were controversial. Some of the controversy was painful for me and for my city. But I believe that most of those bitter or controversial issues—or "sorrows"— became stepping-stones to progress.

Surely my zealous commitment to promoting minority participation was carried out in a fashion that led the U.S. Attorney for the Northern District of Alabama to suspect that there was some illegal motive for my actions and thus some corruption in my administration. He apparently could not bring himself to believe that I would fight such a last-ditch effort to promote minority participation. His skepticism, fueled by incessant complaints from local contractors who had been successful low bidders for city contracts, and upon whom we placed great pressure to include minority subcontractors, led to suspicions of payoffs and kickbacks. It was carried out in an atmosphere of tension and racial division. But in the final analysis it was Birmingham's white corporate community that stepped in to help my administration develop and finance a minority participation program we called the Birmingham Plan. Under that plan the corporate community provided access to capital or finance and training opportunities for minority firms. It was a plan that received national attention and accolades.

There were also disappointments and suspicions that boiled around the development of the Birmingham Civil Rights Institute—a project that our corporate community believed would only serve to reopen the old wounds between the races as had festered during the 1960s civil rights movement and before. But once the institute was in existence, it was the corporate community that stepped in to endow it and serve on its board. Thanks to the leadership of Odessa Woolfolk, Edward Lamonte, Neal Berte, David Vann, and Elmer Harris, the project was finally viewed in a positive light.

Carrying out a court-approved federal consent decree to hire and promote minorities and women spawned bitter division and eventually led to a divided federal court to cite Birmingham for reverse discrimination against whites.

But I would leave city hall a few years later, proud of the fact that Birmingham had the most diverse labor force, based on race, gender, and leadership, of any other government in all of Alabama.

The fight over police brutality and selecting a police chief (and eventually changing the procedures of the Jefferson County Personnel Board in the selection of department heads so that the elected mayors had a stronger voice in shaping the leadership for their departments and cabinets) left a bitter taste in the mouths of some for several years. But as I left city hall in 1999, I had the satisfaction in knowing that police brutality in Birmingham was a thing of the past. There had been no citizen allegations of physical abuse by officers for nearly eight years. In addition, the City of Birmingham Police Department was one of less than seventy in the United States that was certified by the National Accredited Association of Police Departments.

Perhaps there could have been progress without bitter fights but I think not. If it's the end that counts, then it was worth the fight. They were "stepping-stones to higher things."

Like cities worldwide, Birmingham continues to face serious challenges, and just as progress in those cities ebbs and flows, so will the same happen in Birmingham. But Birmingham has turned the corner and its future as one of America's progressive medium-sized cities is assured. In the chamber of the Birmingham City Council, on one of its walls, is the following slogan: "Cities Are What People Make Them." The slogan reminds me of Shakespeare's words from *Coriolanus*, Act III: "What is the city but the people?"

Campaign for a Successor

The campaign to select the city's next mayor began with my announcement of my intent to resign. A couple of weeks before stepping down as mayor, I asked William Bell for the third time if he had called a number of the neighborhood association presidents to ask for their support for him in the upcoming mayoral election. I had been encouraging Bell for several weeks to make these calls and he had politely said that he would. But now a clearly irritated Bell said to me, "Mayor, I'm not going to do everything you want me to do." I quickly apologized and said to him as he left my office, "William, I tell you what, you tell me if you want me to do anything in your campaign. Otherwise I'll have nothing to say." The rift between Bell and me would widen in the days ahead.

It would soon become clear to me that Bell wanted to distance himself from me and my administration. Indeed, I was an albatross around his neck.

With me now out of city hall, the Jimmy Blake-Bernard Kincaid contingent set out to discredit me and my administration and tied Bell, a political ally, to me. Weeks after I left city hall, Blake made a public inquiry about a city purchase of a piece of property made three and a half years earlier. The property was located in the Center Point area. I had recommended the purchase of a 3.3-acre site by the city to be used to entice a city retail business to relocate to the site rather than a site outside of the city. The council had given its approval to a resolution authorizing me to purchase the site. As was routine at city hall, once the purchase was approved, the details of the drawing up of the legal papers for my signature were turned over to the city's legal department. Now, more than three years later, Blake discovered that the council resolution approving the purchase called for a purchase of 30 acres, not the 3.3 acres purchased. The statute of limitations on any perceived violation in connection with the Center Point property purchase had expired. But its use for political fodder and claims of corruption by the Blake-Kincaid allies were repeated daily and the story was carried by the media. At first the assistant city attorney said the resolution approving the purchase had contained a typographical error of 30 instead of 3.3 acres. He later retracted his statement, saying he was uncertain about the typographical error. As the cries about the Center Point property continued, a member of Bell's staff told me that Bell had spoken with the state attorney general about the purchase. The attorney general reportedly told Bell that the statute of limitations on any illegal action that might be connected to the property had expired and the matter would not be pursued by his office. The public furor over the purchase eventually subsided. But just as it did, Bell, now the interim mayor, took an action that really ignited the furor over the land purchase. I learned of that action from the morning edition of the *Birmingham News*. On the front page was the story that Bell had announced that he was appointing a twelve-member blue-ribbon panel to look into the Center Point land purchase. I could hardly believe the story. I wondered why Bell, after being politically flogged with the issue by Blake and Kincaid, would, just as it had been milked for all the negative mileage they could get against Bell, resuscitate the issue. I thought that all Bell needed to do was to make a public statement that he was sending a letter to the state attorney general referring the land purchase to him for any investigation he thought appropriate. Since the attorney general had informed Bell about the statute of limitations, it's highly unlikely that he would turn around and start an investigation. But even if he did, Bell would have done the proper thing—distanced himself from it and put it in an area where it was not a political liability. By appointing the blue-ribbon panel Bell brought the issue back to the center stage of publicity. The media that had written all they could about the deal now had twelve panel members to pursue and a day-to-day hearing.

The appointment of the panel took a further negative turn when Circuit Judge J. Richmond Pearson, who had been asked by Bell to chair the panel, announced that the hearing of witnesses subpoenaed to appear before the committee would be closed to the public. The media reacted angrily about the closed session and questioned whether the panel was part of a cover-up. Blake, who was a panel member, also protested vigorously against the closed hearing, accusing Bell of being party to the cover-up. Bell's move had completely backfired. This panel was now discredited by the media and some of its members. When I first learned about the panel I called an attorney who was a member of Bell's staff. "Why had the mayor made such a move?" I asked. She said she was not sure but thought that he had done so on the advice of one of his political consultants. Bell's political ploy to distance himself from me had backfired. Even when the panel finished its work and found no wrongdoing, it was anticlimactic. The political damage was done. Bell's ploy to distance himself from me had failed miserably.

Having done all they could to incite voters over the Center Point land deal, Blake and Kincaid raised an issue at a council meeting about whether ride equipment purchased over the previous three years by the city for the State Fairgrounds had been legally purchased by me. We had purchased a half-dozen used and reconditioned rides from Murphy Brothers, the nation's largest operator of fairs. The rides had been in use for two and a half years, but now the media, egged on by Blake and Kincaid and leaks from three city employees— two in the finance department and one in the city's law department—carried sensational stories that I had purchased the rides without council authorization. It was totally false and an out-and-out hatchet job. I responded with a letter to the editor spelling out the purchase procedures and noting that an examination of the city budget would clearly show that all expenditures made at the fairgrounds had been legally authorized. The reporter who had been working with the Blake group to put the story together and who made the allegation that I had acted without proper authorization did what such reporters often do when shown that their stories were fabricated. He switched tactics and questioned whether the "authorized purchases" of the ride had been done through public bids. Of course they hadn't. Two city attorneys, Sonny Bass and Pat Burnes, had given my staff a legal opinion that the rides could be purchased through a "sole-source supply" and no bids were required. When I called Terry Burney, who had overseen the purchases at the fairgrounds and suggested he get written statements from the two city attorneys verifying that they had given the sole-source opinions, he attempted to do so. He called back and said Bass and Burnes, while admitting to him that they had given the opinions, said they would not verify it in writing. None of these developments would have occurred had I still been in city hall. But I was gone and not there to fight these carefully crafted political attacks. The reporter then used another journalistic sleight of hand. Had we ever had the rides tested for safety, he asked in his next story. The rides had been in use for more than two years at the fairgrounds and there was no record certifying they had been tested for safety. The groundwork was now laid for the reporter to play his next card.

Bell, in another attempt to distance himself from my administration, canceled the last year of the contract with the fair operator I had hired and entered into a contract with the new operator to operate the upcoming fall fair. As soon as Bell made the decision, the *News* reporter called the new operator, who was in Chicago, and asked if he planned to use any of the rides I had purchased earlier and whose safety the writer had also questioned in several stories. The new operator had not even seen the rides and obviously didn't want to be drawn into the ongoing controversy at the fairgrounds, which was being fanned by the Blake-Kincaid group and the *News*. So he said that he would bring in any rides he used. The reporter was now able to write that the rides were being rejected because of safety concerns. Kincaid, once he became the mayor in 1999, decided that the questionable rides would be shut down and auctioned off. The biggest rip-off of the taxpayers occurred at the auction. According to the *News*, the city auctioned the rides off for $25,000, about $300,000 less than we paid for them. It is my strong belief that the city could have sold the rides for scrap iron and gotten more than $25,000. I wonder what amusement parks are using those same rides today.

The 1999 campaign for mayor of Birmingham hummed along. Fourteen candidates entered the race. Bell fought mightily to put more distance between his campaign and my administration. He forbade his political consultant, Don Jones, to meet with me and I avoided the Bell campaign office. I did approach Bell and asked if he wanted the endorsement of the Jefferson County Citizens Coalition or if he preferred that the coalition not endorse any candidate. He wanted time to think about it and called a few days later to say he wanted the endorsement.

I thought Bell's campaign was awkwardly run at best. Bell's first major fund-raiser for his campaign had been held by me at my home and I invited only those who would commit a minimum of $10,000 contribution each (largely corporate people) to the Bell campaign. It was a very successful event that raised at least $160,000. Most of the attendees had invited me to a meeting at a private home in Mountain Brook a couple of weeks before I retired from office. At that meeting—incidentally I recall only one other black among the thirty to forty persons present—the host group wanted assurance from me that Bell was good mayoral material. I told them that I was sure that once Bell was saddled with the responsibility of mayor he would show his ability to lead. I learned a few weeks later that Bell was invited by the same group to attend a similar meeting.

On October 12, election night, Bell led the fourteen-member field, garnering 49.3 percent (36,277 votes) of the vote in narrowly missing a victory without a runoff. He would go into the runoff with Bernard Kincaid, who had received 27 percent (19,621 votes) of the vote. But the die was cast. Bell would lose. The plan of Kincaid, Blake, and Bill Johnson to force Bell into a runoff had succeeded. The white council members with whom Kincaid was closely allied on the council worked to deliver a large solid block of white voters to Kincaid in the November runoff. In the October primary 71 percent of the city's white voters went to the polls versus 48 percent of the black voters. The turnout was aided by a statewide vote on a state lottery, a very hot issue that would be defeated. I told Bell weeks earlier that I thought it would be a mistake to agree with Governor Don Seigelman that the lottery referendum would be held the same day as the Birmingham mayoral election. I said it would bring out a large white vote opposed to the lottery and those voters would also not vote for him. But he disagreed, saying the lottery vote would increase the turn-out of black voters, who were his base of support.

The runoff election results shocked me and many others. Sixty-seven percent of the city's white voters voted on November 2, casting a solid vote for

Kincaid, and against Bell and Arrington. Only 38 percent of the city's blacks went to the polls for the runoff. Kincaid defeated Bell, 32,174 (50.9 percent) to 31,034 (49.1 percent) votes. In addition to the strong white turnout for Kincaid, he was also helped by the black conservative Jefferson County commissioner, Chris McNair. McNair campaigned hard for Kincaid with black voters and succeeded in helping Kincaid increase his 20 percent black support in October to 30 percent in the runoff, just enough to beat Bell.

I felt that McNair, a longtime acquaintance and friend, was anti-Birmingham in his politics, but I could never forget that he had lost his daughter, Denise, in the heinous act of the bombing of the 16th Street Baptist Church. How he had survived that painful loss without bitterness is hard to understand. From time to time in some of our conversations I thought I detected his hurt and bitterness. Surely if I felt bitter about that crime and thought about it nearly every time I passed the church, it had to weigh heavily on the McNairs. Yet McNair had graciously represented the city in the 1971 national All-American City competition. Birmingham had won the competition and with Chris McNair touting the virtues of Birmingham, the symbolism for Birmingham was very positive. Bear in mind that at this time no one had been charged with the crime that occurred in September 1963.

It was not McNair's support of Kincaid that led me to think of his politics as anti-Birmingham but rather his attitude toward the city during his time on the commission. My perception of his attitude toward the city became an issue with me shortly after he was elected to the commission. For years Jefferson County Commission's three members elected at large were clearly not sympathetic to the city of Birmingham's concerns and rarely supported the city in terms of the way in which it distributed county services to municipalities. When it came to Birmingham the commission would recall that it was elected to represent unincorporated Jefferson County though 60 percent of its revenue came from incorporated areas of the county, with Birmingham being the largest incorporated area. Given the history of the relationship between Birmingham and its county government, I was pleased to offer my support to a federal suit contesting the constitutionality of the county at-large election. A young black attorney named Ronald Spratt filed the suit that led the federal court to require that Jefferson County commissioners be elected from districts. We proposed a district plan that expanded the commission from three to five members. Two of the new five districts were predominantly Birmingham and predominantly black. I was reassured that with two Birmingham district members, the commission would give Birmingham a fairer shake.

McNair was one of the two new black Birmingham representatives elected to the commission. How McNair got to be one of them is worth noting. When the district lines for the new five districts were drawn, McNair's residence was in an overwhelmingly white district in which neither he nor any other black had a ghost of a chance of getting elected. Shortly before we submitted the district plans to federal court, Ron Spratt came to me and said McNair had asked him to adjust the district lines just enough to place his residence inside one of the predominantly black districts. Spratt told me that it was my call as to whether he granted McNair's request. I gave my support to redrawing a small part of the district lines to pick up McNair's home, thus making him eligible to run and get elected from one of the two predominantly black districts. It turned out to be a political mistake on my part: rather than gaining an ally, Birmingham gained an opponent whose politics toward the city were as negative as those of former county commissioners like Tom Gloor, who fought the city on every relevant issue. McNair opposed several important issues for Birmingham when his vote was the critical third vote we needed. For example, I lobbied hard to get the county commission to renovate the large downtown former Pizitz department store building into a county warehouse rather than building a new proposed warehouse outside of the city. Doing that project in Birmingham would have meant more square footage, fewer costs, important jobs for both the city and the county, and a huge boost to Birmingham's downtown renewal efforts. I could not think of a single reason why this would not have been good for Birmingham and the county. Two of the commissioners agreed with me and it appeared that the project would be in Birmingham—until one of the two commissioners approached me and told me that McNair vigorously opposed the plan. I wanted to know why. They did not know the exact reason, but they felt that he did not want to do anything that helped Birmingham and they did not want to do anything to lose his vote on other issues they thought critical. Similar scenarios would occur over the years. McNair became the most anti-Birmingham commissioner on the Jefferson County Commission.

But my successor was now in office—not Bell, the one I banked on, but Kincaid, who had been one of the fiercest opponents of my administration. When I reflected on our poor political relationship I understood why. Back in the

1960s, when I was dean at Miles College in Birmingham, Kincaid was a student and served as student body president. At that time he and I forged a strong relationship. When I entered city politics in 1971, Kincaid was one of my staunchest supporters and workers. A decade later and on several occasions Kincaid had thrown his hat into the political ring, seeking a seat on the City Council and running for state representative. He had appealed to me for support each time and I had backed his opposition each time. He probably thought I was most ungrateful. When he finally succeeded in winning a political race— a seat on the Birmingham City Council—he apparently had no desire to be a political ally of mine. Once on the council he aligned himself with the anti-Arrington coalition led by Jimmy Blake.

It is traditional in American politics for an outgoing executive and an incoming executive to have a transitional meeting face-to-face or to communicate through a transition team for each executive even if the two parties are bitter political foes. This is done, of course, to provide some continuity in government. After I defeated my political ally David Vann in 1979, Vann had his staff prepare a comprehensive transition book for me and was most generous in consulting with me on city matters as they developed during his administration. Kincaid's approach was quite different. Neither he nor his staff expressed any interest in a "transition" meeting. Some members of his staff rejected offers from my staff for a briefing meeting. It's worth noting here that Kincaid, who was elected mayor in 1999, was reelected in 2003. Among the mayoral candidates he defeated was William Bell. In the 2003 runoff for mayor I was an active supporter of Kincaid. Everyone seems to love a winner.

In 2007, Kincaid, the incumbent, and nine other candidates sought the office. Some of the major campaign issues had a very familiar ring. Among the hottest issues were debates about building a dome stadium and how to promote minority participation in city projects. Much of the debate reminded me of the MAPS debate of 1999.

On election day, Birmingham voters chose a new mayor, Larry Langford, who was an unsuccessful mayoral candidate in 1979 when I was first elected mayor. Langford had changed his residence to the suburban city of Fairfield in 1981 and served as that city's mayor for twelve years. He then successfully sought the office of commissioner of Jefferson County and served there for six years before moving his residence back to Birmingham in 2007. He won the mayoral race with 50.3 percent of the vote; Kincaid finished fourth.

On November 6, 2007, Langford took the oath of office as mayor. In the short span of four weeks in office, he succeeded in getting the City Council to adopt his ambitious economic development plan that provides for the construction of a new multimillion-dollar domed stadium, the upgrading of the existing convention center, funds for improving the Public Transit System, and money for Birmingham public schools, including a new scholarship program for city high school graduates. The City Council adopted a $64 million annual tax increase on businesses to underwrite Langford's plan.[1] Successful implementation of this plan will be a giant stepping-stone for Birmingham's progress and, I hope, a major step toward making Birmingham the "Magic City" once again.

Notes

Chapter 1

1. A few months later a group of businessmen, the new mayor, Bernard Kincaid, and some members of the County Commission would lead an unsuccessful, quiet effort to retain the old name for the street, citing the expense of printing stationery with a new street name and possible confusion in finding the new street. They also correctly noted that replacing the former 21st Street (north and south) with Arrington Boulevard interrupted the city's consecutive numbering of the streets running north and south and avenues running east to west. The effort to get rid of Arrington Boulevard and find another suitable honor for its former mayor died quietly after some of the city's black ministers and citizens voiced their opposition to the effort to change the name of Arrington Boulevard.

2. Birmingham Centennial Corporation, *Portrait of Birmingham* (Birmingham: Oxmoor Press, 1971), 5.

3. Leah Rawl Atkins, *The Valley and the Hills* (Birmingham: Birmingham-Jefferson Historical Society, 1981).

4. Sherrel Stewart, "Mayor Arrington to Resign," *Birmingham News,* April 15, 1999.

5. Sherrel Stewart, "Voters Reject MAPS," *Birmingham News,* August 5, 1998.

6. Sherrel Stewart, "No Plan B Anytime Soon," *Birmingham News,* August 5, 1998.

7. William D. Barnard, *Dixiecrats and Democrats: Alabama Politics* (Tuscaloosa: University of Alabama Press, 1974), 112.

8. Michael Tomberlin, "Rules to Grow By" (Study of Growth Strategy for Birmingham), *Birmingham News,* August 9, 1998.

Chapter 2

1. W. E. B. Du Bois, *The Souls of Black Folk* (1903; reprint, New York: Oxford University Press, 2007), 146.

2. Jimmie L. Franklin, *Back to Birmingham: Richard Arrington, Jr. and His Times* (Tuscaloosa: University of Alabama Press, 1989).

3. Virginia Pounds Brown and Laurella Owens, in their book titled *Toting the Lead Row: Ruby Pickens Tartt, Alabama Folklorist* (Tuscaloosa: University of Alabama Press, 1981), tell the story of Alabama folklorist Ruby Pickens Tartt and include the slave narratives she collected, one of which is "Oliver Bell: That Tree Was My Nurse." It is Ms.

Tartt's interview with my maternal great-grandfather, Oliver Bell. In the narrative he speaks about his life during and after slavery.

4. Glen T. Eskew, *But for Birmingham: The Local and National Movements in the Civil Rights Struggle* (Chapel Hill: University of North Carolina Press, 1997).

5. Scott Greendale, "Vann, Arrington, Proctor Win," *Birmingham Post-Herald*, November 3, 1971.

Chapter 3

1. In 1985 the state legislature amended the Alabama Fair Campaign Practices Law to require reporting of contributions and expenditures by candidates for municipal offices.

2. James Lewis, "Arrington Leads Field—44%," *Birmingham Times*, October 10, 1979.

3. Ted Bryant, "Arrington Got Solid Black Vote," *Birmingham Post-Herald*, October 10, 1979.

4. Richard Friedman, "Arrington Edges Parsons," *Birmingham News*, October 31, 1979.

5. Linda Parham, "Carter to Arrington, 'A Great Day,' " *Birmingham Post-Herald*, October 31, 1979.

6. Linda Parham, "I Know Where We Are," *Birmingham Post-Herald*, November 14, 1979.

7. When a young white racist killed two black joggers in Utah and fled law enforcement officers to avoid capture, his journey brought him to Birmingham, where his sister resided. One evening the FBI, who was pursuing him, picked up a phone call from him to his sister, whose phone they had tapped. He was calling her from the Greyhound bus station, which was located directly across the street from Birmingham City Hall. He eluded their effort to capture him in Birmingham. But on the advice of the FBI a local black federal judge and I were put under police security because we fit the profile of his likely targets. Several weeks later the gunman ambushed and shot Urban League director Vernon Jordan in Indiana.

8. Kitty Frieden, "Mayor in Fish Bowl; Under Heavy Guard," *Birmingham News*, March 30, 1980.

9. See Mark Winnie, "60 Jailed in Shothouse Raid," *Birmingham News*, February 16, 1980.

10. Associated Press, "Mayor of Birmingham Targeted in Death Plot," *Atlanta Constitution*, March 24, 1980.

Chapter 4

1. C. H. Milton and Jeanne Halleck, *Police Use of Deadly Force* (New York: National Police Foundation, 1977).

2. *Incident Report, Birmingham Police* (case 5857), July 19, 1975.

3. "Vann Calls Civil Rights Bill a Fraud," *Birmingham News*, March 16, 1969.

4. Franklin, *Back to Birmingham*, 106–7.

5. Ibid., 106–7. I will include only a synopsis of Franklin's account in discussing the case here. Reading Franklin's account is a must for anyone who is interested in the details of the case.

Chapter 5

1. Barnard, *Dixiecrats and Democrats*.

2. Nancy Campbell, "Officer Denies Pistol-Whipping," *Birmingham News*, May 13, 1982.

3. Chris Cook, "Myers to Quit," *Birmingham News*, April 19, 1980.

4. Nancy Campbell, "Fight over Chief Begins," *Birmingham News*, September 4, 1984.

5. The eleventh candidate was Carle Thomas of Dallas. He had been ranked tenth (ahead of Jack Warren) with a score of 70.8, but he withdrew his name before the interview process began.

6. The department used three classifications for its findings on complaints against an officer. The complaint was either "sustained," "not sustained," or "unfounded." The department classified most of its findings after investigation as "not sustained," which meant that the evidence was not sufficient for a conclusive finding.

7. I had come to know Morial when he was general president of my college fraternity, Alpha Phi Alpha, a number of years before he was elected New Orleans's first African American mayor.

8. Gail McCracken, "Parsons' Appeal Rejected," *Birmingham Post-Herald*, July 15, 1981.

9. Editorial, "Parsons' Vendetta," *Birmingham News*, December 3, 1981.

10. Ruth Dunn, "Arrington Attacks Tests," *Birmingham News*, October 20, 1981.

11. Nearly every city case that went to state circuit court was before Judge Carl and he, with seeming delight, ruled against the city. I soon began to criticize him publicly, saying that he was biased against the city. His anti-city rulings only increased. When Carl handed down his first order mandating that I follow personnel board procedures within fourteen days in the police chief selection process, I immediately had city attorneys appeal the ruling to the Alabama Supreme Court. I lost on the appeal in that case. But I also appealed nearly every other subsequent Jack Carl ruling against the city. On several occasions I said to the media that the city had reversed Carl so much that he was now walking backward, which didn't endear me to Carl. We often exchanged dirty looks and silence whenever we met in his courtroom or on the street.

Chapter 6

1. Cindi Lash, "Mayor's Response to Questions on Chief Sought by Council," *Birmingham News*, December 17, 1983.

2. While heading up the Brooklyn precinct of the New York City Police Department, Artie had written and published at least one mystery crime novel. Early in his Birmingham career he would also have a small role in a play or two of the city's annual summer fest program, which included three to four Broadway musicals and performances by some local jazz groups.

3. Dean Burgess, "Reviewing Deutsch—Raves and Pans," *Birmingham News,* July 25, 1982.

4. Don Driver, "Arrington Gets Deal, Testifies for Prosecution," *Birmingham News,* January 31, 1985.

5. Barbara Bryant, "Board Upheld Webb's Firing," *Birmingham Times,* March 3, 1985.

6. Karl Seitz, "The Webb Decision," *Birmingham Post-Herald,* March 1, 1985.

7. Andrew Kilpatrick, "Apologetic Chief Pays City $588 for Phone Calls Home," *Birmingham News,* July 20, 1982.

8. David White, "Mayor Says Money Vanished Long Ago," *Birmingham News,* October 11, 1984.

9. David White, "Property Room Disciplinary Action Promised by Mayor," *Birmingham News,* October 11, 1984.

10. John Archibald, "Barber Says Deutsch May Have Revised Report," *Birmingham News,* March 3, 1991.

11. City of Birmingham Police Department Warrant #999025625, warrant of arrest for Erica Arrington, July 5, 1990.

12. Gail McCracken, "New Chief," *Birmingham Post-Herald,* December 22, 1981. 5.

13. Richard Arrington, "Erica Arrington: A Father's Perspective" (Inside City Hall column), *Birmingham Times,* February 27, 1991.

14. Ibid.

15. Grace Chandler, "Arrington's Son Pleads Guilty in Drug Case," *Birmingham News,* March 20, 1985.

16. Ibid.

Chapter 7

1. Chronology of FBI investigations of Richard Arrington Jr., 1972–82, compiled from FBI FOIPA files. The report contains a summary of key events in the FBI's investigation that led to a federal grand jury investigation of me. City of Birmingham Investigation Files, Book 1, Birmingham Public Library Archives.

2. Donald Watkins, *A Report to the U.S. Senate Judiciary Committee on the Harassment of African-Americans by the Federal Bureau of Investigation,* February 21, 1990, filed under Arrington Federal Investigation Files at the Birmingham Public Library Archives.

3. The phones had been replaced with new phones in upgrading the communication system. In an August 16, 1985, letter to me from Hambric and Associates, the communications systems consultants to the City of Birmingham, I learned that sixteen phones in my office had been bugged. City of Birmingham Investigation Files, Book 2, Birmingham Public Library Archives.

4. Alan Kianoff, "Listening Device Found in Mayor's Car," *Birmingham Post-Herald*, February 14, 1985.

5. Chronology of FBI investigations of Richard Arrington Jr.

6. *The United States v. Marjorie Peters*, case CR 91-4M 1445 (records of the City of Birmingham and FBI investigation files on Peters), U.S. Federal Bureau of Investigation, Richard Arrington Jr. Files, Book 5, Birmingham Public Library Archives.

7. Ibid.

8. Some of the firm's other projects included the following: Martin Luther King Center for Social Change (Atlanta); Bolgatanga Library of Ghana; Lionel Hampton Houses (New York); Equitable Corporate Complex (Milford, Connecticut); Schomburg Library (Harlem, New York); Studio Museum (Harlem, New York); Battery Park Housing (New York); and Hunts Point Multi-Purpose Center (New York).

9. Peggy Sanford, "Juror Felt Coerced in Peters Case," *Birmingham News*, November 27, 1991.

10. Bob Blalock, "Peters Investigation to Bring Down Blacks, Watkins Says," *Birmingham News*, September 8, 1991.

11. Cathy Donelson, "Black Senator Says Majority of Black Officials Being Probed," *Montgomery Advertiser*, June 4, 1989.

12. "FBI and IRS Investigation of the Harassment of Black Elected Officials," Books 1 and 2, Birmingham Public Library Archives. This report also contains the articles of incorporation of the Alabama Black Elected and Appointed Officials Legal Defense Fund.

13. Watkins, *A Report*.

14. "FBI and IRS Investigation of the Harassment of Black Elected Officials."

15. The details of these investigations are too lengthy for me to discuss them in their entirety. Anyone interested in the details should review archives, available to the public at the Birmingham Public Library Archives, and David Burnham's *Above the Law: Secret Deals, Political Fixes, and Other Misadventures of the U.S. Department of Justice* (New York: Scribner, 1996). What I have chosen to do is to comment on certain selected investigation activities. See also Bob Blalock, "Shocking Tone of FBI Memo Bothers Arrington," *Birmingham News*, October 18, 1990. The article notes that the *News* examined 518 pages of my FBI FOIPA files.

16. Today Mafundi is confined to state prison under the state's three-time felony or habitual felony act. His third alleged felony was the sexual abuse of his alleged

girlfriend—a charge he denied. But in the end—and no doubt to the satisfaction of some Birmingham police officers—Mafundi ended up the big loser.

Chapter 8

1. Freedom of Information Files of U.S. Justice Department on Richard Arrington Jr. (1972–92), City of Birmingham Public Library Archives.

2. The dates, times, and names used by these agents are part of my schedule kept by my executive secretary, Caroline Knowles. All visitors to my office during my twenty years as mayor are in the archive files.

3. Affidavits of Mousallem and Arrington, City of Birmingham Special Investigation Report, Book 5, Birmingham Public Library Archives.

4. Reports on the "Solicitation of Creative Evidence by FBI," City of Birmingham Special Investigation Report, Book 6, Birmingham Public Library Archives.

5. Affidavits of Mousallem.

6. "Fatal Shooting of Robert Mousallem," City of Birmingham Special Investigation Report, Book 5, Birmingham Public Library Archives.

7. Ibid.

8. Michelle Chapman, "Pat Davis Gets 6 1/2 Year Prison Term," February 2, 1990.

9. Ibid.

Chapter 9

1. Mayor Arrington to U.S. District Attorney Frank Donaldson, January 11, 1992, City of Birmingham Federal Investigation Files on Richard Arrington Jr., Book 2, Birmingham Public Library Archives.

2. Peggy Sanford, "Arrington Allegations Rankle Kelly," *Birmingham News*, October 26, 1991.

3. "Tarlee Brown: Charges and Plea Agreement," City of Birmingham Federal Investigation Files on Richard Arrington Jr., Book 3, Birmingham Public Library Archives; "Background Reports on Milkey and Brown Associates," City of Birmingham Federal Investigation Files on Richard Arrington Jr., Book 4, Birmingham Public Library Archives.

4. Nancy Berekis, "Watkins Adamantly Rebuts Kickback Allegations," *Birmingham Post-Herald*, October 31, 1991.

5. Appointment diaries of Mayor Arrington, 1979–99, Archives of Arrington Administration, Birmingham Public Library Archives.

6. Several years later, in February 1988, Tarlee Brown, Willie Davis, and I incorporated ABD Marketing Corporation, an energy conservation firm subcontracted with Time Energy Systems of Houston, Texas. The firm was only formed after the Alabama

Ethics Commission authorized my participation. In the one year of its existence ABD earned each of us about $39,000 from its contracts.

7. *The United States v. Marjorie Peters.* This file contains the sworn affidavit and testimony of Cecil Jones.

8. Peggy Sanford, "Judge—Tarlee Brown Told the Truth," *Birmingham News*, August 2, 1993.

9. *United States v. Tarlee Brown,* case no. CR 91111805, Birmingham Public Library Archives.

10. Bob Blalock, "City Hall Fights Back," *Birmingham News*, November 11, 1990. More daily schedules and diaries, including those for the period 1979–99, are now available at the Birmingham Public Library Archives in the Arrington Administration Files and at the Birmingham Civil Rights Institute.

11. John Archibald, "Upset But Not Humiliated Mayor Prepares for Prison," *Birmingham News*, January 23, 1992.

12. Bob Blalock, "Grand Jury Ends Arrington Probe," *Birmingham News*, November 12, 1992.

13. Peggy Sanford, "Justice Department, Mayor Make Peace," *Birmingham News*, July 30, 1993. In *Above the Law*, Burnham devotes several pages of chapter 8, titled "Uncivil Wrongs and Civil Rights," to the Justice Department's mistreatment of me.

14. Peggy Sanford, "Arrington Fundraiser Success," *Birmingham News*, September 8, 1991.

15. Peggy Sanford, "Scrushy Supports Arrington," *Birmingham News*, September 9, 1991.

16. Frank Donaldson retired in March 1992 at the age of seventy while his grand jury was still investigating me but not without telling the *Birmingham News* that I was "the most prominent racist" he'd ever met.

17. John Staed, "Jack Selden's Days Numbered," *Birmingham Post-Herald*, November 10, 1992.

18. Is this federal harassment of me really eternal? Well, maybe not when I'm dead. But I wouldn't bet my estate on it. In 2006 local FBI agents have attempted to subpoena records of some of my personal investments. My attorney complained to their superiors and the subpoenas were withdrawn. In August 2006 the local U.S. attorney labeled me "a person of interest" in an ongoing federal investigation. I'm sure the feds have an explanation for these recent actions—they "just go where the evidence leads them."

Chapter 10

1. City of Birmingham reference files on "Development of the Birmingham Civil Rights Institute," Birmingham Public Library Archives. This report includes (1) the

original copy of the Vann proposal for the institute; (2) progress reports from Odessa Woolfolk on the development of the institute; (3) appointment letter for the architect of the institute; (4) a list of members of the BCRI task force; (5) the program for the dedication of the institute; (6) Ambassador Andy Young's handwritten letter commending the city on the institute; and (7) the chronology of the federal investigation related to the institute.

2. I wrestled with the question of whether my discussion about the BCRI in this book should even mention the city's painful experience with a federal investigation of the BCRI project by U.S. Attorney Frank Donaldson (see chapter 7). But I believe that some brief overview of this bitter experience is warranted as a part of my comments on the BCRI. So, I have decided to provide this overview by including relevant excerpts from the findings set forth in "The Report of the City of Birmingham, Alabama to the Alabama Attorney General Regarding Certain Allegations of Fraudulent Activities—in connection with The Birmingham Civil Rights Institute Project."

3. "Vann Calls Civil Rights Bill a Fraud," *Birmingham News,* March 16, 1969.

4. Nancy Berekis, "Museum Site Price Double Appraisal," *Birmingham Post-Herald,* April 19, 1990.

5. The Birmingham corporate community, most of whom opposed the idea of this project right from the start, would later establish a $7 million endowment for the BCRI. Credit goes to Odessa Woolfolk, Ed Lamonte, and David Vann, all members of the BCRI's Board of Directors, for the about-face by our corporate community.

Chapter 11

1. "State Law Makers Introduce 10 Annexation Bills," *Birmingham News,* January 1, 1985.

2. Michele McDonald, "Annexation Bills Birmingham Priority," *Birmingham News,* January 20, 1985.

3. Alan Kianoff, "Annexation May Open Track," *Birmingham Post-Herald,* October 19, 1984.

4. David White, "City Council Delays Vote on Annexation," *Birmingham News,* March 12, 1988.

5. Sherrell Wheeler, "Fultondale, Birmingham Same Land," *Birmingham News,* March 12, 1985.

6. David White, "City Girth to Stretch," *Birmingham News,* March 10, 1985.

7. J. L. Lewis, "Block 60," *Birmingham Times,* March 24, 1982.

8. Phil Shook, "Too Soon to Talk about Block 60 Washout," *Birmingham News,* January 9, 1983.

9. Gail McCracken, "Katopodis Clashes with Mayor on Annexation," *Birmingham Post,* January 7, 1981.

10. Stan Bailey, "No Quick Decision on Block 60," *Birmingham News,* November 13, 1984.

11. Terry Horne, "Block 60 Lives On," *Birmingham Post-Herald,* August 25, 1983.

Chapter 12

1. Mitch Mendelson, "By Any Name, It's a Political Machine," *Birmingham Post-Herald,* September 20, 1987.

2. Ingrid Kindred, "All Black Slate Endorsed by Arrington Coalition," *Birmingham News,* October 12, 1981.

3. Our prominence as the "black political machine" also made us the target of FBI undercover agents and informers—a story I tell in greater detail in chapter 5.

4. Kindred, "All Black Slate."

5. "Notes and Proceedings of the Alabama New South Coalition (ANSC)," Birmingham Public Library Archives (compiled by Richard Arrington Jr.).

Chapter 13

1. Notes/files on the Arrington administration's negotiations (1980–99) with the football programs of the Universities of Alabama, Auburn, Alabama at Birmingham, Alabama A&M, and Alabama State (compiled by Richard Arrington Jr.). This is a complete collection of the letters and negotiations between the City of Birmingham and the universities regarding scheduling of games at Legion Field in Birmingham, dating from the Bear Bryant era through the Bockrath era.

Chapter 14

1. Joseph Bryant, "Langford Tax Plan Set to Start January 1," *Birmingham News,* December 5, 2007.

Index